Body, Mind, and Soul

The Teachings of Kabbalah Series
by Rabbi Yitzchak Ginsburgh

The Hebrew Letters
Channels of Creative Consciousness

The Mystery of Marriage
How to Find True Love and Happiness in Married Life

Awakening the Spark Within
Five Dynamics of Leadership that can Change the World

Transforming Darkness into Light
Kabbalah and Psychology

Rectifying the State of Israel
A Political Platform based on Kabbalah

Living in Divine Space
Kabbalah and Meditation

Body, Mind, and Soul
Kabbalah on Human Physiology, Disease, and Healing

Consciousness & Choice
Finding Your Soulmate

The Art of Education
Internalizing Ever-New Horizons

What You Need to Know About Kabbalah

Kabbalah and Meditation for the Nations

Anatomy of the Soul

A Sense of the Supernatural
Interpretation of Dreams and Paranormal Experiences

THE TEACHINGS OF KABBALAH SERIES

Body, Mind, and Soul

Kabbalah on Human Physiology, Disease, and Healing

Rabbi Yitzchak Ginsburgh

Gal Einai

Jerusalem • New York • Los Angeles

Body, Mind and Soul

Rabbi Yitzchak Ginsburgh

Printed in the United States of America and Israel
First Edition

Copyright © 5764 (2004) by GAL EINAI

All rights reserved. No part of this publication may be reproduced or transmitted in any form or by any means electronic or mechanical, including photocopying, recording, or any information storage and retrieval system, without written permission, except in the case of brief quotations in critical articles and reviews.
For information:

Israel: GAL EINAI
          PO Box 1015
          Kfar Chabad 72915
          tel. (in Israel): 1-700-700-966
          tel. (from abroad): 972-3-9608008
email: books@inner.org
Web: www.inner.org

GAL EINAI produces and publishes books, pamphlets, audiocassettes and videocassettes by Rabbi Yitzchak Ginsburgh. To receive a catalog of our products in English and/or Hebrew, please contact us at any of the above addresses, email orders@inner.org or call our orders department in Israel.

ISBN: 978-965-7146-08-8

cover design: Shmuel Kaffe

THIS BOOK IS DEDICATED TO

OUR BELOVED FAMILY IN ISRAEL

MAY THE ALMIGHTY BRING THE
TRUE AND COMPLETE REDEMPTION
WITH THE COMING OF MOSHIACH
TO ISRAEL AND THE ENTIRE
WORLD SPEEDILY IN OUR DAYS

BILL, EILEEN, AND PHILIP WELLS.

"...נכון שיכתוב השיעורים שלומר בצורת ספר. בברכה להצלחה..."

"...It would be proper to publish your classes in book form. With blessings for success..."

— *from a letter from the Lubavitcher Rebbe to the author, Elul 5741*

Table of Contents

Preface **1**

PART ONE: HUMAN ANATOMY AND PHYSIOLOGY **9**

1. Soul and Body **11**
    In the Image of God 11
    The *Sefirot* 13
    The Four Letters of God's Name 20
    Powers of the Soul and Human Anatomy 23
    Spiritual Holism 26
    Building Blocks of Creation 27
    In Summary 31

2. Mystical Anatomy **33**
    The Eye 33
    Fingers—Tongue; Toes—*Brit* 41
        The Principle of Balance 41
        "Five Opposite Five"—from Mind to Toes 43
        How the Sefirot divide into "Five opposite Five" 45
        The Tablets of the Covenant 47
        Procreation 48
        The Sense of Touch and the Higher and Lower Unions 50
        Two Levels of Da'at 54
    Three Stages of Spiritual Growth 56
    Higher and Lower Worlds 58
    The Mouth 65

3. Mystical Physiology **69**
    The Vision of Ezekiel 69
    The Physiological Systems of the Body 73

PART TWO: KABBALISTIC UNDERSTANDING OF DISEASE — 89

4. Origins of Disease — 91
  Evil, Disease, and Fear 91
    The Three Primal Fears 92
  Fear of the Wolf 98
  Fear of the Lion 109
  Fear of the Snake 113
  Gold, Silver, and Copper 118

5. Understanding Illness — 123
  Allostasis and Disease 123
  The Transforming Power of Disease 127
  Illness as Spiritual Lack 138
  Illness as Spiritual Estrangement 142
  Malfunctions of the Immune System 147

6. Lupus — 151
  The Dimensions of the Disease 151
  Collagen Disease 154
  Fatigue and Perseverance 155
  Treatments of Lupus 157
    An Ancient Remedy 158
    Remission 159
    Meditation, Positive Thinking, and Support 160

PART THREE: KABBALISTIC UNDERSTANDING OF HEALING — 163

7. Methods of Healing — 165
  The Power of the Physician 165
    The Physician's Eyes 165
    The Physician's Hands 168
    The Physician's Mouth 174

Table of Contents ix

    Eyes, Hands, and Mouth 176
  Contemporary Medical Practice 178
    1. Homeopathy 179
    2. Allopathy (conventional medicine) 179
    3. Osteopathy 180
    4. Naturopathy 180
    Four Methods as One 183
  Healing and the Soul 184
    1. Healing at the level of Nefesh 185
    2. Healing at the level of Ruach 187
    3. Healing at the level of Neshamah 189
    4. Healing at the level of Chayah 190
    5. Healing at the level of Yechidah 192
    6. Healing at the level of Etzem HaNeshamah 192

8. The Healing Power of Prayer   195

  Drawing Down Healing Power 195
    The Prayer of the Sick Person 196
    The Prayer of a Wise Man 197
    The Thought of a Tzadik 198
    The Priestly Blessing 199
    Infinite Patience 202
  Forms of Prayer 203
  The Healing Power of *Teshuvah* 205

Supplementary Essays   209

  1. Right and Left 211
  2. Three Planes 213
  3. Six 215
  4. Basic Colors 217
  5. Sight and Shabbat 220
  6. Implications of Nakedness 222

7. The Thirty-two Pathways 225
8. The Five Fingers 228
9. *Partzufim* and Contact Points 231
10. Contraction and Relaxation 235
11. Light, Water, Firmament 237
12. Spirituality and Reproduction 240
13. Regularity and Health 242
14. Six Permutations 247
15. Death and Life 249
16. Expert Healing 251
17. Healing and the Torah 253
18. The Indestructible Bone 257

Endnotes   **259**

Glossary   **313**

Index   **333**

Preface

In our modern day and age, new ideas on health and healing are being sparked—both with regard to applied techniques and to the theoretical basis of healing itself—not only by scientists and medical professionals, but also by educated and perceptive laymen.

The conventional methodology of diagnosis and treatment has traditionally focused on determining the immediate cause of an illness by empirical observation of its symptoms. However, interest in the psychological and spiritual origins of disease has begun to have a great impact on the way physicians practice modern medicine. Current physical diagnosis and treatment have begun to take into account the spiritual anatomy of the inner person. In addition, the growth and success of alternative medical therapy, as well as consumer education and sophistication in the Information Age, have challenged the very bases of health and healing.

Separation of the body and its physical systems from the inner person was once a medical axiom. However, this presumption has begun to change. Recent scientific research notes fundamental relationships between the mind and the body, connections that were known and described hundreds of years ago by scholars of the Torah and Kabbalah. In fact, a survey of modern research on "mind-body connections" suggests that these are attempts to describe, categorize, and understand the *soul*.

It seems most appropriate, therefore, to introduce the public to the long-standing tradition of healing and medical practice within Judaism in general, and Kabbalah in particular. This work has been written for the person who wishes to develop an understanding of this tradition and its wisdom regarding the nature of the body and its soul-roots.

In Kabbalah's perception of spiritual physiology, the health and maintenance of the body is dependent upon that of the *soul*, a spiritual entity not traditionally recognized or related to in medicine. Kabbalah teaches us how to heal the spiritual afflictions of the soul together with the physical afflictions of the body; how to better understand the one from the other and thereby to bridge the soul to the body.

ชิ   ชิ   ชิ

In order to better appreciate the insights Kabbalah can offer in our understanding of physiology and medicine, and how we will see these insights unfold in the present work, we shall briefly consider a few introductory points regarding the nature of Kabbalah and its methodology.

The word "Kabbalah" derives from the Hebrew root whose original meaning in the Bible is "to parallel." Kabbalah analyzes all of reality in "parallel" to basic spiritual/Divine models or frames of reference.

Together with the principle of parallelism, one of the most basic teachings of Kabbalah is that every well-defined set of objects appears as a hologram, where each element of the set reflects all of the others. This phenomenon is referred to as "inter-inclusion."

The parallel principle and the inter-inclusion principle are interdependent, for when the proper parallels (one-to-one correspondences) are made between two sets, the inherent wealth of significance possessed by each member of the two sets is brought into relief. The property of inter-inclusion is thus better revealed within each set.

In order to apply these two inter-related principles of parallelism and inter-inclusion in any given context, we must possess a number of Kabbalah's most basic sets of concepts. These fundamental conceptual sets will serve as models or frames of reference, which, through applying the principles of parallelism and inter-inclusion, will help us structure our understanding of the concepts discussed.

The three most basic models of Kabbalah, defined in detail in the first part of this book and employed throughout its remainder, are the four letters of God's essential Name, the ten *sefirot*, and the twenty-two letters of the Hebrew alphabet. These will be seen to correspond to the properties of our souls and to the limbs and physiological systems of our bodies. During the course of our discussion, they will be helpful in our quest for understanding how to maintain good health and heal states of disease.

ත   ත   ත

The material presented here is divided into three parts:

Part I: Human Anatomy and Physiology through the Eyes of Kabbalah

Part II: Kabbalistic Understanding of Disease

Part III: Kabbalistic Understanding of Healing

As medical practice is generally seen as consisting of diagnosis and treatment, the first two parts of the book deal with diagnosis, while the third deals with treatment. When we speak of healing, we tend to think of an illness of the body that requires a remedy. However, as we have noted, in Kabbalah no physical illness is separate from a spiritual illness, and spiritual illness often (though not always) manifests itself as a physical ailment.

Rabbi Dov Ber, the Maggid of Mezritch,[1] once said that "a small hole in the body causes a large hole in the soul."[2] Therefore, we can sometimes understand the "small hole" in our bodies by examining its result, the corresponding "large hole" in our souls.

Thus, we begin this book with a look at the mystical perception of human anatomy/physiology.

Part I—a reference guide to body and soul interaction—presents a mystical map of the body as follows:

Chapter 1, "Soul and Body," provides an overview of some of the most basic vocabulary in Kabbalah—the Divine channels of energy and the corresponding powers of the soul. Afterwards, this chapter moves on to draw associations between these spiritual powers and the physical structure of the body.

Chapter 2, "Mystical Anatomy," begins a systematic (though not exhaustive) mystical examination of various parts of the body—such as the eyes, the fingers, and the procreative organ (*brit*).

Chapter 3, "Mystical Physiology," continues the mystical examination of the body, focusing on systems such as the respiratory system, the circulatory system, and the immune system.

Part II focuses on disease and the Kabbalistic understanding of its causes, as follows:

Chapter 4, "Origins of Disease," examines the phenomenon of the primal fear of death and its relationship to illness, in its three symbolic manifestations, the fear of the wolf, the fear of the lion, and the fear of the snake.

Chapter 5, "Understanding Illness," considers the transformational power of illness and looks at illness as a spiritual lack and as spiritual estrangement. It focuses in particular on the immune system, which is shown to be central in understanding disease and developing the ability to fight it.

Chapter 6, "Lupus: A Case Study," examines an example of an autoimmune disease, applying the above models to an understanding of a particular illness.

Part III discusses healing as follows:

Chapter 7, "Methods of Healing," looks at the power of the physician and considers various forms of contemporary medical practice—including homeopathy, allopathy, osteopathy, and naturopathy—and their mystical correspondences.

Chapter 8, "The Healing Power of Prayer," explains how healing power can be drawn down through various spiritual practices, and especially through the most potent healing tool of all—that of *teshuvah* ("return to God").

If "understanding an illness is half its cure,"[3] then giving full expression to one's existential longing to become one with the ultimate source of life, the Creator of the universe, through heartfelt prayer and *teshuvah* (return to God), is the other half. Would both halves be complete, one would have no need for external remedies. When external remedies are indeed required, with greater understanding of the illness comes the insight to discover new, better methods for its cure.

                                                                   ❦   ❦   ❦

In this book, Rabbi Ginsburgh has compiled material he originally presented in lectures on human physiology, medicine, and healing, in various cities in Israel and America, including Jerusalem, Shechem (at Yeshivat Od Yosef Chai), Rehovot, New York, and Los Angeles.

In addition to the main flow of ideas in the text, *Body, Mind, and Soul* contains a wealth of more advanced material intended for seasoned students of Kabbalah and Hassidism. These expositions are appended as supplementary essays and endnotes, and even the beginner will be enriched by perusing them.

                                                             ❦   ❦   ❦

We have observed the following conventions in this book:

Several Names for God are used in the Bible and referred to here. Because of their holiness and spiritual power, it is forbidden to pronounce these Names other than in prayer or when reciting a complete Biblical verse. Therefore, we have deliberately altered the transliteration of these Names, in accordance with the time-honored practice of how observant Jews pronounce them in non-liturgical contexts.

The unique, four-letter Name of God is known generally as the Tetragrammaton and is referred to in Jewish writings (and in this book, as well) as "the Name *Havayah*." We are forbidden to pronounce this Name altogether, and indeed, its correct pronunciation is not known nowadays. In liturgical concepts, the Name *Adni* is pronounced in its place; in non-liturgical contexts, the word *Hashem* ("the Name") is substituted. Due to its special sanctity, it has been intentionally abbreviated (or hyphenated) when a verse is written in Hebrew. In English, we have spelled it with large and small capitals ("GOD") in order to distinguish it from all the other Names of God except for *Shakai*, which we translate as "the Almighty."

The term "Bible" (*Tanach*) comprises the Torah (the Five Books of Moses); the Prophets (consisting of eight books: Joshua, Judges, Samuel, Kings, Isaiah, Jeremiah, Ezekiel, and the Twelve Prophets); and the Writings (consisting of eleven books: Psalms, Proverbs, Job, Ruth, the Song of Songs, Ecclesiastes, Lamentations, Esther, Daniel, Ezra-Nehemiah, and Chronicles).

The term "Torah" must be understood according to the context: in its narrowest sense, it refers to the Five Books of Moses, but more generally, it can refer to the entirety of God's written and orally transmitted teachings to Israel and all of humanity.

The term "Kabbalah" is sometimes used in its specific sense, to refer to the classic texts of the ancient Jewish mystical tradition, and sometimes in its more general sense, to refer to the whole of the inner dimension of the Torah, including the teachings of Hassidism. Indeed, Hassidism is referred to in Hassidic texts as "the Kabbalah of the Ba'al Shem Tov,"[4] inasmuch as its revelation of the innermost core of faith and wisdom lies at the base of all the classic texts of Kabbalah.

∂ ∂ ∂

We wish to thank here a number of individuals for their contribution to this book:

Mr. Avichai Madmoni, for inspiring us to undertake this work.

Our medical advisor, Dr. Yosef Lev (Jeffry Lee) Kashuk M.D., F.A.C.S., for his professional comments and insights.[5]

Mr. Yechezkel Anis, Rabbi Asher and Mrs. Sara Esther Crispe, Rabbi Moshe Genuth, Mrs. Rachel Gordon, Mr. Uri Kaploun, Mrs. Uriela Sagiv, and Rabbi Moshe Wisnefsky, for their invaluable editorial assistance.

Our hope and prayer is to continue to shed light on the field of medicine from a traditional Jewish perspective, opening up the wellsprings of the Kabbalistic tradition for the benefit of all mankind.

Gal Einai Publications
Jerusalem
10 Shevat 5764

PART ONE

Human Anatomy and Physiology

ויברא אלהים את האדם בצלמו

And God created man in His image

Genesis 1:27

1

Soul and Body

IN THE IMAGE OF GOD

And God said,
Let us make man in our image,
after our likeness."[1]

The Torah begins with the account of creation, the apex of which is the creation of the human being, who alone was created "in the image of God."[2] By creating us in His image, God imbued us with an innate affinity to Him, which manifests itself as our ability to consciously connect to our Divine source, our Creator, in faith and knowledge. Our belief in Him and knowledge of His presence in all aspects of our lives are the keys to our spiritual and physical well-being.

Just as God's initial creation of the universe was twofold—"In the beginning God created the heavens and the earth"[3]—so did He create the human being in a twofold manner, body and soul. In man, his "heavenly" part, the soul, so permeates his "earthly" part, the body, that they appear to be one entity. In truth, the physical body perfectly mirrors the spiritual soul vested in it. This is why Kabbalah views physical health to be inseparable from spiritual health.

Since in Kabbalah body and soul function as a unit, in order to access the mystical understanding of human anatomy and physiology, we must first understand how Kabbalah perceives the soul and the soul's interaction with the body.

In this regard, one of the most fundamental teachings of Kabbalah is the system of the ten *sefirot*, the channels of Divine life-force or energy. These ten *sefirot* are sometimes eleven, when both the super-conscious *keter* and its conscious counterpart, *da'at*, are counted.

The meaning of the term *sefirot* fluctuates according to the context in which it is used. The ten *sefirot* can refer to the ten manifestations of God, the ten powers of the soul, or the ten structural forces of reality.[4] All of the worlds that we inhabit, whether spiritual or physical, display the same array of supernal characteristics. Thus, each *sefirah*, or channel of Divine energy, can be understood as a creative force at work behind the scenes, forming worlds, or, at the most personal level of manifestation, forming the basic intellectual and emotive properties of our souls.

First of all, we will examine the Kabbalistic model known as the "Tree of Life" (portrayed on the next page) and explain how its *sefirot* manifest as powers of the soul that relate to all facets of the human condition.

The *Sefirot*

left axis	middle axis	right axis
	keter "crown"	
binah "understanding"		*chochmah* "wisdom"
	da'at "knowledge"	
gevurah "might"		*chesed* "loving-kindness"
	tiferet "beauty"	
hod "thanksgiving"		*netzach* "victory"
	yesod "foundation"	
	malchut "kingdom"	

The first of the properties of the soul, *keter* (lit., "crown"), is the super-conscious experience of the soul. Just as a crown sits above the head, so too, *keter* reflects the power in the soul to connect to a transcendent region that is beyond the horizon of the conscious mind, a region outside the domain of normative logic and reason. In Hassidic thought,[5] the realm of the super-conscious is broken down into three distinct super-conscious experiences: faith, pleasure, and will.

In the context of healing, one must first *believe* in God the Creator,[6] "who heals all flesh and acts wondrously."[7] One must then connect to the innate *pleasure* of life and the *will* to be healed.

Next, there are three intellectual properties of the soul called:

- *chochmah* ("wisdom")
- *binah* ("understanding"), and
- *da'at* ("knowledge").

The first intellectual property of the soul, *chochmah* (lit., "wisdom"), refers to the mind's intuitive ability to uncover and perceive new insights. By introducing new flashes of insight into a person's consciousness, *chochmah* provides the mind with the conceptual seed or kernel idea from which all cognition sprouts. The manifestation of *chochmah* in the soul depends upon the degree to which one possesses an inner state of *selflessness*.

Selflessness creates the concave vessel in the soul that, like a vacuum, draws into itself spiritual light and life-force.

Binah (lit., "understanding"), the second intellectual property of the soul, reflects the native analytical ability of the mind, which processes and structures new insights by means of contrast and comparison. This logical construction process yields fully matured and developed states of consciousness. The inner psychological experience of *binah* in the soul is one of *joy*.

Joy in the service of God comes from a full understanding of the great merit afforded to a mortal, finite human given the opportunity to serve the Infinite One, blessed be He. Hassidism teaches that joy, the inner experience of understanding, fuels the soul's longing to return and become one with God (*teshuvah*). In Isaiah, we find: "and his heart shall understand, and he shall return [to God] and become healed."[8] This is the power of understanding (and joy) to heal.

The third intellectual property of the soul, *da'at* (lit., "knowledge"), is the ability to unite the two previous mental processes of *chochmah* and *binah*, and is dependent on the power of concentration. *Da'at* relates to the truth that it perceives as a unified whole,[9] and is thus an inner psychological experience of *unification*.

The experience of unification is the conscious counterpart of the highest of the three super-conscious levels of the soul, faith. Knowledge of God the Healer reflects one's absolute faith in Him and in His power to heal. By connecting to Him consciously we draw His healing power into our entire being.

After this, come three emotive properties of the soul, called:

- *chesed* ("loving-kindness")
- *gevurah* ("might"), and
- *tiferet* ("beauty").

Chesed (lit., "loving-kindness") denotes the expansive state of the heart, in which it is emotionally open and eager to give. Motivated by *love*, the attribute of *chesed* expresses itself as giving to another out of concern for the other's spiritual growth.

By contrast, *gevurah* (lit., "might") falls into the category of restraint, causing one to withhold. It is motivated by *fear*.

In the context of health, love motivates one to feel concern for the well-being of others, as well as for one's own well-being,[10] and seek means to improve physical health. The fear of illness, on the other hand, augments one's conscious drive to maintain good health. It provides one with a balanced (not over-exaggerated) sense of caution and restraint with regard to unhealthy items or situations. Ideally, both the love of good health and the fear of disease should exist for God's sake, in order to best fulfill one's purpose in life.[11]

The third emotive property arrives as the synthesis between the first two. *Tiferet* (lit., "beauty") denotes the beautiful effect of combining many colors. Balancing between the extremes of loving-kindness and restraint/judgment, *tiferet* is identified with *mercy* or *compassion*.

Compassion is one's sense of sincere empathy with another. Here, healing another's illness is experienced as healing oneself. One feels, on his flesh, the illness of the other and rejoices in his recovery. In Kabbalah, this is seen as the most essential spiritual property of the dedicated physician.

Next, come the three operative or behavioral properties of the soul. Described by the functions they perform, they serve to direct the energy and output of the mind and heart into action. They are:

- *netzach* ("victory")
- *hod* ("thanksgiving"), and

- *yesod* ("foundation").

Netzach (lit., "victory") refers to the ability to overcome obstacles in executing an action. This depends upon one's sense of *confidence*.

With regard to healing, we are confident that, with God's help, the efforts made to facilitate our cure will bear fruit. In times of illness, the Torah instructs us to seek the aid of the most expert physician available and to follow his or her advice. God is the true Healer, but His emissary is the expert physician. While seeing a doctor and making every effort to cure ourselves and lead a healthy life, we anchor our trust in God alone.

Hod (lit., "thanksgiving") is the power to persevere by acknowledging God as the source of all of one's abilities and thanking God for all that He bestows. Here, one walks a path of simplicity[12] and *sincerity*.

Here, together with his complete faith in God who will surely heal him, he accepts the pain he experiences with love for God, remembering that "he whom He loves does God chastise."[13] His complete faith assures him that his temporary suffering is in fact a cleansing, rectifying process for both soul and body.

The third property in this group, *yesod* (lit., "foundation"), is the power of self-actualization and sense of self-fulfillment. Self-fulfillment is known in Kabbalah and Hassidism as the attribute of *truth*, for it is dependent upon one's devoted effort to "validate" oneself, both to oneself within and to the world at large.

Here, one reaches the apex of one's drive to be healthy and sound in body and soul. Truth brings *keter*'s super-conscious sense of the innate pleasure of life to its consummate state of experiential fulfillment. Sound health becomes one's true reality.

The final property of the soul is called *malchut* (lit., "kingdom"). A kingdom is a person's domain of influence. Likewise, a kingdom is the expression of all the powers of the soul as they become manifest in outer reality and actually affect the world. Hassidism teaches that true sensitivity to one's domain of influence, one's kingdom, depends upon one's sense of *lowliness*, as expressed by King David, the archetypal soul of *malchut*: "And I shall [always] be lowly in my own eyes."[14]

In lowliness, one says to himself: "I do not deserve to be healthy. As is the case with regard to all the gifts of life, good health is a gratis gift of God. I must try my best to emulate God and bestow the gratis gift of whatever may advance good health upon all those in my circle of influence."

In summary:

Chapter One: Soul and Body

sefirah or property of the soul		power of the soul	inner (psychological) experience	in the context of health
	keter "crown"	super-consciousness	faith, pleasure, will	belief in God the Healer, connection to the innate pleasure of life, and the will to be healed
intellectual properties	*chochmah* "wisdom"	insight	selflessness	the vessel drawing healing power into itself
	binah "understanding"	analysis	joy	the healing that comes with returning to God in joy
	da'at "knowledge"	concentration	unification	to know God, the Healer, is to become healed
emotive properties	*chesed* "loving-kindness"	giving	love	sincere concern for the well-being of others
	gevurah "might"	restraint	fear	caution with regard to anything unhealthy
	tiferet "beauty"	balance	compassion	true empathy with the sick
behavioral properties	*netzach* "victory"	overcoming obstacles	confidence	one's efforts to become well will surely bear fruit
	hod "thanksgiving"	perseverance	sincerity	whatever God bestows in one's life is surely for his own good
	yesod "foundation"	self-fulfillment	truth	the apex of the drive to be healthy
	malchut "kingdom"	influence on one's environment	lowliness	good health is a gratis gift of God

THE FOUR LETTERS OF GOD'S NAME

The ten *sefirot* may also be organized by their relationship to the four Hebrew letters of the essential, unpronounceable Name of God known as the Name *Havayah*, which in itself represents perhaps the most fundamental model of Kabbalah. Indeed, the ten *sefirot* are but a manifestation of the Divine process encoded in these four holy letters.

Although the essence of this Name of God is above meaning, etymologically it is derived from the Hebrew root that means "existence," and can be read as either "He who was, is, and will be" (essentially above time), or as "He who continuously brings [all reality] into existence."[15] According to this latter reading, the four letters of this Name teach us that we may conceive of "existence" or "life" in terms of a four-stage unfolding structure.

The transcendent *sefirah* of *keter* ("crown") is alluded to by the upper tip of the first letter of God's Name, the *yud*. The *yud* itself corresponds to the seminal *sefirah* of *chochmah* ("wisdom"). The first *hei* corresponds to the expansive comprehension of the *sefirah* of *binah* ("understanding"). The *vav* corresponds to the next six[16] *sefirot*—from *chesed* to *yesod*—which are collectively known as the *midot* ("characteristics"). The final *hei* corresponds to the domain of the *sefirah* of *malchut* ("kingdom").

The full correspondence of the letters of the Divine Name to the ten *sefirot* is thus:

Chapter One: Soul and Body

׳ upper tip of *yud*	*keter*	"crown"
׳ *yud*	*chochmah*	"wisdom"
ה *hei*	*binah*	"understanding"
ו *vav*	*midot*	"emotions"
ה *hei*	*malchut*	"kingdom"

We will see later how these five levels manifest themselves in all aspects of human anatomy. In relation to the creative process or the healing process ("creation" in Hebrew is cognate to "healing"[17]), these five levels are known as the five stages of:

- infinite, absolutely concealed Divine light
- contraction of the infinite light into one point of creative potential
- expansion of the point to create "hidden worlds"
- linear projection of the hidden reality toward revealed reality
- expansion of the projected line to create "revealed worlds"

Vis-à-vis the healing process, one must first connect in faith to God's infinite light, the source of all healing. Then, through selflessness, one contracts the infinite light into a single point of healing potential (intended to heal a specific soul and body). The healing energy must then expand, by means of a detailed understanding of the problem at hand and the joy that comes with understanding, to create anew—to heal—one's inner self, the "hidden worlds" of the soul (one's mindsets, opinions, and thoughts in general). By the means of the emotive attributes of the soul, one projects his inner image—"And He created him in the image of God"[18]—toward his outer image (the body). Finally, one integrates the healing energy into the body itself, recreating the body by means of lowliness: "I deserve nothing; all is a gratis gift of God."

To summarize:

׳ upper tip of *yud*	*keter* "crown"	connection to source of healing
׳ *yud*	*chochmah* "wisdom"	contraction to single point of healing potential
ה *hei*	*binah* "understanding"	creating anew one's inner self
ו *vav*	*midot* "emotions"	projecting one's inner self on one's outer self
ה *hei*	*malchut* "kingdom"	integrating the healing energy into one's body

POWERS OF THE SOUL AND HUMAN ANATOMY

Now that we have a picture of the powers of the soul, we shall take a look at how Kabbalah relates these spiritual powers to aspects of the human anatomy.

(In the traditional Kabbalistic literature, great emphasis is placed on the correlation between the ten *sefirot* and the physical limbs and organs of the human body, skipping directly from the plane of the Divine to the plane of the physical. Only at a later stage in the historical unfolding of the revelation of the Torah's hidden wisdom did the Ba'al Shem Tov, the 18th-century founder of Hassidism, and his disciples come to ascribe the psychological correlates noted above to both the supernal *sefirot* and their physical parallels. These psychological correlates (love, fear, joy etc.), serve as the spiritual intermediaries by means of which the Divine *sefirot* become reflected in the physical limbs of the body.)

Identifying powers of the soul with parts of the body illustrates the Kabbalistic idea of *hitlabshut* ("enclothement"), wherein a higher reality is vested in a lower one. In this instance, a power of the soul is the higher reality that expresses itself through the medium of a lower reality, a limb or organ of the body.[19]

The correspondence presented in Kabbalah between the *sefirot* and the limbs of the body can be summarized as follows:

	left axis	middle axis	right axis
		keter "crown" **skull**	
intellectual properties	*binah* "understanding" **left hemisphere of brain**	*da'at* "knowledge" **posterior of brain**	*chochmah* "wisdom" **right hemisphere of brain**
emotive properties	*gevurah* "might" **left arm**	*tiferet* "beauty" **torso**	*chesed* "loving-kindness" **right arm**
behavioral properties	*hod* "thanksgiving" **left leg**	*yesod* "foundation" ***brit***	*netzach* "victory" **right leg**
		malchut "kingdom" **mouth**	

Keter ("crown") is manifest in the body as the skull. Just as a crown encircles the head, so the skull encircles the brain. The skull further suggests the erection of a physical border around our field of conscious experience. Consciousness, which gives definition to the mind and places limits on its ability to expand and inflate, is itself always surrounded by a border of unconscious experience that, in turn, gives it shape.

Chochmah ("wisdom") is considered to be the essential mind or the "mind within the mind," while *binah* ("understanding") can be regarded as the "heart within the mind." (In addition, *binah* is reflected in the heart itself, the physical seat of emotive experience born of the understanding of the mind.) This distinction also plays itself out in the body, where *chochmah* is positioned in the right hemisphere and *binah* in the left hemisphere of the brain,[20] while *da'at* ("knowledge") is located in the posterior region of the brain.

With regard to the three emotive properties of the soul, we find that the right arm embodies *chesed* ("loving-kindness" and the left arm *gevurah* ("might"). This is alluded to in the verse from the Song of Songs,[21] "His left arm is under my head, and his right arm embraces me" and in the saying of the sages,[22] "let the left arm reject and the right arm draw near." To "reject" in this context means to disengage, granting the other a sense of independence before drawing him near. Similarly, the imagery of "his left arm is under my head" means that he nurtures my sense of independence before embracing me with his right arm. The torso is the balancing position of *tiferet* ("beauty"), which incorporates all the parts of the body, and is centered between the body's two arms.[23]

Of the behavioral properties of the soul, those of *netzach* ("victory") and *hod* ("thanksgiving") correspond to the legs of the body. Legs represent one's first and most continual contact with outer reality. Moreover, the legs facilitate the movement of the body as a whole, bringing a person where he or she wants to go. *Netzach* is the quality of putting "one's best foot forward" in an assertive posture. *Hod* is the left leg, which keeps a person's movement on course by monitoring and validating his or her assertive thrust. Finally, the property of *yesod* ("foundation") corresponds to the male and female reproductive organs. Referred to as the "conclusion of the body,"[24] *yesod* is the body's physical manifestation of its own ability to actualize and fulfill itself in procreation, as well as to connect and communicate with others.

The last power of the soul is manifest in the mouth. *Malchut* ("kingdom") is the domain of a person's influence. As it is written, "the word of the king is his authority,"[25] meaning that the extent of the king's rule is marked by how far his word travels. The ability of the mouth to speak is the power to affect one's environment, one's world.

SPIRITUAL HOLISM

From the analysis above, we see that the powers of the soul are divided into three general levels of consciousness: intellectual, emotive, and behavioral characteristics.

(Above the intellectual characteristics is the super-conscious *keter*, which in Kabbalah is considered an adjunct to them.[26] Similarly, below the behavioral characteristics is *malchut*, which is also considered an adjunct to them.[27])

Each of these three groupings further divides into three axes—right, left, and middle.

This basic division of the powers of the soul into three, and three into three, is mirrored in the human body in several ways. For example, we are taught in Kabbalah that the human body as a whole and each of its limbs divides into three segments or joints.

With regard to the complete stature of the human being, these are the head, the body, and the legs. Each of these further subdivides into three: the head has a brain with three regions; the body has two arms and the torso; the legs consist of two plus the procreative organ, which is considered in Kabbalah to be a "third leg."

And so it is with respect to each one of the limbs in particular. If we look at the arm, we see that it consists of the upper arm, the forearm, and the hand. The hand consists of the wrist, the palm, and the fingers. Each finger is made up of three joints (the thumb's third joint is in the hand, below the palm). And so it is with all the parts of the body, which can be divided into smaller and smaller parts.

In Kabbalah, this general phenomenon is understood to indicate that each part of the body possesses a beginning, middle, and end, or "a head, a body, and feet." It is considered to be one of the most important indications of the intrinsic holism of the human body.

Spiritually, this means that every limb possesses characteristics that are intellectual (head), emotive (body), and behavioral (feet).[28]

BUILDING BLOCKS OF CREATION

The Hebrew word *Kabbalah* derives from the root *k-b-l* whose original meaning in the Bible is "to parallel." This is because Kabbalah analyzes all of reality in "parallel" to basic models or frames of reference. Thus far, we have looked at two such models: one consisting of ten levels or developmental stages, the ten *sefirot* (and its division into three and into three again); and a second, an even more fundamental frame of reference, known as the "seal of creation," the four Hebrew letters of God's essential Name, *Havayah*.

The third basic model is represented by the twenty-two letters of the Hebrew alphabet.[29] Relative to one another, the ten *sefirot*, which most simply correspond to the ten numbers from 1 to 10, the basis of all abstract thought, are referred to as "lights" (whose inner essence is God's essential Name, *Havayah*), while the twenty-two letters, the building blocks of intelligible language, are referred to as "vessels." Together, the ten *sefirot* and twenty-two letters become the "thirty-two pathways of wisdom" through which God created the world.[30]

The classic Kabbalistic text, *Sefer Yetzirah*, the "Book of Formation,"[31] describes the twenty-two Hebrew letters as the building blocks of creation and divides them into sub-groups based on both grammatical/phonetic and spiritual considerations. There are three sub-groups:

- three "mother" letters: *alef, mem, shin*
- seven "double" letters: *beit, gimel, dalet, kaf, pei, reish, tav*
- twelve "simple" letters: *hei, vav, zayin, chet, tet, yud, lamed, nun, samech, ayin, tzadik, kuf*

The terms "mother," "double," and "simple" refer to the phonetic properties of the letters. "Mother," *aim* in Hebrew, means both "womb" and "source." The three "mother" letters define the phonetic parameters or extremes of the alphabet—the three corners of the phonetic triangle: The *alef* is "pure voice," the *mem* "soft voice," and the *shin* "sharp voice." Each of the seven "doubles" possesses two phonetic forms. The "simples" possess only one such form.

Sefer Yetzirah further identifies each letter with a part of the body. In the healing process, meditation on a specific letter draws spiritual energy and healing power into its corresponding limb.

The three "mother" letters correspond to the three primal elements of creation—air, water, and fire—and the three general divisions of the body respectively: chest corresponds to air; abdomen to water; and head to fire.[32]

letter		element of creation	part of body
alef	א	air	chest
mem	מ	water	abdomen
shin	ש	fire	head

The seven "double" letters correspond in the body to the seven "gateways" of the head. Each one serves as a gateway for the senses of sight, hearing, smell, and taste—the sensations of external reality—to enter the consciousness of the soul. Each gateway, when sanctified, serves as a portal through which a Divine gift or blessing can be received, as follows:

letter		gift	gateway of head
beit	ב	wisdom	right eye (sight)
gimel	ג	wealth	right ear (hearing)
dalet	ד	children	right nostril (smell)
kaf	כ	life	left eye (sight)
pei	פ	rule	left ear (hearing)
reish	ר	peace	left nostril (smell)
tav	ת	favor	mouth (taste)

The twelve "simple" letters correspond to twelve basic limbs and organs of the body. Each of these "controls" (often in a most mysterious way, for no overt relationship is apparent) a spiritual sense or talent of the soul, each of which corresponds to one of the twelve tribes of Israel:

letter		Tribe	sense/talent	Limb/organ
hei	ה	Judah	speech, expression	right leg
vav	ו	Issachar	thought, contemplation	right kidney
zayin	ז	Zebulun	walking, progress	left leg
chet	ח	Reuben	sight, perception	right hand
tet	ט	Simon	hearing, understanding	left kidney
yud	י	Gad	action, rectification	left hand
lamed	ל	Ephraim	touching, sexuality	gall bladder
nun	נ	Menasheh	smell, sensitivity	intestines
samech	ס	Benjamin	sleep, dreaming	lower stomach
ayin	ע	Dan	anger, indignation	liver
tzadik	צ	Asher	eating, taste	higher stomach
kuf	ק	Naphtali	laughter, exuberance	spleen

IN SUMMARY

Thus far, we have examined three basic Kabbalistic models that are the foundations of all creation (including, of course, the creation of the human being who was formed in the image of God). As *Sefer Yetzirah* tells us in its very opening sentence:

> With thirty-two wondrous pathways of wisdom, God engraved...and He created His world with three books (*sefarim*): "scribe" (*sofer*), "book" (*sefer*), and "story" (*sipur*).

The three primordial "books" of creation referred to in the first sentence—the "scribe," the "book," and the "story"—correspond to the models of four, of ten and of twenty-two which we have discussed above. The model of four is that of the Name of God, who is the author, or "scribe," of creation. The model of ten is that of the ten *sefirot*, as inscribed in the "book" of creation. (The ten correspond to the ten sayings of creation, the essence of the book of Genesis. They also correspond to the Ten Commandments, the essence of God's entire book, the Torah.) The model of twenty-two is that of the twenty-two letters of the Hebrew alphabet, which relate the "story" of creation.

With these foundational models in mind, we are now ready to look more closely at the human body—its parts, limbs, organs, and systems. To examine the body in detail would take a textbook of hundreds of pages, an undertaking outside the scope of this work. Instead, we will look at a sampling of phenomena that illustrate the mystical correspondences enumerated above, which will lay the groundwork for our subsequent discussion of disease and healing.[33]

2

Mystical Anatomy

One of the most basic teachings of Kabbalah is that every well-defined set of objects possesses the property of "inter-inclusion," appearing as a hologram where each element of the set reflects and manifests all of the others in itself. Based upon this principle, Kabbalah sees in each one of the parts or limbs or organs of the body a reflection and manifestation of the entire body. Indeed, we can now more readily understand the recently revealed biological phenomenon that the genes of each cell of the body encode the entire body.

Keeping this in mind, we will now analyze several parts of the body: the eyes, the fingers and the toes, the tongue and the *brit*, and the mouth.

THE EYE

In Kabbalah, we are taught that the eye is a miniature mirror that reflects the entire human being, both body and soul, as created in the image of God.[1] Our sages compare God's gift of sight ("light") to the eye—to His gift of the soul to the body.[2]

With regard to a bride, our sages say that the beauty of a bride's eyes reflect the beauty of her whole body.[3] True Torah sages, likened to the beautiful eyes of a bride, are called "the eyes of the congregation."[4] In addition to their insight into the Torah and their foresight with regard to worldly events, their unblemished beauty, the infinite depth of personality shining from their own eyes, reflects the innermost beauty of the Jewish people as a whole.

In a similar vein, the Torah speaks of guarding one's most beloved as "guarding the apple of the eye."[5]

The eye possesses four colors that correspond to the four letters of God's essential Name, *Havayah*, as well as to the four legs of the "Divine throne" and of the "Divine chariot" described in the mystical vision of the prophet Ezekiel.[6] These four colors are the white of the eye, the red blood vessels visible in the eye, the color of the iris, and the black pupil of the eye.

White contains, as one, all colors. The white of the eye reflects the initial, all-inclusive point of the *yud* of God's Name. It corresponds to the right axis of the Tree of Life, namely the intellectual property of *chochmah*, the faculty of wisdom or Divine insight, and to its derivative along the right axis, the emotive property of *chesed*, the attribute of lovingkindness. Notably, these are the spiritual attributes of Abraham.

Around and penetrating the white of the eye, wisdom, are tiny but visible red blood vessels.[7]

In his blessing to his twelve sons before his passing, Jacob blessed Judah that his eyes should become red from good wine.[8] From this we understand that wine, which itself is red and is even referred to in the Torah as the "blood of grapes,"⁹ brings out the red in the eyes. The red in the eyes reflects the first *hei* of God's Name and corresponds to the left axis of the Tree of Life, namely, the intellectual property of *binah*, the faculty of understanding or the ability of the soul to meditate on the Divine (the spiritual service described metaphorically in Hassidism as "drinking wine"). The red of the eye also corresponds to the derivative of *binah* along the left axis, the emotive property of *gevurah*, the attribute of might, together with its inner characteristic, the attribute of awe. Notably, these are the spiritual attributes of Isaac.

When we speak of the color of the eye, which distinguishes one individual from another, we refer to the color of the iris. The iris can be blue, brown, or yellow-green, with various shades in between such as hazel, which is a yellow-brown. The particular color of each individual's eyes reflects the *vav* of God's Name and corresponds to the central faculty of the mind, knowledge or *da'at*. The sages teach that it is each individual's *da'at* that distinguishes his or her personality from that of another: "Just as each individual's face is unlike another's, so is each individual's *da'at* unlike another's."¹⁰

Da'at is referred to as the "key" that opens all of the six chambers, i.e., attributes of the heart, including the three emotive properties and the three behavioral properties, collectively known as the *midot*. These in turn correspond to the full spectrum of the colors of the rainbow.

With respect to the particular colors of the iris, the various shades of blue correspond to the emotive and behavioral attributes of the right axis (in contrast to the intellectual faculty situated at the apex of the right axis, *chochmah*—white), *chesed* ("loving-kindness") and *netzach* ("victory"); the various shades of brown correspond to the emotive and behavioral attributes of the left axis (in contrast to the intellectual faculty situated at the apex of the left axis, *binah*—red), *gevurah* ("might") and *hod* ("thanksgiving"); the various shades of yellow-green correspond to the middle axis, *tiferet* ("beauty") and *yesod* ("foundation").[11]

Although *da'at* opens all the chambers of the heart, its major derivative along the middle axis, its primary manifestation in the emotions, is the attribute of *tiferet* (yellow) and its immediate and direct derivative, the attribute of *yesod* (green). In the terminology of the Torah, yellow and green are considered different shades of the same primary color, yellow-green (*yarok*).[12] Yellow is the color of the sun and green is the color of vegetation nourished by the sun's light rays by the process of photosynthesis.

Tiferet ("beauty") is defined in Kabbalah as the harmonious blending of colors. This initially refers to the harmonious blending of *chesed* (blue) and *gevurah* (brown), but in a larger sense means that *tiferet* comprises all the colors. With regard to the color of the iris, then, this means that even the various shades of blue and brown may ultimately be considered shades of yellow-green.[13]

Since the colors of the iris correspond to the *midot*, and the central, all-inclusive *midah* is *tiferet*, the primary color, it follows that the particular color of an individual's eye in a certain sense reflects or suggests the full spectrum of the rainbow.

The spiritual attributes corresponding to the colors of the iris are those of Jacob of whom it is said that "his bed was complete."[14] Jacob's twelve sons, the progenitors of the twelve tribes of Israel, were identified with the complete spectrum of colors. Each tribe possessed its own color, which was displayed on its tribal flag and represented as one of the twelve gems on the breastplate of the High Priest.[15]

Finally, we come to the pupil of the eye, whose color, or rather, absence of color, is black.[16] The pupil is referred to in the Torah idiomatically as the "daughter of the eye," the most precious and guarded part of the eye. In Kabbalah, the "daughter" figure is associated with *malchut* ("kingdom"), the last of the ten *sefirot*. *Malchut*, "possessing nothing of its own,"[17] only that which it receives from above, corresponds to black, the experience of existential lowliness and distance from God, which is *malchut*'s inner characteristic.

This is also the character trait identified with the archetypal soul of *malchut*, King David, who said, "and I shall [always] be lowly in my own eyes."[18]

The power of sight itself emanates from the inner point of the pupil. Sight occurs when external, physical light hits the eye, activating the eye's innate power to emanate its own spiritual light, which then "photographs" the scene of its field of vision.[19]

As in the beginning of creation, light shines in the darkness.[20] The prophet Jeremiah states, "from afar God appears to me."[21] It is from the innermost point of the existential state of feeling "afar" from God (the inner point of the black pupil of the eye) that God's light shines in the eyes of man.

In the next chapter, we will explore a Kabbalistic analysis of Ezekiel's vision of the "dry bones." According to this analysis, the four components of the human body—bones, blood vessels, flesh, and skin—correspond to the four Hebrew letters of God's essential Name, *Havayah*. The fifth, spiritual level that gives life to the body, the spirit—as the verse states, "from four directions, come, O spirit, and blow into these corpses, that they may live"[22]—corresponds to the fifth, transcendent level of God's Name, the upper tip of the *yud*.

As we have seen above, the four colors of the eye correspond to the four letters of God's Name, moreover, since the eye encapsulates the entire physical body and spirit of life, its four colors also correspond to the four components of the human body as follows:

׳ upper tip of *yud*	power of sight	spirit of life
י *yud*	white of eye	bones
ה *hei*	red of eye	blood vessels
ו *vav*	colors of iris	flesh
ה *hei*	black pupil	skin

In the following description of the formation of man, the sages establish the correspondence of the spirit of life to the sight of the eye,[23] as well as that of the father (associated with *chochmah*) to the color white, and that of the mother (associated with *binah*) to the color red:[24]

> There are three partners in [the formation of] man: the Holy One, blessed be He, the father, and the mother.
>
> The father contributes the whiteness, which becomes the bones, the sinews, the nails, the brain in the head, and *the white of the eye.*
>
> The mother contributes the redness, which becomes the blood, the skin, the flesh, the hair, and *the black [pupil] of the eye.*
>
> And the Holy One, blessed be He, contributes the spirit [of life], the soul, the form of the face, *the sight of the eyes*, the hearing of the ears, the speech of the mouth, the raising of the hands, the walking of the legs, understanding, and intellect.[25]

׳ upper tip of *yud*	*keter* "crown"	power of sight	God's light
׳ *yud*	*chochmah* "wisdom"	white of eye	Abraham
ה *hei*	*binah* "understanding"	red of eye	Isaac
ו *vav*	*midot* (and *da'at*) "emotions"	colors of iris	Jacob
ה *hei*	*malchut* "kingdom"	black pupil	David

As stated above, the power of sight emanates from the pupil. This is an instance of the principle that "the end is wedged in the beginning and the beginning in the end."[26]

In order to refine and heal our eyes we must guard them from seeing evil.[27] We must attune our eyesight to seek only the good in the world around us. If evil enters our field of vision, we must be quick to turn our eyes away. Even of God, it is said, "He sees iniquity but does not dwell on it."[28] King David beseeches God in the Book of Psalms, "Turn my eyes away from seeing vanity."[29]

In addition to guarding our eyes from evil, we must always make a conscious effort to focus our eyesight on God's presence before us, as reflected in His providence over us, as it is said, "I place God in front of me always."[30] Ideally, guarding one's eyesight and focusing at all times on God finds its expression in the teaching of the sages that the truly righteous would never look outside the four cubits around them. These four cubits allude to the "four cubits of *halachah*,"[31] which themselves allude, as taught in Kabbalah, to the four letters of the Name *Havayah*.

When studying Torah, one should concentrate and consciously focus his eyesight on the holy letters of the Torah. We are taught that "letters [i.e., looking at the letters in the Torah] make wise."[32] The insight of *chochmah* (especially with regard to the Divine wisdom of the Torah) relates in general to the sight of the eyes.

As we will see later, with regard to the eyes of the physician, the deepest expression of love is through the eyes. Therefore, to heal one's eyes one should always intend to look at all those with whom he comes in contact with love (so much the more with regard to his beloved ones—his spouse, his family, and so on).

Fingers—Tongue; Toes—*Brit*

The Principle of Balance

King David envisions the creation as the working of God's fingers: "When I see Your heavens, the working of Your fingers, the moon and the stars that You have established...."[33]

Certainly, the most evident allusion to the ten *sefirot* in the human body is the ten fingers. Indeed, we find at the beginning of *Sefer Yetzirah*,[34] the first Kabbalistic text:

> The ten ineffable *sefirot* correspond to the ten fingers—five opposite five—and the single covenant[35] is placed in the middle, in the word of the tongue and the circumcision of the *brit*.[36]

Here, we find the first explicit portrayal or tangible model of the ten *sefirot* in Kabbalah.[37] We also find the first presentation of the most fundamental principle of *tikun* ("rectification") in Kabbalah in the qualities of balance and equilibrium.[38] Balance between the right and left axes of the *sefirot* is dependent upon the middle axis of the *sefirot* in general, and upon the faculty of *da'at* ("knowledge") in particular. *Da'at* is the seat of the soul's power of sensitivity.

Physically, sensitivity becomes manifest as the sense of touch in the fingers. In Kabbalah, establishing perfect balance and equilibrium is a function of "touching and not touching," gentle "touching" relating in particular to the innate sensitivity of the five fingers of the right hand and sublime "not touching" relating to the innate sensitivity of the five fingers of the left hand.[39]

(Further on, in our discussion of the healing energy latent in the hands of the physician, we will explain how he must reach the perfect state of balance in his hands, applying the principle of "touching and not touching" in treating his patients.)

Da'at serves to balance the creative tension produced between the two symmetric groups of five *sefirot* each. *Da'at* is able to balance and regulate the two groups of five because it itself subdivides into two categories of five. These two categories of *da'at* are described in Kabbalah as the "two crowns" of *da'at*:

- the "crown of *chasadim*" possesses five levels of *chesed* ("loving-kindness")—the "positive" powers of attraction at the level of mind, corresponding to the five fingers of the right hand;

- the "crown of *gevurot*" possesses five levels of *gevurah* ("might")—the "negative" powers of repulsion at the level of mind, corresponding to the five fingers of the left hand.

"Five Opposite Five"—from Mind to Toes

These two sets of five inherent to *da'at*, "five opposite five," prevail throughout creation. They extend from the mind to permeate the first five emotive and behavioral characteristics of the heart (from *chesed* to *hod*). Each of these five characteristics becomes energized with the vitality necessary to express itself in reality by one *chesed* of *da'at* (positive, attractive force) and one *gevurah* of *da'at* (negative, repellent force).

The reason that only the first five of the six characteristics of the heart described above need to be individually energized by the *chasadim* and *gevurot* of *da'at*, and not the sixth, is that the first five are particular, individual attributes of the heart. By contrast, the sixth, *yesod*, is the comprehensive sense of equilibrium and balance—"foundation" (i.e., a sense of being grounded)—which concentrates and fuses the five particular attributes that precede it into one holistic experience.

From the heart, these ten individual forces—five and five—extend to manifest themselves, physically, in the five fingers of the right hand (corresponding to the five *chasadim* of *da'at*) and the five fingers of the left hand (corresponding to the five *gevurot* of *da'at*). The energies descend in the body to manifest once more, at the very extremity of the body, in the five toes of the right foot and five toes of the left foot.

Thus, there are four levels of manifestation of the five *chasadim* and five *gevurot* of *da'at*: in their origin in the mind, in the heart, in the fingers, and in the toes. The first two of these levels, in the mind and in the heart, are concealed, while the latter two levels, in the fingers and toes, are revealed. This, then, suggests that these four levels of manifestation may be seen to correspond to the four letters of the Name *Havayah*.

The mind corresponds to the *yud* of the Name, which, in particular, relates to *chochmah*, as is said, "*chochmah* is the mind."[40] Likewise, the heart corresponds to the first *hei* of the Name, which, in particular, relates to *binah*, as is said, "*binah* is the heart."[40] The fingers correspond to the *vav* of the Name, which, in particular, relates to the *midot*, seen as extensions of *tiferet*. The toes correspond to the latter *hei* of the Name, which, in particular, relates to *malchut*; they are extensions of the feet, the lowest part of the body (the contact point of the body to the earth), which are often seen to signify *malchut*.

י *yud*	*chochmah*	five mental attractive forces and five mental repellent forces	mind
ה *hei*	*binah*	these forces as they permeate the attributes of the heart	heart
ו *vav*	*midot*	these forces as they find physical expression in the hands	fingers
ה *hei*	*malchut*	these forces as they find physical expression in the feet	toes

As the ten *chasadim* and *gevurot* of *da'at* become manifest at four distinct levels, we have, in total, forty forces, twenty attractive forces and twenty repellent forces, the first two sets of ten manifest spiritually (in the mind and heart) and the latter two sets of ten manifest physically (in the fingers and toes). These forty individual forces correspond to the forty days of the giving of the Torah to Moses—the personification of *da'at*—on Mt. Sinai.[41] The Ten Commandments were engraved on two tablets—"five opposite five," as we shall see.

How the *Sefirot* divide into "Five opposite Five"

In Hebrew, each one of the fingers possesses an individual name: the thumb is *agudal*; the index finger is *etzba*; the middle finger is *amah*; the ring finger is *kemitzah*; the little finger is *zeret*. The name of the thumb, *agudal*, derives from the word for "greatness" (*gedulah*), a synonym in Kabbalah for "loving-kindness" (*chesed*), as in the verse from the Book of Chronicles[42] that explicitly enumerates the five attributes of the heart (the remaining four fingers corresponding to the four subsequent attributes):

To you, O God, are the greatness [loving-kindness], and the might, and the beauty, and the victory, and the glory, for all is in heaven and earth.

left hand	gevurot	chasadim	right hand
agudal thumb	repellent force of *chesed*	attractive force of *chesed*	*agudal* thumb
etzba index finger	repellent force of *gevurah*	attractive force of *gevurah*	*etzba* index finger
amah middle finger	repellent force of *tiferet*	attractive force of *tiferet*	*amah* middle finger
kemitzah ring finger	repellent force of *netzach*	attractive force of *netzach*	*kemitzah* ring finger
zeret little finger	repellent force of *hod*	attractive force of *hod*	*zeret* little finger

Furthermore, we are taught in Kabbalah that the five *chasadim* and five *gevurot* of *da'at* correspond to the ten *sefirot*—for *da'at*, whose inner essence is the power of "unification," which unites the intellectual faculties of the mind and unites the mind with the heart, crystallizes in itself all of the ten *sefirot*. These can be seen to divide into two groups of five in two distinct fashions:

- the first five, more spiritually oriented *sefirot* (from *keter* to *gevurah*) are considered "right" relative to the latter five, more physically oriented *sefirot* (from *tiferet* to *malchut*);
- the five *sefirot* of *keter*, *chochmah*, *chesed*, *tiferet*, and *netzach* all tend to the right, the *chesed* principle, whereas the five *sefirot* of *binah*, *gevurah*, *hod*, *yesod*, and *malchut* all tend to the left, the *gevurah* principle. (The middle axis of the *sefirot* is seen to descend diagonally, from right to left, placing its two higher *sefirot*, *keter* and *tiferet*, to the right, and its two lower *sefirot*, *yesod* and *malchut*, to the left.)

According to the first scheme, we have:

Chapter Two: Mystical Anatomy

left hand	gevurot
agudal thumb	tiferet "beauty"
etzba index finger	netzach "victory"
amah middle finger	hod "thanksgiving"
kemitzah ring finger	yesod "foundation"
zeret little finger	malchut "kingdom"

chasadim	right hand
keter "crown"	agudal thumb
chochmah "wisdom"	etzba index finger
binah "understanding"	amah middle finger
chesed "loving-kindness"	kemitzah ring finger
gevurah "might"	zeret little finger

According to the second scheme, we have:

left hand	gevurot
agudal thumb	binah "understanding"
etzba index finger	gevurah "might"
amah middle finger	hod "thanksgiving"
kemitzah ring finger	yesod "foundation"
zeret little finger	malchut "kingdom"

chasadim	right hand
keter "crown"	agudal thumb
chochmah "wisdom"	etzba index finger
chesed "loving-kindness"	amah middle finger
tiferet "beauty"	kemitzah ring finger
netzach "victory"	zeret little finger

The Tablets of the Covenant

As noted above, *Sefer Yetzirah*'s model of the ten *sefirot* as "five opposite five" finds its most significant expression in the two tablets of the covenant given to Moses at Mt. Sinai, upon which were engraved the Ten Commandments.

The Ten Commandments are the foundation of all of the 613 commandments of the Torah, which divide into positive, attractive forces—the 248 active commandments (the *do's*, each of which entails a spiritual, attractive force toward good)—and negative, repellent forces—the 365 prohibitive commandments (the *don't's*, each of which entails a spiritual, repellent force away from evil). In general, the five *chasadim* of *da'at* motivate the performance of the active commandments, while the five *gevurot* of *da'at* fortify the soul to refrain from wrongdoing and thereby observe the prohibitive commandments.

The tablets are called "the tablets of the covenant," alluding to the "single covenant," situated between the "five opposite five." The higher covenant of "the word of the tongue" corresponds to the *sefirah* of *da'at* above the five *sefirot* from *chesed* to *hod*. The lower covenant of "the circumcision of the *brit*" corresponds to the *sefirah* of *yesod*, the sixth of the characteristics of the heart, which concentrates and fuses the five *sefirot* above it into one, holistic experience. *Yesod*, the unifying power in the heart, reflects *da'at*, the unifying power in the mind. Implicit in the two tablets of the covenant are these two covenants.

Procreation

Da'at and *yesod* are alluded to by the word "all" in the above verse from the Book of Chronicles: "for *all* is in heaven and earth." "All" in heaven above (in the soul, the mind) refers to *da'at*, the power that concentrates all the intellectual faculties and connects them to the heart; "all" on earth below (in the soul, the heart) refers to *yesod*, the power that concentrates all the emotive and behavioral attributes and connects them to *malchut*, the ultimate reality of "earth" below.

Significantly, the average numerical value of the two words *da'at* (474) and *yesod* (80) is the same as that of the word for "seed" (*zera*, 277). The procreative seed of new life is drawn from *da'at* to *yesod*. Indeed, the *brit* of *yesod* cannot be actualized without being aroused by the power of *da'at*.[43]

In Kabbalah, we are taught that the six days of creation correspond to the six emotive attributes of the heart. Adam was created on the sixth day and was intended to be the "righteous one, the foundation (*yesod*) of the world."[44] The very essence of human existence is to "balance" and thereby rectify all of reality. For this reason the human being, and only the human being among all creation, was given the power of *da'at*.

Adam was told to "be fruitful and multiply and fill the earth."[45] As noted above, in our discussion of eye-color, the sages teach us that there are "three partners in man: the Holy One, blessed be He, the father, and the mother." The father and the mother each contribute five properties to their child. The father provides: (1) the bones, (2) the sinews, (3) the nails, (4) the brain, and (5) the white of the eyes. The mother provides: (1) the blood, (2) the flesh, (3) the hair, (4) the skin and (5) the black of the eyes. God contributes an additional ten properties, including the soul.

From this model, we may infer that the five *chasadim* represented by the five fingers of the right hand correspond to the five contributions of the father (the five *chasadim* of *da'at* derive from the "father"-image in Kabbalah) and that the five *gevurot* of the left hand correspond to the five contributions of the mother (as the five *gevurot* of *da'at* derive from the "mother"-image in Kabbalah). The "single covenant" that is placed in the middle is the gift of God, the soul of life.[46]

We are able to create new life only when we reach the age of puberty, when we first receive the faculty of *da'at*. Furthermore, *yesod* itself is stimulated to awaken only through the force of *da'at*, as noted above. As *da'at* is the seat of all the senses of the soul, it arouses sensitivity in general, and the sensitivity of *yesod* in particular.

The Sense of Touch and the Higher and Lower Unions

Just as there are the five physical senses of sight, hearing, smell, taste, and touch, so are there five corresponding spiritual senses of sight, hearing, smell, taste, and touch (as experienced in a meditative or dream state). The five spiritual senses correspond to the five fingers of the right hand, while the five physical senses correspond to the five fingers of the left hand. All proceed from and are aroused by *da'at*, including the sense of touch—the kiss of the tongue and the conjunction of marital union—and it is *da'at* that serves to balance and unite all in the experience of the Divine.

This is aptly demonstrated in *gematria*.[47] As enumerated in the *Mishnah*,[48] each hand possesses 30 bones— 14 revealed joints and 16 concealed joints. These are 30 of the 248 bones that compose the skeleton and correspond to the 248 positive commandments. Together, the two hands possess 60 bones, corresponding to the 60 Hebrew letters of the Priestly Blessing:

> *May God bless you and protect you.*
> *May God shine His countenance upon you and be gracious to you.*
> *May God turn His countenance toward you and grant you peace.*[49]

The priests recite this blessing with their hands raised (the blessing itself is referred to as "the raising of the palms"). The light of the 60 letters emanates from the 60 bones of the two hands.[50]

The letter *lamed*, whose numerical value is 30, represents the 30 bones of each hand. The two *lamed*'s of the two hands, when facing each other, form an image of the heart. The word for "heart" (*lev*) is spelled *lamed beit*—*beit* signifying "two"—thus implying "two *lamed*'s."[51]

The heart, which is "in the middle" of the two hands, ascends to express itself in the "word of the tongue" and descends to express itself in the "circumcision of the *brit*."[52]

In Kabbalah, the right hand is called "the great hand"[53] and the left hand is called "the strong hand."[54] The body itself is in the middle, between the two hands, and is aroused by their union as in two hands clapping; this is why the body is called the "middle hand" or "uplifted hand."[55] The power of the "uplifted hand" is to ascend, thereby elevating the emotive attributes of the heart to the inner consciousness and perception of the mind, which finds expression in the covenant of the "word of the tongue."

The "five fingers" of the "uplifted hand" are, in fact, the five phonetic origins of speech in the mouth:

1. the throat (from which emerge the four letters *alef, hei, chet,* and *ayin*),
2. the palate (from which emerge the four letters *gimel, yud, kaf,* and *kuf*),
3. the tongue (from which emerge the five letters *dalet, tet, lamed, nun, tav*),
4. the teeth (from which emerge the five letters *zayin, samech, tzadik, reish, shin*), and
5. the lips (from which emerge the four letters *beit, vav, mem,* and *pei*).

(As we shall see, the mouth also contains all of the ten *sefirot*—with the tongue corresponding to the middle axis of *da'at, tiferet,* and *yesod*. Thus, it is clear why the tongue in particular, represents the "single covenant" in the mouth.)

The five phonetic origins of speech in the mouth together with the ten fingers of the hands equal 15. These are the 15 "fingers" of the "three hands"—"the great hand," "the strong hand," and "the uplifted hand." Relative to the mouth (which possesses five origins of speech), the *brit* is singular in the sense that it possesses one origin of procreative energy. This 1 together with the 10 toes of the feet equal 11.

We thus see how the "higher union" and "lower union" of God's Name *Havayah* is most beautifully reflected by the human model portrayed in *Sefer Yetzirah*. The "higher union" appears in the first two letters of the Name *Havayah* (*yud*, *hei*), which equal 15. The "lower union" appears in the last two letters of the Name *Havayah* (*vav*, *hei*) which equal 11.

In Kabbalah, the "higher union" is referred to as the "union of kissing," while the "lower union" is referred to as the "union of body." In the supernal worlds, the "higher union of kissing"[56] gives birth to angels[57] (which are without bodies), while the "lower union of body" gives birth to souls (that enter physical bodies).[58]

The tongue and the *brit* are the body's two essential points of "intercourse"—that is, they are the two primary energy centers or contact points, situated along the middle line of the body. In Kabbalah, the energy issued from each of these centers or contact points merges with that of one's soul-mate to procreate. The power to procreate physically issues from the lower of these points, while the power to procreate spiritually (i.e., to give birth to energies that can surface as ideas or impulses, or, in the higher spiritual worlds, to give birth to angels) issues from the higher point of the mouth and tongue.

We are further taught in Kabbalah that there exists an additional energy center/contact point—the middle point of the chest, the contact point of "embrace." This point, relative to the points above and below it, represents an intermediate level of connective energy—more material than that of the point above it, yet more spiritual than that of the point below it.[59]

Kabbalah teaches that meditative practice—the soul's spiritual endeavor to contact and become one with God—is similar to the physical union of soul-mates. Physical union begins from the middle point, the point of embrace, ascends to the higher point, the kiss, and finally descends to the lower point, the actual state of cleaving to one's beloved to become one. (As the Book of Genesis states: "And he shall cleave to his wife and they shall become one flesh."[60])

Two Levels of *Da'at*

As we saw above, the balancing power of the soul is manifest in the secret of the "single covenant," which appears at two levels—in the tongue (to balance the ten fingers), the faculty of *da'at*, and in the *brit* (to balance the ten toes), the attribute of *yesod*. On a deeper level, these two covenants correspond to the two levels of *da'at* itself—*da'at elyon* ("higher *da'at*") and *da'at tachton* ("lower *da'at*)."

Da'at elyon is the perspective of all of created reality from a vantage point from "above." From this perspective, the Creator Himself is the one and only true essence of all being, and reality is perceived as having no independent existence outside its Creator. *Da'at tachton* is creation's perspective of its Creator from its vantage point "below," that is, from within created reality. From this perspective, creation recognizes the existence of its Creator but is unable to truly know Him.

Of all the leaders of the Jewish people, it was Moses, the greatest of all men, who fully united and integrated the two levels of *da'at*. In the Torah, he is called "the man of God,"[61] which is interpreted by the sages[62] as follows:

- "from mid-point and above [he was] God," meaning that he had the power to perceive reality through the "eyes" of God;

- "from mid-point and below [he was] man," meaning that he had the power to humbly know God, man's Creator, through the eyes of man.

Furthermore, it is said of Moses that "the *Shechinah* [Divine Presence] speaks through the throat of Moses."[63] From this we learn that the external expression of *da'at elyon* is through "the words of the tongue," especially in speaking words of Torah in general and revealing the inner mysteries of the Torah in particular.

The external expression of *da'at tachton* is through the union of husband and wife, as referred to in the original union of man and woman: "and Adam *knew* Eve, his wife."[64] The modesty necessary in the union of husband and wife reflects our inability to know the Creator's essence,[65] especially at that very moment in which we most emulate our Creator—the moment of creating new life.

Thus, we can see how the tongue and the *brit*, the two manifestations of the "single covenant" which represents the union of God and humanity, are interrelated in essence, both emanating from *da'at*.

We may further infer that their rectification is also interdependent. The rectification of the faculty of speech (to speak only good and sweet words) and the guarding of the covenant of the *brit* (to express only true love for one's spouse in marital relations) depend upon and influence one another. For this reason, the two terms—"the word [*milah*] of the tongue" and "the circumcision [*milah*] of the *brit*"—are the same.

Three Stages of Spiritual Growth

The Ba'al Shem Tov links these concepts to the vision of the prophet Ezekiel. This vision, which encompasses the first chapter of the Book of Ezekiel, is considered the most mystical passage of the Bible:

> *And I saw, and behold, a stormy wind came out of the north,*
> *a great cloud, and a flashing fire,*
> *and a translucent glow surrounded it,*
> *and out of the midst of it, out of the midst of the fire,*
> *was something like the* chashmal.[66]

The Hebrew word *chashmal* appears only in the context of this vision,[67] and is understood by tradition to be a type of light or energy that is also personified as a specific type of angel. The word is a compound of the words *chash*, meaning "silent" and *mal*, meaning "speaking." Therefore, these angels are said to be "sometimes silent, sometimes speaking."[68]

Between the two extremes of silence and speech, Kabbalah identifies a third, intermediary stage. The allusion to this stage is in the double meaning of the second syllable, *mal*, which can also be translated as "circumcision." We thus have three stages: silence, circumcision, and speech.

The Ba'al Shem Tov then connects these three stages with his three-stage process of spiritual growth, called "submission," "separation," and "sweetening." We can chart these correspondences as follows:

chash	silence	submission
mal	circumcision	separation
mal	speech	sweetening

The first stage of spiritual growth—*chash* or "silence"—is also alluded to in the opening sentences of *Sefer Yetzirah* (segments of which were quoted above):

> With thirty-two wondrous pathways of wisdom, God engraved...and He created His world with three books: "scribe," "book," and "story." [These are] the ten ineffable *sefirot* and the twenty-two letters of foundation.... The ten ineffable *sefirot* correspond to the ten fingers—five opposite five—and the single covenant is placed in the middle, in the word of the tongue and the circumcision of the *brit*.

The root of the word for "ineffable" or "unutterable" (*blimah*) is subsequently used in *Sefer Yetzirah* in the phrase, "*shut* [*belom*] your mouth from speaking," thus referring to the phase of silence (*chash*). We can discern from this that in order to proceed on a path of spiritual growth we must first meditate in silence on the mysteries of the "ten ineffable *sefirot"* and then actualize the potential of our lower (human-like) *da'at* and our higher (God-like) *da'at*.

HIGHER AND LOWER WORLDS

The higher and lower *da'at* further correspond to the higher and lower worlds, which are also alluded to in the opening of *Sefer Yetzirah*:

- the ten fingers correspond to the ten *sefirot* of the world of *Atzilut*,[69] the higher world, whose consciousness is exclusively that of *da'at elyon*;
- the ten toes correspond to the ten *sefirot* of the world of *Beriah*, the lower world, whose consciousness is that of *da'at tachton*.

These twenty elements of the human body, together with the two balance-points—the tongue and the *brit*—are associated with the twenty-two Hebrew letters, as we can see by drawing the following representation, in which the tongue is above the ten fingers and the *brit* is above the ten toes:

Chapter Two: Mystical Anatomy

The two letters that correspond to the "single covenant," manifest at its two levels, are *alef* and *lamed*. These two letters combine to form the two-letter Name of God, pronounced *Kel*. This Name appears in the song of Hannah with reference to the two levels of *da'at*: "for GOD is a God [*Kel*] of [two levels of] knowledge."[70]

Hannah, who was barren for many years, had prayed silently to conceive a son, whom she promised to dedicate to God's service. When she finally conceived and gave birth to the prophet Samuel, she sang this song of thanksgiving.

Hannah's song is the Biblical source for the existence of the two levels of *da'at* described above. These two levels are alluded to in the two letters of God's Name *Kel* as portrayed above:

- *Alef* corresponds to the intuitive wisdom and insight of the mind, as it is written: "I will teach you [*aalefcha*] wisdom."[71]

- *Lamed* corresponds to the emotive power of the heart, for the letter *lamed* represents the "heart" (*lev*) throughout the Torah, as we saw earlier.[72]

Thus, we learn that the inner insight of the mind (the consciousness of *da'at elyon*) finds its external expression in the tongue, whereas the inner emotion of the heart (the consciousness of *da'at tachton*) finds its external expression in the *brit*.

When the hands are raised—as in the recitation of the Priestly Blessing—the tongue that blesses is situated between the ten fingers. When the hands are lowered, it is the *brit* that is between the ten fingers.[73]

It was stated above that *da'at elyon* serves to balance the ten fingers (the ten *sefirot* of the world of *Atzilut*) and that *da'at tachton* serves to balance the ten toes (the ten *sefirot* of the world of *Beriah*). However, when the fingers are lowered, we now see that it is *da'at tachton* (the covenant of the *brit*) that balances the ten fingers. This teaches us that the union of the supernal *sefirot* of *Atzilut* gives birth to the consciousness of *da'at tachton* in *Beriah* and below.

Furthermore, there is also a relation between *da'at elyon* (the tongue) and the lower worlds (the toes): the Divine service of souls in the lower worlds reveals, ultimately, *da'at elyon* on earth.

Moreover, *da'at elyon* and *da'at tachton* of the tongue and the *brit* at times invert. The emotions of the heart find their expression in the words of the tongue. The seminal essence of the mind contracts into the seed of the *brit*.[74] Ultimately, the revelation of the Divine essence on earth depends upon

Chapter Two: Mystical Anatomy 61

the rectification and sanctification of "the circumcision of the *brit*."

To summarize our discussion thus far, let us quote the end of *Sefer Yetzirah*,[75] which summarizes the content of the entire book:

> These are the twenty-two letters with which [ten Names of God] were engraved. And with them He made the three books and with them He created His Universe…and when our father Abraham of blessed memory came, he looked and observed, and understood and studied, and engraved and carved; he succeeded in creation…. Immediately, the Master of All, blessed be His Name forever, revealed Himself to him, and seated him in His bosom and kissed him on his head and called him "Abraham, the one who loves Me." And He made a covenant with him and his seed forever…. And He made a covenant between the ten fingers—the covenant of the tongue, and between the ten toes—the covenant of circumcision. And He bound the twenty-two letters of the Torah to his tongue and revealed to him His secret. He drew them with water, ignited them with fire, blasted them with wind, burned them with seven, and led them with twelve constellations.

As we see, the ending of *Sefer Yetzirah* returns to its opening. This phenomenon of making a full circle is described in *Sefer Yetzirah* itself (as noted above): "Its end is wedged in its beginning."

The Talmud[76] mirrors this concept when it declares that "all goes after the seal": the final statement of a Torah text encapsulates the entire content of the text, while especially relating to its beginning (which as well contains the essential seed of all to follow).

The all-inclusive power of the beginning itself reflects the principle of *da'at elyon* (since the term "higher" [*elyon*] in Hebrew also implies "earlier," in the sense of "beginning"), the higher covenant of the tongue. The all-inclusive power of the end corresponds to *da'at tachton* (since "lower" [*tachton*] implies "later," in the sense of "end"), the lower covenant of circumcision.

This relates to the fact that in the Book of Genesis, the covenant that God made with Abraham had two stages or manifestations:

1. the first was the "covenant between the pieces," in which God promised Abraham and his descendants the entire Land of Israel;[77]
2. the second was the covenant of circumcision, in which God promised Abraham that he would become the father of many nations.[78]

The first, "higher" covenant, the spiritual power of the Jewish people to inherit the Promised Land, "the land of the living,"[79] depends upon the articulation of the words of the Torah.[80] The tongue is situated between the ten fingers of the hands, which represent the ability "to do." Thus, the relationship of tongue to fingers is seen to reflect the principle of studying the words of the Torah in order to behave according to its teachings.

The second, "lower" covenant, that of circumcision, is situated between the ten toes, which represent the ability which children inherit from their parents, to continue along their path. Thus, the relationship of circumcision to toes is seen to reflect the parents' firm commitment to educate their offspring to follow along their positive path of life.

After describing the two manifestations of the single covenant as given to Abraham, *Sefer Yetzirah* concludes by reviewing the basic secrets and groupings of the twenty-two letters of the Hebrew alphabet, which it had previously described as "bound one to the other."[81] The power that binds them all together is the power of the "one" above the twenty-two. The absolute "one" both encompasses the twenty-two from above and permeates them from within.

These two manifestations of the "one," as transcendent (*sovev kol almin*) and as immanent (*memalei kol almin*), also correspond to the two manifestations of the single covenant, the hovering spirit that issues from the tongue and the essential seed that is drawn by the *brit*.[82]

The Single Covenant	
word of the tongue	*brit*
da'at elyon	*da'at tachton*
"covenant of the pieces," promise of the Land of Israel	covenant of circumcision, promise of many descendants
manifestation of "one" as transcendent	manifestation of "one" as immanent

Tongue (social intercourse) and *brit* (marital intercourse) are two manifestations of the one concept of covenant. When we connect, in covenant, to God, by correct speech and correct use of our procreative organs as defined in Jewish law, we are sound and healthy.[83] With connection comes stability and vitality. Severance of the bond of love to God (His Torah, His people, and His land), by incorrect use of our tongue and *brit*, creates imbalance in our psychological and physiological systems.[84] Healing power comes with the reinforcement of the consciousness of the "single covenant."

The Mouth

Our analysis of the mouth is based on the following correlations:

left axis	middle axis	right axis
binah "understanding" **throat**		*chochmah* "wisdom" **palate**
	da'at "knowledge" **tongue, back of**	
gevurah "might" **lower jaw/teeth**		*chesed* "loving-kindness" **upper jaw/teeth**
	tiferet "beauty" **tongue, length of**	
hod "thanksgiving" **lower lip**		*netzach* "victory" **upper lip**
	yesod "foundation" **tongue, tip of**	
	malchut "kingdom" **oral cavity**	

In the mouth, the palate corresponds to the *sefirah* of *chochmah* ("wisdom"). Just as the inner eye of wisdom experiences new flashes of insight, so do the taste buds of the palate, on the inner spiritual plane, experience new tastes of truth. (The taste buds of the tongue integrate the taste of truth to influence one's character.) In Psalms we read, "Taste and see that God is good."[85] The very word *chochmah* is read in Kabbalah as *cheich-mah*, "the palate of the sublime."

Just as the palate is the lower extension or reflection of the brain, generally identified with *chochmah*, so is the throat understood to be the higher extension or reflection of the heart, generally identified with *binah* ("understanding").[86] The throat is thus understood to be the *binah* of the mouth. In Kabbalah, we speak of the union of the palate and the throat, reflecting the supernal union of *chochmah* and *binah*[87] in the mouth.

The tongue, which in the mouth corresponds to the middle axis of the *sefirot*, possesses three "centers of energy": its back, its length, and its tip, corresponding to the three *sefirot* along the middle axis: *da'at*, ("knowledge") *tiferet*, ("beauty") and *yesod* ("foundation").

At the back of the tongue, where the tongue is attached to the throat, lies its power to connect—the point of *da'at*. Of this point it is said, "if there is no *da'at* there is no *binah*; if there is no *binah* there is no *da'at*."[88]

The length of the tongue itself corresponds to the *sefirah* of *tiferet* ("beauty"). Here lies the power of "language" or "tongue." In the tongue lies the beauty of self-expression, the eloquent blend of rich vocabulary.

The tip of the tongue corresponds to the *sefirah* of *yesod* ("foundation"), the holy covenant in the mouth. Of this oral energy center it is said, "the covenant of the tongue corresponds to the covenant of the flesh [i.e., the *brit*]."⁸⁹ We have addressed at length this correspondence of tongue to *brit* above.

At its tip, the tongue touches, as it were, the empty cavity of the mouth itself. The oral cavity is indeed the essence of the mouth, for as the mouth in general corresponds to the *sefirah* of *malchut* ("kingdom"), the empty vessel that receives the lights of all the higher *sefirot*, so, in the detailed analysis of the mouth, the cavity is its own particular level of *malchut*, the very end of the middle axis of the *sefirot*. The touching of the tip of the tongue to the mouth's cavity is thus an analog to the marital union of husband and wife, *yesod* and *malchut*.

The upper and lower jaws with their two rows of teeth correspond to the two *sefirot* of *chesed* ("loving-kindness") and *gevurah* ("might"). Chewing food is like processing an idea to make it digestible. This process depends upon the two primary emotive attributes of the soul. *Chesed* motivates the desire of the soul to "integrate" the sparks present in external reality, to elevate the Divine life-force contained within the food to enliven man, while *gevurah* performs the actual grinding of the teeth, breaking the food into digestible particles, of which is said, "*malchut* [in our context, the mouth] is built [made able to perform its function to eat] out of *gevurah*."⁹⁰

Similar to the upper and lower jaws and teeth, the upper and lower lips correspond to the two *sefirot* of *netzach* ("victory") and *hod* ("thanksgiving"). These guard the entrance to the mouth from the outside.⁹¹ In addition, the lips—through a kiss—serve to convey an expression of the soul deeper than words. In a kiss, they join the tip of the tongue to form the union of the triplet *netzach-hod-yesod* within the mouth.[92]

In the Torah, we find that disease results from the misuse of the mouth: incorrect eating[93] and incorrect speaking.[94] The Torah defines the parameters of what is permissible (spiritually and physically healthy) to eat and what is permissible and proper to speak.

With regard to speech, we find in the Book of Proverbs that "death and life are in the hand of the tongue."[95] As we have seen, it is the tongue in particular that connects the three levels—the intellectual, the emotive, and the behavioral—all within the mouth itself, as the middle axis.

In the previous section, we saw that the tongue corresponds to *da'at elyon*. When rectified, the tongue is able to express the concept that God is the one and only true reality; when blemished, it gives expression only to one's own ego. When rectified, it is the tongue that, by speaking words of Torah and expressing love for others, conveys the healing, life-giving power inherent in the Divine soul to the physical body as a whole.

3

Mystical Physiology

THE VISION OF EZEKIEL

In one of the visions of Ezekiel,[1] the prophet finds himself in valley full of "dry bones." He is commanded to prophesy over the bones that they should hear the word of God and live:

> *So said God to these bones,*
> *"Behold, I shall bring spirit into you and you shall live.*
> *And I shall place blood vessels on you*
> *and raise flesh upon you, and cover you with skin.*
> *And I shall breathe spirit into you and you shall live,*
> *and you shall know that I am God."*

Ezekiel watches as, incredibly, the bones come together and become covered with blood vessels, flesh, and skin. "But there was no breath in them." Ezekiel is again commanded to prophesy:

> *Thus says God:*
> *"Come from four directions, come, O spirit,*
> *and blow into these corpses, that they may live."*

Finally, the corpses come to life and Ezekiel finds standing before him "a very large army...the whole House of Israel," whom God promises to bring back to its rightful home.

In Ezekiel's vision, which alludes to the resurrection of the dead at the End of Days, we find a four-level depiction of the body—bones, blood vessels, flesh, and skin—and a fifth, spiritual level that gives life to the body, the spirit. The model most fitting for a comparative analysis of this structure, implied in the phrase "come from four directions, O spirit," is God's four-letter essential Name *Havayah*, which we discussed earlier.

The bones, blood vessels, flesh, and skin correspond to the four letters of the Divine Name, with the upper tip of the *yud* corresponding to the fifth, transcendent level of the spirit.[2]

The first letter of the Divine Name, *yud*, alludes to the seminal, essential point of consciousness, inasmuch as the form of the letter *yud* is the most compact of all the Hebrew letters, serving as their structural core. The letter *yud* of the Name *Havayah* corresponds to *chochmah*, the seminal essence of created reality, as it is written, "You made them all with *chochmah*."[3] Thus, the *yud* may be seen as the seed of life. Similarly, the bones may be seen as the body's self-regenerating seed, as blood cells are produced in the bone marrow. Indeed, the word for "bone marrow" in Hebrew is the same as that for "brain" (*mo'ach*), the seat of *chochmah*, as it is said, "*chochmah* is the brain."[4]

The skeletal system, the most basic frame of the body, supports all the additional physiological systems—such as the muscular system, the circulatory system, the nervous system, etc.—that are layered upon it. This is alluded to by the fact that the word for "bone" (*etzem*) also means "self" or "essence," that is, the core of one's being.

The second letter of the Divine Name, *hei*, is visualized in Kabbalah as a three-dimensional letter—with the two attached sides projecting length and width, while the third dimension is suggested in the detached foot that we are taught to imagine as a line running through the page, thus manifesting the dimension of depth. Overall, the letter *hei* refers to expansion, in all three dimensions of the physical body, starting from the point of essence, which here is seen as the skeletal system. In spiritual terms, *hei* corresponds to *binah*, the understanding in the heart that spreads out to animate the entire body and to motivate its myriad functions. Thus, physically, the first *hei* of God's Name reflects the circulatory system, which can be described as the basic inner communication of life-force within the body. The circulatory system provides all the limbs and organs of the body with a sense of togetherness and interdependence—"we are all part of the same organism"—and is thus the body's internal "understanding" of self.

The third letter of the Divine Name, *vav*, refers to the basic emotive characteristics—the *midot*—of which there are six, the numerical equivalent of the letter *vav*. (The *vav* most particularly corresponds to *tiferet*, which, as we saw in chapter 1, signifies the torso, the "trunk" of the body.) One's character attributes relative to one's understanding are like the flesh that fills out the body, which in turn is filled with and enclothes the blood vessels. In terms of consciousness, the flesh signifies our normative self-awareness, the way we normally feel ourselves (in contrast to the skeleton and circulatory system, which signify our relationship to our inner core and motivations).

The fourth letter of the Divine Name, the final *hei*, refers to the skin, the most exterior layer and outer clothing of the body. Skin serves as the body's sensor and protector and is responsible for the body's surface appearance, thus fittingly serving as the "kingdom" (*malchut*) of the four general divisions of the body. *Malchut* is termed "the revealed world," the way things appear.

Whenever this four-level system is used to contemplate existence, there is always a fifth, higher and all-inclusive level that animates the other four. This fifth level is seen as the source of existence, and in the case of the body is the spirit of life, which comes to breathe life into all the other levels. Similarly, the *sefirah* of *keter*, the all-inclusive source of all the other *sefirot*, is referred to as "the source of life."[5]

׳ upper tip of *yud*	*keter* "crown"	spirit of life	source of existence
י *yud*	*chochmah* "wisdom"	bones	inner core of self
ה *hei*	*binah* "understanding"	blood vessels	inner motivations
ו *vav*	*midot* six "emotive attributes"	flesh	normative self-awareness
ה *hei*	*malchut* "kingdom"	skin	exterior protection

The Physiological Systems of the Body

Open any basic text of human physiology and you will find the functions of the body divided into systems such as: the nervous system, the respiratory system, the circulatory system, the digestive system, the reproductive system, etc. And so it is from the viewpoint of Kabbalah.

As we have seen above, an analysis of the body using the basic model of the Name *Havayah*, based on the vision of Ezekiel, allows us a glimpse into the spiritual connections for the respiratory system (spirit or breath of life), the skeletal system (bones), the circulatory system (blood vessels), the muscular system (flesh), and the protective system of the skin.

From this basic analysis of the body, we can proceed to a more detailed analysis in which each of the ten properties of the soul relates explicitly to a physiological system in the body.[6]

left axis	middle axis	right axis
	keter "crown" **respiratory system**	
binah "understanding" **blood**		*chochmah* "wisdom" **bone marrow**
	da'at "knowledge" **nervous system**	
gevurah "might" **circulatory system**		*chesed* "loving-kindness" **skeletal system**
	tiferet "beauty" **muscular system**	
hod "thanksgiving" **immune system**		*netzach* "victory" **endocrine system**
	yesod "foundation" **reproductive system**	
	ateret hayesod source of *malchut* **skin**	
	malchut "kingdom" **digestive system**	

The first property, that of the *keter*, the superconscious "crown," corresponds to the respiratory system, the physical conduit through which the spirit of life enters the body.

When God created Adam, He "formed man of the dust of the ground, and breathed into his nostrils the breath of life."[7] Thus, we learn that the breath of life comes from God on high, the source of all life. In breathing, we internalize that which is exterior to us; we inhale from that which is above us.

The Hebrew word for "inhaling" (*she'ifah*) also means "aspiration." Thus, breathing is an expression of the soul's innate desire to ascend and go beyond its conscious self into the realm of its super-conscious link to God, as experienced in its super-rational faith, pleasure, and will.

Thus, a lack of pleasure and will in life (reflecting a lack of faith in the Divine purpose of life) may well result in dysfunction of the respiratory system. One should attempt to "breathe" into his being newly inspired aspiration to live.

Chochmah ("wisdom") corresponds to the bone marrow. Major medical research now regards bone marrow as a system in its own right. As stated above, bone marrow is responsible for producing blood cells—the most basic biological unit in the body. Just as every aspect of the body depends on the bone marrow, so too, all of existence depends on *chochmah*, as King David teaches us: "[God,] You have made all [of Your creations] with wisdom."[8]

A lack of insightfulness may indicate a weak bone-marrow system. The answer lies in the devoted study of the inner dimension of the Torah, namely Kabbalah and Hassidism, which awakens the soul's innate faculty of *chochmah*. The production of blood cells from the bone marrow resembles, on the physical plane, a creative process of "something from nothing." On the spiritual plane, experiencing oneself continuously being created *ex nihilo* may well serve to strengthen one's bone-marrow system.

Binah ("understanding") is associated with the blood itself, now also considered a physiological system in its own right, in addition to the circulatory system of the blood vessels. *Binah*, which is cognate to the root *b-n-h* ("to build"), receives its raw material from *chochmah*, the bone marrow, expanding its encoded information. In Kabbalah, *binah* is referred to as the "mother," whose primary contributions to the formation of her child are the red aspects of his or her body, as we saw earlier in our discussion of the eye. In contrast, *chochmah* is referred to as the "father," who generates the white aspects of the body, such as the bones.

Of the mother, it is said, "the mother of the children is joyful."[9] A lack of joy in life may reflect a problem in the blood. In Hassidism, we are taught that a deep, inner sense of joy comes from meditating on God's Divine providence over all His creations. Similar to the effect of the blood on the limbs of the body, Divine providence links together God's creations to experience themselves as one organism. With the sense of God's care for all comes joy. Providence channels Divine life-force to each of God's creations, and as blood in a living organism, the life-force flows freely from one being to another, from the healthy limb to heal the diseased limb. The joy of witnessing Divine providence in one's life may thus serve to cure ailments relating to the blood.

These two relatively abstract physiological systems—the bone marrow and the blood—assume the roles of "father" and "mother" in the body and function together in perfect union. In Kabbalah, the continual union of the "father" and "mother" principles is responsible for the ongoing creation of reality. In the words of the *Zohar*: "the father [here, the bone marrow] and the mother [here, the blood] are two partners that never separate."[10] Their union, expressing the inner creative power of the living soul, is continuous, as illustrated by the fact that the bone marrow continuously creates new blood cells.

Before proceeding to describe the physiological system that corresponds to the third intellectual property of the soul, *da'at* (situated below *keter* on the middle axis of the Tree of Life), we will present the two systems that correspond to *chesed* and *gevurah*. These systems are situated below *chochmah* and *binah*, respectively, on the right and left axes of the Tree of Life. As they are directly related to their "parent" systems and function together with them, it is appropriate to discuss them at this point.

The *sefirah* directly under *chochmah* is *chesed* ("loving-kindness"). *Chesed* is personified by Abraham, as in the words of the prophet Micah, "give loving-kindness to Abraham."[11] The numerical value of Abraham's name (248) is equivalent to the number of bones in the body[12] and the number of positive, active commandments of the Torah, as stated above. Consequently, *chesed*, the attribute of Abraham, is identified with the skeletal system.

The inner, emotive experience of *chesed* is love. God calls Abraham "the one who loves Me."[13] Love of God and man, who is created in the image of God, may well serve as a spiritual remedy for skeletal diseases. To love God is to perform, in love, all of the 248 active commandments of the Torah.[14] To love one's fellow man is to help him in every way possible.

The phrase in the Torah "the God of Abraham,"[15] is understood in Kabbalah to refer to the overarching, Divine life-force of Abraham, the faculty of *chochmah* above the attribute of *chesed*. The bones of the body act as the vessels or containers for the bone marrow. Thus, the physiological analogy to the spiritual level referred to as "the God of Abraham" is the system of the bone marrow above the system of the skeleton.

Similarly, while *binah* refers to the blood, it is the property of *gevurah* ("might"), located directly beneath *binah* on the Tree of Life, that gives "shape" and direction to the blood, controlling its circulation throughout the body. It channels the blood and directs it into specific vessels (which it itself creates), the blood vessels of the circulatory system. According to Kabbalah, there are 365 major blood vessels in the human body, which correspond to the 365 prohibitive commandments of the Torah.

The 365 blood vessels correspond as well to the 365 days of the solar year. Each one of these blood vessels includes both an artery and its related vein. The distinction between arteries and veins is made as follows: the arteries (which pulsate) are likened to the days of the year (which are characterized by activity/pulsation) while the veins (which do not pulsate) are likened to the nights (which are characterized by rest). Each complete blood vessel thus includes a full circuit, a day and a night.

While we might first regard the blood and blood vessels as a single system, they are now understood to be two separate systems, as mentioned above. In Hassidic thought, the force of contraction (*gevurah*) that the blood vessels exert on the blood itself serves to strengthen the life-force inherent in the blood.[16]

Contraction is an act of "might," the basic meaning of *gevurah*. Its inner experience is awe in the presence of God and fear of the consequences of disobeying Him. With awe comes the might to control and direct the life-force flowing, in the form of blood, through the body.[17] The archetypal soul in the Torah that personifies *gevurah* is Isaac, who, amongst the patriarchs, lived a full life of 180 years—180 "days" (summers) and 180 "nights" (winters)—in the Torah, a year is called a "day" (of "night," winter, and "day," summer)—completing a full cycle of 360 degrees. A healthy circulatory system is thus dependent upon "the fear/awe of Isaac,"[18] the source of might in the soul.

We will now return to the third intellectual property of the soul, *da'at* ("knowledge"), and its physiological system.

The faculty of *da'at* ("knowledge") in the soul corresponds to the nervous system in the body. *Da'at* is understood in Kabbalah to be the seat of all of the soul's sensitivity and feeling. The body's sensors are its nerves.

In Kabbalah, we are taught that *da'at* possesses two seemingly antithetical but ultimately complementary sides. The first appearance of *da'at* in the Torah is in reference to "the Tree of Knowledge [*da'at*] of Good and Evil." From this we understand that *da'at* is a sense of spiritual or moral polarity. The soul's power to sense good and to be attracted to it is referred to as the "right side" of *da'at*, whereas the soul's power to sense evil and to repel it is referred to as the "left side" of *da'at*. In a rectified soul, the attraction to good entails conscious self-awareness of loving good, whereas the soul's fear of evil, responsible for repelling and fighting off the evil, operates at the unconscious level of the soul.

Abstracting and extending this understanding, the right side of *da'at* corresponds to all of one's conscious sensations and voluntary reactions, while the left side of *da'at* corresponds to all one's unconscious sensations and involuntary reactions.

In terms of the nervous system, the right side of *da'at* corresponds to the voluntary nervous system, referred to as the cerebrospinal nervous system. Here, conscious sensation and control of the body implies self-awareness, knowing oneself. In a rectified personality, knowing oneself is necessary in order to act constructively in the world and help others. For this reason, this side of *da'at* is identified with the right.

The left side of *da'at* corresponds to the involuntary nervous system, the autonomic nervous system, which itself divides into the sympathetic and parasympathetic systems. The parasympathetic system serves to slow the heart, dilate the blood vessels, increase the activity of the glands, constrict the pupils of the eyes, etc., whereas the sympathetic system does the opposite.

Serving as the unconscious side of *da'at*, the involuntary nervous system allows all of the body's necessary functions to perform automatically. Naturally occurring processes such as digestion and respiration function without a person's conscious involvement. Such functions are necessary in order for the body to sustain itself.

Since *da'at* entails the dual sensitivity of attraction to good and repulsion from evil, we must properly balance the tensions created by these two opposite forces. Therefore, it is here that we find the seat of free choice in the soul. To strengthen one's nervous system is to strengthen one's power of free choice, to be clear and unequivocal about choosing good and the same for repelling evil. In the words of the Torah, "See, I have given you this day life and good, death and evil…and you shall choose life."[19]

By choosing good as defined by the Torah, God's word to man, one unites with God, the ultimate, absolute good. The inner experience of *da'at* is union. It is the experience of union that creates the balance between the two opposing sides of *da'at*, the attraction to good and the repulsion from evil. To strengthen one's power of free choice, and thereby one's nervous system, one must strengthen his consciousness of union with God and the Divine souls of Israel, "an actual part of God."[20]

Directly below *da'at* on the middle axis of the Tree of Life, the *sefirah* of *tiferet* ("beauty") corresponds to the muscular system of the body. The heart, which belongs both to the muscular system as well as to the circulatory system, tends to the left side of the body, alluding to the combined forces of *gevurah* and *tiferet*. In general, a sound, well-developed muscular system makes for a beautiful body. Muscles are the seat of the body's physical strength. Here also, we see the combined forces of the spiritual attributes of *gevurah* and *tiferet*.

The inner experience of *tiferet* is compassion. In Kabbalah, we are taught that in the Divine soul, characterized in particular by its property of *da'at* (its power to choose good), its attribute of compassion (*tiferet*, directly below *da'at*) is most potent. (This is in contrast to those souls that lack the faculty of *da'at*. Their feeling of mercy on others is mere pity, and they are unable to bring this feeling to its actualization.) Potent compassion begins with a sense of true empathy for the other, and possesses the strength of character necessary to succeed in extending one's hand to the other to extricate him from his troubles. On the spiritual plane, potent compassion reflects a strong heart and a strong muscular system.[21]

Before describing the physiological systems that correspond to the two *sefirot* following *tiferet*—*netzach* (to the right) and *hod* (to the left)—we will continue along the middle axis of the Tree of Life.

Yesod ("foundation"), the continuation and extension of *tiferet*, is the power of self-actualization in the soul. Here, on the physical plane it manifests itself as the reproductive system, the innate capacity to re-produce or re-create one's own self in the form of progeny.[22]

The inner experience of *yesod* is truth or verification, in the sense of realization or self-fulfillment. Clearly, there is no greater self-fulfillment than physical reproduction,[23] bringing into the world another soul, a reflection of oneself, created in the image of God.[24] Thus, to strengthen one's reproductive system, one must make every effort to realize his life's dreams in general. This is the power of the soul of Joseph, the archetypal soul of *yesod* in Kabbalah, who saw his dreams come true.

(In modern society, the mistake is often made that pursuing a career in order to fulfill oneself in life contradicts devoting oneself to marriage and raising a family. In truth, self-fulfillment in all avenues of life and devotion to raising a family are interdependent. Realizing oneself in the world begins with the conscious realization that the greatest possible self-fulfillment is reproduction and raising a family—fulfilling the blessing that God gave man on the day of his creation: "Be fruitful and multiply and fill the earth and conquer it..."[25]—and that this does not prevent one from simultaneously pursuing a career.)

Upon further reflection, it can be seen that an additional property of the soul and an additional physiological system issues from *yesod* to become the source of *malchut*, the *sefirah* immediately below it. The source of *malchut* in *yesod* is known as *ateret hayesod*, literally, "the crown of the *yesod* [i.e., of the *brit*]." This property of the soul corresponds to the sign of the covenant of circumcision—the *brit milah*.

The act of circumcision is a two-fold process performed on the skin of the male *brit*: removal of the foreskin and the peeling back of the mucous membrane to reveal the crown of the organ. This process refines the initially coarse physical skin, making it capable of reflecting spiritual light. This is alluded to in the phonetic affinity in Hebrew of the words for "skin" (*or*, with an *ayin*) and "light" (*or*, with a *alef*).[26] Hence, the *brit milah*, specifically the manifestation of the crown of the organ—*ateret hayesod*—is regarded as the origin of the physiological system of the skin.[27]

Additionally, the word chosen in *Sefer Yetzirah* for the *brit* is *maor*, cognate to the word for "skin" (*or*). Not by coincidence is the skin that must be removed in circumcision called, in English, the "foreskin." In Hebrew, it is called the *orlah*, also from the sub-root *or* ("skin").

As taught in Kabbalah and known especially in homeopathy, healthy skin relates to a healthy sexual life. For a Jew this means "guarding of the *brit*" and leading a healthy sexual life according to the parameters of the Torah.

Like the first *sefirah* of *keter*, the final *sefirah* of *malchut* ("kingdom") also relates to internalizing a necessary component of life from the external world. Extracting the spiritual and physical "sparks" of nourishment from the lower realms of reality (the mineral, vegetable, and animal kingdoms), and ingesting them, transforms them into vital human energy. Digestion operates as a clarification process whereby useful elements from the environment are assimilated into the body, while waste products are expelled.[28]

However, in contrast to *keter*—which represents the respiratory system and involves a dynamic of descent whereby vital energy (oxygen) is drawn down into the body from the air or heavens above—*malchut*, which represents digestion, involves the opposite dynamic, that is, the elevation into the body of "fallen sparks" of energy (nourishment), extracted from the products of the earth below. A feminine image in Kabbalah, *malchut* alludes to the digestive system, as in King Solomon's description of the "woman of valor" who "gives food to her house [body]."[29]

The inner experience of rectified *malchut* is a feeling of existential lowliness, of being far from God and longing to return to Him (in contrast to the inner experience of *chochmah*, pure and simple selflessness). Lowliness also implies the power to lower oneself to those below one. This power is especially necessary for a king. (In Kabbalah, the king's sitting on his throne is his lowering himself to judge and provide for his people.)

As above, one eats in order to elevate fallen sparks, to find, identify and redeem, sparks of Godliness in levels of creation below oneself. This requires a spiritual service of lowering oneself in order to uplift the fallen sparks. In expelling waste products from the body, one is to meditate on his own state of existential lowliness. Thus, on the spiritual plane, a healthy digestive system depends upon a sense of lowliness, the power to lower oneself to that which is below him, and the longing to return to God with one's booty of fallen sparks.

We will now return to the two remaining *sefirot*, *netzach* and *hod*. (Normally, in the order of the *sefirot*, *netzach* and *hod* come before *yesod* and *malchut*. However, in relation to the body, the *sefirot* of *netzach* and *hod*, which correspond to the legs, extend below *yesod* and *malchut*, for which reason they are the last physiological systems to be described here.)

Netzach ("victory") corresponds to the endocrine system, comprising glands and hormones, while *hod* ("thanksgiving") represents the immune system. Of all the systems in the body, these are the two most recently understood in the medical world to function together. So too, *netzach* and *hod*, the two legs, function together. In the words of Kabbalah, *netzach* and *hod* are "two halves of the same body," or, colloquially, "two sides of the same coin."

Netzach, situated under *chesed* on the right axis of the Tree of Life, means both "victory" and also "eternity." It is the ability to overcome obstacles that stand in the way of the body's growth and development processes, those processes that ensure sound health and longevity. Working to generate new cells and structures within the body, the hormones of the endocrine system perpetuate the life of the body and aid it to overcome the obstacles of time. *Netzach* is also understood in Kabbalah as the "milk" that nurtures the growth and development motivated by *chesed* from which it branches out.

The inner experience of *netzach* is (self-)confidence, the confidence that God always stands at our side to give us the power to succeed in all of our *self-initiated* endeavors.[30] In order to grow and develop spiritually, a youth must be taught[31] to acquire a balanced, rectified sense of self-confidence.[32] This must be nurtured in his consciousness just as an infant nurses on his mother's milk. An imbalance in one's hormones may reflect an imbalance in one's inner sense of confidence. In order for one's hormones to properly regulate one's metabolism, one must learn how to manifest and regulate, control and orchestrate, one's energies. One of the meanings of *netzach* is "orchestration."

Finally, we turn to *hod*, which corresponds to the immune system, the physiological system that fights disease. The immune system monitors that which properly belongs in the body and that which is a foreign invader. A healthy immune system annihilates destructive foreign intrusions into the body; an unhealthy immune system turns on the body itself. In Part II, when we discuss illness and healing, we will focus on the immune system and examine it in detail.

The inner experience of *hod* is sincerity. Sincerity implies honesty in all one's social transactions. The word *hod* means "acknowledgement" and "thanksgiving." To strengthen one's immune system, one must cultivate in his soul a sense of thanks to all those benevolent to him, and acknowledge his indebtedness to others, both for their physical as well as spiritual gifts to him (as when one acknowledges the truth of another's words, thanking him for enlightening him and correcting his previous mistaken assumption). With sincere acknowledgement of one's indebtedness to others, transcending egocentric subjectivity, one reaches the objectivity necessary to recognize an ally or a foe, to link to the ally and fight off the foe, both on the spiritual and physical planes.

PART TWO

Kabbalistic Understanding of Disease

שכינתא מרעא בגלותא

The Divine Presence is Ill in the Exile

Tikunei Zohar 142b

4

Origins of Disease

Evil, Disease, and Fear

According to Kabbalah, disease is a phenomenon of the unbalanced left side of the *sefirot* and the properties of the soul. As we saw above in our discussion of *da'at*, the right side of *da'at* is the (conscious) attraction to good, while the left side of *da'at* is the (unconscious) repulsion of evil. In *Sefer Yetzirah*, evil and disease are identified as the same: "there is no more evil than disease."[1] The left side senses evil for, in a certain respect, it is the ultimate origin of evil, i.e., evil or disease is a degenerate manifestation of the left. This is so for the left, in Kabbalah, signifies contraction (*tzimtzum*) or concealment of Divine light and life-force, ultimately resulting in a frightening experience of the darkness of night; i.e., absence of the revelation of God's presence and providence in the world. In the soul, the central experience of the left (the inner experience of *gevurah*, the middle point of the left axis, its center of gravity), is fear. Any fear, other than the fear of God, is a source of disease.

The human psyche is full of fears. Some are conscious; others are unconscious. Some have developed over one's lifetime; others are innate, inherited from parents or experiences in the mother's womb; yet others derive from previous lifetimes. With progressive stages in maturity come the insight and spiritual power to identify and overcome fears, even those most deeply rooted in one's psyche.

A weakness in any one of the spiritual attributes that correlate to the physiological systems of the body is a contraction (*tzimtzum*) of that particular attribute. That is to say, that if a particular attribute is strong and complete, it is "right," while if it is weak and incomplete, it is "left." The result: fear, at that level of the soul.

For example, if one's spiritual attribute of compassion (correlating to the muscular system of the body) is weak, one becomes afraid, whether consciously or unconsciously, to express compassion toward another, lest he cause damage to himself. This fear, in turn, may result in heart disease or some other disease relating to the muscular system. And so it is with regard to the other attributes of the soul and physiological systems of the body. Each individual fear reflects a syndrome, from weakness to fear to disease. Preventive medicine seeks to catch and treat the weakness before it develops into a psychological phobia and a physical illness.

The Three Primal Fears

The origins of disease can generally be traced to three primal fears, three focal points of fear or core traumas in the human psyche:

Chapter Four: Origins of Disease

- fear of rape
- fear of murder, and
- fear of insanity.

Underlying all of these fears is the fear of death, but each one anticipates death by a different route.

For the *collective* consciousness of the Jewish people ("the community does not die,"[2] so its underlying fear is not death in the normal sense of the word), the focus of fear is the fear of exile—the communal state of disease, as will be explained at length in Chapter 5. The Talmud likens the three major exiles of the Jewish people—Egyptian, Babylonian, and Roman (known as the exile of Edom)—to a man being attacked by a wolf, a lion, and a snake, respectively:

> A man was on a journey and a wolf attacked him, but he escaped unharmed. Continuing his journey, he told the story of the wolf until a lion attacked him and he escaped unharmed. Continuing his journey, he told the story of the lion until a snake attacked him and he escaped unharmed. He then forgot about the first two assaults and told only the story of the snake. So it is with Israel: their more recent troubles make them forget their earlier troubles.[3]

The fear of the wolf alludes, in particular, to the fear of rape or any other form of sexual molestation.

The fear of rape refers, in an extended way, to any compulsory invasion of oneself by something other than oneself. This fear exists on all levels, both physically and psychologically. While primarily a feminine manifestation of fear, the fear of the wolf and all of its implications can also manifest itself in the male—as a man can also fear rape to a certain degree. Labeling this fear as feminine only means that it is more pronounced in women. Finally, the association of the wolf with the rapist is not restricted to the Talmud; in modern media, too, the sexual predator is often symbolized as a wolf.

The fear of the lion is linked to the primal fear of murder, the fear of death. People who harbor this fear in their heart unconsciously fear the lion figure, lurking in the dark, about to consume them. While the fear of the wolf is the fear of being attacked and harmed, the fear of the lion is the fear of being consumed.

The fear of the snake, whose venom affects the mind—as did the words spoken by the primordial snake to Eve in the Garden of Eden—is the fear of insanity. As in the case of the primordial sin, temporary insanity can be identified as the cause of all wrongdoing. Losing one's mind, or a loss of attention to one's deeds, opens up the possibility of sin, for if people were truly to know what they were doing, they would be aware of the implications and consequences of their actions, and they would never transgress.[4] In the words of the sages, "no one commits a sin unless he has been overtaken by temporary insanity [literally, 'a spirit of folly']."[5]

This is alluded to in the Talmudic passage quoted above, in which the man on the journey forgets his previous traumas only when attacked by the snake. It is not stated that he *forgets* the story of the wolf when attacked by the lion, just that he does not tell it. Only the trauma of the snake so affects the mind to the extent that all previous impressions are blotted out.

These three syndromes, the fear of the wolf, lion, and snake, correspond to the three levels of the soul discussed above. The "wolf syndrome" corresponds to the behavioral properties of the soul (the three *sefirot* of *netzach*, *hod*, and *yesod*). The "lion syndrome" corresponds to the emotive properties of the soul (the three *sefirot* of *chesed*, *gevurah*, and *tiferet*). The "snake syndrome" corresponds to the intellectual properties of the soul (the three *sefirot* of *chochmah*, *binah*, and *da'at*).

Each triplet of *sefirot* comprises a *sefirah* of the right axis, a *sefirah* of the left axis, and a *sefirah* of the middle axis. "Right" implies attraction or love; "left" implies repulsion or fear; "center" implies a sense of self that may tend either to the right or to the left.[6] Each of the three syndromes of fear described above reflects an exaggerated tendency of the self toward the left, toward fear.

	left axis fear	middle axis sense of self	right axis love
		keter skull **respiratory system**	
intellectual properties **snake syndrome**	*binah* left hemisphere of brain **blood**	*da'at* posterior of brain **nervous system**	*chochmah* right hemisphere of brain **bone marrow**
emotive properties **lion syndrome**	*gevurah* left arm **circulatory system**	*tiferet* torso **muscular system**	*chesed* right arm **skeletal system**
behavioral properties **wolf syndrome**	*hod* left leg **immune system**	*yesod* brit **reproductive system**	*netzach* right leg **endocrine system**
		malchut mouth **digestive system**	

The wolf syndrome, the fear of rape, as well as the act of rape itself, relates to the *sefirah* of *yesod* ("foundation"), the *brit* in the body. The fear of rape preys, like a wolf, upon the *sefirah* of *hod* ("thanksgiving"), the immune system, which is the defense mechanism of the body against foreign invasion.

This syndrome may thereby be understood as *yesod* inclined "left" toward *hod*.

The lion syndrome, the fear of murder, relates to the middle part of the body, the torso, *tiferet* ("beauty"), the location of the heart. In particular, however, the physical heart is situated on the left side of the body, in the realm of *gevurah* ("might"). As stated earlier, the heart belongs to two of the physiological systems, the circulatory (*gevurah*) and the muscular (*tiferet*), being the body's major muscle. A further indication of the relation of the lion to *gevurah* is that in Hebrew the word for "lion" (*aryeh*) and *gevurah* possess the same numerical value (216). Thus, the fear of the lion consuming one's heart may be understood as *tiferet* inclined "left" toward *gevurah*.[7]

Finally, the snake syndrome, the fear of insanity, attacks the intellectual properties of the mind. The snake (and the soul's sensitivity to the snake which is the soul's archenemy) corresponds to the *sefirah* of *da'at* ("knowledge"), as in the episode of the Tree of Knowledge of Good and Evil, where the snake tempts Eve. The snake is the personification of the evil *da'at* and Eve is the personification of *binah* ("understanding"). Thus, the fear of insanity is *da'at* inclined "left" toward *binah*.[8]

To summarize:

snake syndrome	fear of insanity	*da'at* tending toward *binah*
lion syndrome	fear of murder	*tiferet* tending toward *gevurah*
wolf syndrome	fear of rape	*yesod* tending toward *hod*

Images of wolf, lion, and snake appear abundantly throughout the Bible. Though they generally represent negative forces (as described above), each symbol also possesses a positive side. The negative side represents the origin of the disease, while the positive side points to its cure. For example, the evil, primordial snake is the origin of insanity—any transgression of the Torah's laws being a temporary state of insanity, as mentioned above—while the positive snake-figure, the Messiah, as will be explained, possesses the cure for all forms of insanity.

A symbol is most potent when it becomes personified, as we saw with the snake and Eve above. According to Kabbalah, a living figure or character in a previous age may become, at a later stage in history, a psychological or physical condition whose ramifications affect all of humanity.

Let us now examine each syndrome in detail, focusing on the negative, the disease, as well as the positive, the cure.

Fear of the Wolf

As told in the parable of the Talmud quoted above, the wolf's attack on the traveler symbolizes the Egyptian exile of the Jewish people.

The sages teach that "in the merit of the righteous women of Israel our forefathers were redeemed from Egypt."[9] The Torah testifies to the fact that though the Jewish males were in bondage to the Egyptians, the Egyptians were unable to enslave, that is to seduce, the Jewish women.[10]

Only in one case did Jewish immunity to foreign invasion in the realm of marital relations fail. Often, an exception proves the rule. The exception was the case of Shlomit, the daughter of Divri.[11] These two names allude to the reason that she became vulnerable to be defiled, unknowingly, by an Egyptian oppressor, the very Egyptian that Moses killed the following day.[12] The name *Shlomit* derives from *shalom*, "peace" or "greetings," and the name *Divri* derives from *dibur*, "speech." She exaggerated in her seemingly innocent greeting of *shalom* ("peace be with you") to every Egyptian passer-by.[13] (This itself derived from her unconscious, exaggerated fear of rape. Often, unconscious fear of the other becomes conscious attraction and attempt to find favor in the eyes of the other. On the spiritual plane, this parallels a malfunctioning immune system.) Later, in the wilderness, her son, born of the Egyptian father, blasphemed the Name of God.[14] This transgression relates in Kabbalah to the *sefirah* of *hod*, which corresponds to the immune system and the wolf syndrome.

After they had escaped from Egyptian bondage and were making their way through the wilderness to the Land of Israel, with the Egyptian wolf still lurking in the back of their consciousness, the Jewish people succumbed to the seduction of the Moabite women. This caused a plague that claimed 24,000 lives.[15] Here, the evil inclination of sexual lust, which in turn led to the worship of Ba'al Peor, a particularly hideous form of idolatry,[16] reached its peak.

In the Torah, we are taught that Divine punishment reflects the nature of the transgression.[17] The punishment in this case was death by plague; the transgression was sexual lust for idolatrous women. The sages liken the punishment for this sin to a wolf entering and devouring a flock of sheep.[18] Thus, we may conclude that sexual lust, as well as the fear of sexual abuse, relates to the image of a wolf threatening sheep.

In addition to the wolf symbolizing the Egyptian exile,[19] the evil wolf (*ze'ev*) of the Bible is personified in the Book of Judges as a minister of Midian who waged war against Israel in the 12th century BCE.[20] During a key battle, the Israelites, led by Gideon, were outnumbered 450 to 1, but they were miraculously victorious. The officers of Midian, Orev and Ze'ev, literally "raven" and "wolf," were captured and executed.[21]

The raven also symbolizes strong sexual impulses. The Hebrew word for "raven" (*orev*) is phonetically related to the word for "ambush" (*arav*). Thus, the raven, the first officer of Midian to be mentioned, represents the ambush of the rapist, while the wolf, the second officer of Midian, represents the rapist's assault. The fear of rape includes the fear of both the raven and the wolf.

The initial letters of the two officers' names, *ayin* and *zayin*, can be read *az*, meaning "bold," or *eiz*, meaning "goat." The evil goat symbolizes a demon in the Torah.[22] As explained above, the fear of rape may be generalized to refer to the fear of any compulsory invasion of oneself by something other than oneself. The demonic goat symbolizes invasion into the private domain.[23] Physiologically, such invasion may refer to any disease associated with one of the systems of the body that relate to the wolf syndrome, as described above.

These two officers, Ze'ev and Orev, served the two kings of Midian, Zevach and Tzalmuna. The name Zevach, which means "slaughter," begins with the two primary letters of Ze'ev. Rape is a form of slaughter or murder, as will be further explained. Orev serves, in particular, Tzalmuna, whose name means "a moving shadow-image" as in "the shadows of evening" described by the prophet Jeremiah.[24] (We will presently see that the name Orev derives from the same root as the word *erev*, meaning "evening.") Sexual lust as well as the fear of sexual abuse epitomize the psychological state of the unrectified power of imagination (personified by Tzalmuna and his minister Orev, the shadow-image of evening).[25]

All four appear together in Psalm 83, which, significantly, is the number of diseases in the world, according to the sages,[26] in the context of a fervent prayer to God to eradicate the nations that plot the destruction of Israel: "Make their nobles like Orev and Ze'ev, all their princes like Zevach and Tzalmuna."[27]

On the other hand, the tribe of Benjamin personifies the good wolf of the Torah. When blessing his sons before his death, Jacob identified his youngest son Benjamin as a "preying wolf."[28] Here, Jacob prophetically alluded to the episode recorded at the end of the Book of Judges,[29] which relates the travails of a man from a tribe of Levi who, together with his concubine, took lodging in the Benjaminite town of Gibeah.

While there, the concubine was taken by the men of the town, raped, abused and left to die. The Levite cut up the woman's corpse into twelve pieces and sent them along with a report of the atrocity to each of the tribes. Incensed at the brutality of the men of Gibeah, the tribes took up arms against the tribe of Benjamin, swearing also not to give their daughters in marriage to Benjaminite men.

After much warfare, however, the tribes regretted that Israel was about to lose one of its integral units and agreed that the men of Benjamin should be allowed to "snatch" wives for themselves from "the daughters of Shiloh" as they dance in the vineyards; thus, they circumvented their own oath not to give their daughters freely.

So we see here that although at first the tribe of Benjamin sinned sexually, in the end, after most of the tribe had been wiped out, the remainder was allowed to snatch, like wolves, wives from amongst the dancing maidens. The very evil inclination of the wolf was here elevated and rectified, for both the young men and women participated voluntarily in the play, for the sake of Heaven; the fear of rape was overcome and sweetened at its source. The tribe of Benjamin, from whom would come the first king of Israel, Saul—who "snatched the kingdom" like a wolf[30]—was thus reestablished.

The sages teach[31] that the wolf of Benjamin symbolizes the altar in the Temple (the altar was in the territory of Benjamin), upon which the animal sacrifices were offered. The altar, where the sacrifices were slaughtered and consumed by fire, can be compared to a wolf that consumes its prey. The Hebrew word for "altar" (*mizbeiach*) shares its root with the word for "slaughter" (*zevach*), the name of the king of Midian served by Ze'ev, the wolf, as mentioned above. On the altar, both the wolf-image and the inclination to slaughter find their ultimate rectification.

When we examine the blessing of Jacob to Benjamin more closely, we find more fascinating allusions. The full blessing reads:

> *Benjamin is a preying wolf:*
> *in the morning he shall eat booty,*
> *and in the evening he shall divide the spoils.*[32]

Rashi, quoting the sages,[33] interprets "in the morning he shall eat booty" as referring to the "morning and sunrise" of the Jewish kingdom, the kingdom of Saul. "And in the evening he shall divide the spoils," he interprets as referring to the story of Mordechai and Esther—also from the tribe of Benjamin—who divided the spoils of the evil Haman in the "evening…even after the sun set" on the Jewish monarchy.

The blessing of Benjamin clearly links the image of the wolf with the turning points of the daily cycle, morning and evening. Above, we saw that the companion of the wolf (*ze'ev*) is the raven (*orev*). The word *orev* shares its root with the word for "evening" (*erev*). "Evening" first appears in the Torah's story of creation, where evening and morning are juxtaposed: "and there was evening, and there was morning.…"

The raven is called *orev* for it is as black as the evening. In the Book of Habbakuk,[34] we find the idiom "evening wolves," a clear allusion to the relationship of the wolf to the raven: "His horses are faster than leopards, and more sharp-toothed than evening wolves.…"

In the Book of Zephaniah,[35] we find the juxtaposition of the evening wolves to the morning: "...its judges [devour it] like evening wolves, that do not leave any bones till the morning."

The words for raven (*orev*) and evening (*erev*) are related to the word for "plain" (*arav*). In the Book of Jeremiah,[36] we find the idiomatic juxtaposition of the wolf with "plains": "Therefore the lion of the forest will strike them, and the wolf of the plains will despoil them."

As a rapist, the wolf strikes at eve[37] or at dawn, when he can first identify his prey. The location of his assault is the plain or the field:

> *But if a man finds a betrothed girl in the field,*
> *and the man forces her, and lies with her;*
> *then the man only who lay with her shall die.*
> *But to the girl you shall do nothing;*
> *there is in the girl no sin deserving death,*
> *for as when a man rises against his neighbor,*
> *and slays him, so is this matter.*
> *For he found her in the field,*
> *and the betrothed girl cried out,*
> *and there was no one to save her;*
> *there was no one to rescue her.*[38]

Here, the Torah likens rape to murder,[39] implying that the fear of rape, the fear of the wolf, entails the fear of the lion as well.[40]

In contrast, the prophet Isaiah[41] envisions the universal peace of the Messianic Era as a time when "the wolf will live with the lamb." Indeed, this is the first in a series of images that continues: "...and the lion will eat straw like the cow. A suckling will play at the hole of the snake and a child will place his hand over the lair of the serpent." Note that the order is wolf, lion, snake.

The Jewish people are likened by the sages to a lamb surrounded by seventy wolves,[42] that is, the seventy gentile nations of the earth, whose desire it is to rape and devour us, to seduce us to assimilate into their culture.[43] With the coming of the End of Days, true and lasting peace will be established between Israel and the nations, with Israel serving as the light to the nations. At a later stage in the Messianic Era, the natural order itself will metamorphose to a world where the physical wolf and lamb will lie down together and live in peace.[44]

If the Jewish people are likened to a lamb surrounded by wolves, then Benjamin—symbolized as the "preying wolf"—is the "wolf within the lamb." In Kabbalah, he represents the fertile feminine womb of the collective soul of Israel (in the terminology of Kabbalah, the *yesod* of *malchut*), the rectified receptive power of the soul that guards itself from foreign invasion and fights off enemies, while sanctifying itself to receive and nurture the holy seed given it from above. Ultimately, impregnated with the seed of Divine light and life-force, this is the spiritual power of the Jewish people to become a light to the nations and achieve, forever, peace between wolf and lamb.[45]

The Land of Israel is described in the Torah as "a land that flows [*zavat*] with milk and honey."[46] The word *zavat*, from *zov* meaning "flow," is related to *ze'ev*, meaning "wolf."[47] On the negative side, "flow" is a symptom of gonorrhea (*zivah*), a disease described explicitly in the Torah.[48] Although both males and females may be afflicted by this disease and experience its chief symptom, a purulent discharge or flow, a more common symptom for the female is experiencing a flow of blood like that of menstruation, but not at its proper time. In any event, this clearly relates the wolf-image and syndrome to sexual disease.

(Significantly, in homeopathy, all disease is seen to derive from the itch of the skin, here associated with the crown of the *brit*, as explained above, and with the sexual diseases of gonorrhea and syphilis. All disease begins with the wolf syndrome; all exiles originate in the Egyptian exile, as taught by the sages.[49])

On the positive side, the Torah speaks of the "flow" of seven liquids: water, wine, dew, milk, blood, olive oil, and honey.[50] In Kabbalah, these correspond to the seven attributes of the heart, from *chesed* to *malchut*, as follows:

gevurah "might" **wine**		*chesed* "loving-kindness" **water**
	tiferet "beauty" **dew**	
hod "thanksgiving" **blood**		*netzach* "victory" **milk**
	yesod "foundation" **olive oil**	
	malchut "kingdom" **honey**	

Let us note that here, blood is associated with the *sefirah* of *hod*, whereas in our analysis of the physiological systems, blood was associated with the *sefirah* of *binah*. *Binah* is not related to the seven liquids; however, it represents the mental origin of the emotion of *hod*, as stated in Kabbalah: "*binah* extends until *hod*."[51]

Good health is supported by the flow of the blood—in the circulating state referred to as "run and return"[52]—throughout all the limbs of the body.[53] The fact that here the blood corresponds to *hod* reinforces our identification of disease and cure in general with *hod*, the seat of the immune system.[54]

The Land of Israel is described throughout the Bible as "a land flowing with milk and honey." The "flow" of milk and honey alludes to another liquid, blood, inasmuch as the essential life-flow in the body is its blood, as stated. The tribe that, more than all the others, is innately associated with the Land of Israel is Benjamin, for Benjamin was the only one of Jacob's sons born in Israel. His positive "wolf"-image, the source of cure for all diseases affecting the physiological systems related to the wolf-syndrome, is symbolized by the "flow" (*zav*, cognate to *ze'ev*—"wolf," as above) of milk and honey in the Land of Israel.

Milk alludes to the endocrine system, the physiological system responsible for growth (the power of mother's milk) and associated with the *sefirah* of *netzach* on the right axis (as explained above), the complementary *sefirah* to *hod* on the left axis. Also as explained above, the rectification of each of the *sefirot* on the left axis is its inclusion and union with the respective *sefirah* on the right, thereby achieving balance and equilibrium. Our sages actually state that lactation transforms menstrual blood (*hod*) into mother's milk (*netzach*).⁵⁵ The union of the endocrine system (*netzach*) and the immune system (*hod*) is related in the *Zohar* to the image of marital union: "[In marital union,] he is in *netzach*, she is in *hod*."⁵⁶

Honey corresponds to *malchut*, the digestive system. The very substance of honey is a product of the digestive system of bees. In the phrase "a land flowing with milk and honey," "honey" refers to bees' honey, whereas in the context of the seven fruits with which the Land of Israel is blessed,⁵⁷ "honey" refers to date-honey. The proper amount of honey in one's diet, in accordance with one's age and state of health,⁵⁸ aids the digestive process.

The numerical value of the word for "honey" (*devash*) equals that of the word for "woman" (*ishah*, 306), who, in Kabbalah, is the symbol of *malchut* and who ascends, in marital union, to *hod*. Thus, we have completed a cycle: the rectification of blood (*hod*) depends upon its union (or inter-inclusion) with milk (*netzach*); milk combines with honey (*malchut*), which then ascends to purify the blood (*hod*). This rectification process is an inherent property of the Holy Land, the Land of Israel, which flows (alluding to the flow of the blood) with milk and honey.

Amazingly, the combined numerical value of the names of these three liquids ("milk," *chalav*, 40; "blood," *dam*, 44; and "honey," *devash*, 306) exactly equals that of the word for "[olive] oil" (*shemen*, 390), the liquid associated with the *sefirah* of *yesod*, the unifying link in this cycle.⁵⁹

This rectification process is associated with the tribe of Benjamin. In Kabbalah, Benjamin is known as the "lower *tzadik,*" corresponding, in human physiology, to the woman's womb, the physical location that experiences the fear of the wolf. The soul-root of Benjamin present within every Jew is able to overcome this fear and fight off the diseases associated with it.

FEAR OF THE LION

As related in the Talmudic parable quoted above, the attack of the lion on the traveler symbolizes the Babylonian exile of the Jewish people. And indeed, the personification of the evil lion in the Book of Jeremiah is Nebuchadnezzar, the king of Babylonia who destroyed the first Temple, laid waste to the Jewish people, and exiled them from the Land of Israel, as it is written, "The lion has ascended from his thicket to destroy nations...."[60]

Nebuchadnezzar destroyed the Temple on the 9th day of *Av*, the Hebrew month aligned with the zodiac sign Leo, the lion. The holy Temple in Jerusalem is referred to as "the lion of God" (*ariel*)—"O Ariel, Ariel, the city where David resided..."[61]—as is the Temple altar itself.[62] Our sages teach us that fire from heaven descended upon the Temple's altar in the form of a lion to consume the sacrifices.[63] Even God Himself is referred to in the Book of Amos as a lion—"The lion roars, who shall not fear? God has spoken, who shall not prophesy?"[64] All of these images of the lion are brought together in the cryptic saying of the sages:

> The lion ascended in the sign of the lion to destroy the lion, in order that the Lion ascend in the sign of the lion to rebuild the lion.[65]

This saying refers to Nebuchadnezzar's destruction of the Temple; it implies that it was, in fact, necessary for the man-made Temple to be destroyed by the evil lion in order that God, the Divine Lion, rebuild it to stand forever.

In addition to Nebuchadnezzar, the evil lion refers to the nation of Moab (in particular, to the mighty warriors of Moab): "Benaiah ben Jehoyada...smote the two lion-men of Moab..."[66]

Above, we saw that the evil wolf-image relates to the nation of Midian; here we see that the evil lion-image relates to the nation of Moab. In Kabbalah, these two related nations, who made peace between themselves in order to wage war on Israel,[67] pertain to the *sefirah* of *chochmah*; they are both perversions of true wisdom.[68]

In Hassidic thought, the inner soul-quality of *chochmah* is *bitul*, "self-nullification," the opposite of which is an exaggerated sense of self that brings one to be continually in conflict with others. This is the characteristic of Midian, whose name means "conflict" and "quarrel."[69]

The intellectual experience of wisdom is that of a new flash of insight, a new intuitive vision of reality. If one's faculty of wisdom is rectified, one's insights will be true. If not, one intuits erroneously. This tendency to err at the intuitive level of wisdom is depicted as the nation of Moab.

Midian and Moab, representing an exaggerated sense of self and intuitive error, are dependent upon one another—lack of *bitul* leads one to false intuition. The wolf gives rise to the lion. Physical wolf-syndrome diseases, when untreated at the level of behavioristic characteristics of the soul, give rise to physical lion-syndrome diseases, at the level of the emotive characteristics of the soul.

When blessing his sons before his death, Jacob blessed the tribe of Judah with kingship, noting: "Judah is a lion cub."[70] He blessed the tribe of Dan with judgeship, noting, "Dan shall be a snake on the way, a serpent on the path."[71] Jacob stated as well, in his blessing to Dan, that he would resemble the tribe of Judah: "Dan will judge his people like the one [i.e., the king] of the tribes of Israel."

The two tribes are further linked in the blessings that Moses gave before his death, when Moses blessed the tribe of Dan to be "a lion cub."[72] So we see that Dan connects the lion to the snake, to the kingdom of David (who came from the tribe of Judah), and also to the son of David, *Mashiach ben David*, known as "the holy snake," as we will see presently. Indeed, the *Zohar* states that from the tribe of Dan will come the commander-in-chief of the army of the Messiah.

The one man in the Bible who personifies the union of Judah and Dan is Daniel. The name Daniel means "judge of God," but Daniel came, in fact, from the tribe of Judah and from the royal lineage of King David. Daniel was thrown into the lion's den and emerged unscathed for he symbolizes the holy lion, the power to overcome the evil lion. The sages say that of all Biblical figures, Daniel is the closest to personifying the Messiah.⁷³ Thus Daniel unites, in holiness, the lion with the snake.

The Code of Jewish Law begins with the injunction that one should be as "courageous as a lion."⁷⁴ Like a lion, poised to pounce on its prey, one ought to pounce out of bed in the morning with renewed vitality and confidence to conquer all the enemies of the day ahead. With the courage of a lion in one's service of God one overcomes the fear of the lion.

In the Book of Proverbs, it is stated that the fear of the lion, the fear of murder, is what keeps one at home, in bed:

> *The lazy man says,*
> *"There is a lion outside!*
> *I will be murdered in the street!"*⁷⁵

One must combat this evil psychological fear of the lion by means of the holy psychological lion—the power to get up, go out, and get things done.⁷⁶

To cure those diseases affecting the body's skeleton, circulatory system, and muscular system (i.e., those systems related to the lion-syndrome), one must become as agile and courageous as a lion. In Hassidism, we are taught that agility characterizes *chesed*,⁷⁷ corresponding to the healthy skeletal system of the body. Courage is, of course, the property of *gevurah*, corresponding to the circulatory system. The vital energies of both of these systems permeate the muscular system, the essence and heart—lion-heart—of the body itself.

FEAR OF THE SNAKE

The archenemy of the Jewish people, and the quintessential representation of evil in the Torah, Amalek (a grandson of Esau), personifies the primordial snake of the Garden of Eden.

The Ba'al Shem Tov teaches that the numerical value of the Hebrew word *Amalek* (240) is identical to that of *safek*, meaning "doubt." Spiritually, Amalek attacks the mind and the inner point of faith in God, innate in the Divinely-inspired intelligence of the Jewish soul. The venom of Amalek seeks to cause the soul to "lose its mind."

Another figure who most personifies the snake (and who is a descendent of Amalek) is Titus, the Roman emperor who destroyed the second Temple. (His successor, Hadrian, exiled the Jewish people from the Land of Israel, beginning the present exile.) When Titus entered the Temple, he mocked God and the Divine service of the Jewish people, attempting to poison others with the venom of doubt. The sages relate that he himself was killed by a mosquito that entered his nose.[78]

This odd story takes on new meaning when we consider the teaching of the sages that God created everything in this world, even those creatures that appear to be of no use to humanity (such as the mosquito), for a good purpose—to heal human ailments. The very word for "a creature" in Hebrew (*beriah*) is cognate with "sound health" (*beriut*), thus implying that every creature possesses some healing power.

The Talmud[79] states that the mosquito (*yitush*) was created to heal the bite of the snake (*nachash*). The numerical value of *yitush* (716) is twice that of *nachash* (358), implying that on a spiritual plane, there is something about a mosquito bite that is twice as potent as that of a snake.[80]

Another explicit Biblical personification of the snake is Nachash, the king of Ammon, who besieged the Jewish settlement of Jabesh-Gilead. When the inhabitants offered to make a treaty with him and serve him, he demanded:

> *"On this [condition] I will seal a [covenant] with you:*
> *When the right eye of each of you is put out.*
> *It will be a sign of shame for all of Israel."*[81]

When the primordial snake seduced Eve to partake of the forbidden fruit of the Tree of Knowledge of Good and Evil, his venom went straight to her eyes:

> *And the snake said to the woman,*
> *"You shall surely not die.*
> *For God knows that on the day the you will eat of its*
>   *fruit,*
> *your eyes will be opened, and you will become as God,*
> *knowing good and evil."*
> *And the woman saw that the tree was good to eat*
> *and desirable to the eyes....*[82]

The eye is the seat of the sense of sight, the sense that most reflects the inner perception of the mind. As is stated in the Biblical account of Adam, Eve, the snake, and the primordial sin, lacking sight, even in one eye, implies lacking

Chapter Four: Origins of Disease

the knowledge that one is naked (either in the physical sense or in the spiritual sense, "naked of *mitzvot*"[83]).[84] One whose eyes, or eyesight, have been blemished by the venom of the snake lacks the knowledge that he is unclothed, and so becomes subject to shame. This is especially true with regard to the people of Israel, whom God cares for and protects "as the pupil of His eye."[85] The shame that comes with nakedness, as is most often reflected in dreams, is the beginning of mental disorder.

The people of Jabesh-Gilead sent out an urgent appeal for help that was heard by Saul, the newly appointed king of Israel, who rallied a supportive force that defeated Nachash and saved the inhabitants of Jabesh-Gilead. By virtue of his display of courage and leadership, his kingship became firmly established and accepted by all of Israel.

By Divine providence, the initial test of the new king of Israel, King Saul, was similar to the initial test of humanity in the Garden of Eden: to resist the temptation of the snake. Fired by the zealous spirit of God to defend Israel, King Saul withstood the test and so established his kingdom by conscripting all the tribes of Israel to fight Nachash, king of Ammon. The holy wolf killed the evil snake.[86]

(This supports the notion that will be explained later: in a certain sense, the wolf-figure, which corresponds to the immune system[87] of the body, includes all three figures—wolf, lion, and snake—and so is able to overcome the snake.)

Just as Amalek, the evil snake, represents the epitome of evil, so does the positive snake represent the epitome of good. As noted above, the Messiah himself is referred to in the *Zohar* as "the holy snake." This association is alluded to by the numerical equivalence of the Hebrew words *Mashiach* (358) and *nachash*, "snake." The *Zohar* further states that the Messiah, the holy snake, will kill the evil snake by overcoming the fear of insanity, thereby overcoming insanity itself, and filling human consciousness solely with the knowledge of God.[88] His reward will be to marry the Divine princess, the "congregation of Israel," to unite with the point of origin of the souls of Israel, thus bringing redemption to the world.

In particular, that aspect of the personality of the Messiah that engages in battle against the evil snake, Amalek, is known as the Messiah, the son of Joseph.[89] Joseph, the great dreamer and dream interpreter, personifies the soul gifted with the ability to properly diagnose and heal the ailments and malfunctions of the mind, to reach deep into the subconscious realms of the soul and there to retie wrongly connected wiring.[90]

As explained above, the snake-image connects with that of the wolf insofar as both manifest sexual impulse. Joseph epitomizes the rectification of the sexual drive, because he refused the sexual advances of Potiphar's wife.

The connection of the snake to Joseph is seen in the relationship between the Hebrew word for "snake" (*nachash*) and the word for "guess" (*nacheish*).

Guessing the future is a forbidden practice, according to the Torah, which brands it as a form of witchcraft. Guessing is a distortion of the mind, a psychological manifestation of the venom of the snake that goes directly to the mind.

Yet Joseph was able to interpret dreams and accurately forecast the future, as in his interpretation of Pharaoh's dream of seven fat cows and seven lean cows, which foreshadowed seven years of plenty and seven years of famine.

Joseph was able to do this because, as the holy "guesser," the holy snake, he possessed the Divine inspiration to always intuit the truth. Thus Joseph said of himself: "For a man as myself shall surely guess [correctly]!"[91]

Another example of a holy snake was Samson, who came from the tribe of Dan. As stated above, the tribe of Dan was blessed by Jacob to inherit judicious leadership and to be a snake. Samson was the descendant of Dan who fulfilled Jacob's blessing—that "Dan shall be a snake on the way, a serpent on the path,"[92] and that "Dan shall judge his people like one of the tribes of Israel."[93]

Samson, the judge of Israel, is the spiritual precursor of David, the king of Israel. On the spiritual plane, we see here an example of the holy snake (Samson) giving birth to the holy lion (David). This is supported as well by the fact that David's own father, Jesse, is referred to as "the snake."[94]

In the Book of Judges,[95] we read of Samson's sexual impulsiveness as well as of his incredible strength. The sages teach that no one ever possessed such seminal prowess as Samson.[96] Samson (as later did David) killed a lion, whose carcass became a honeycomb. In his riddle to the Philistines, he drew on this image when he challenged them to figure out who is meant by the metaphors, "From the eater came forth the food; from the bold came forth the sweet."[97] Here, the boldness and strength of the lion, the eater, are converted into sustenance—food—and sweetness by the holy snake.

All three images of wolf, lion, and snake converge in the person of Samson, who, according to Kabbalah, is an essential, although premature Messianic figure of the Bible.

GOLD, SILVER, AND COPPER

In one incident during the forty years of wandering in the desert, poisonous snakes attacked the Israelites, as a punishment for their complaints against God.

Moses prayed to God for forgiveness and was instructed to make a snake out of copper, so that people could look at it and be healed.

> *Moses made a snake out of copper*
> *and placed it on the pole;*
> *so it was that if a snake bit a man,*
> *he would gaze at the copper snake and live.*[98]

The snake placed upon a pole has thus become the universal symbol of healing, the caduceus.

The Hebrew root of the word for "snake" (*nachash*) is the same as that of the word for "copper" (*nechoshet*). The Hebrew word for "wolf" (*ze'ev*) is related to the word for "gold" (*zahav*). The three primary metals of the Torah, from which the Tabernacle and Temple were constructed, were "gold, silver, and copper."[99] If gold alludes to the wolf and copper to the snake, this would seem to imply that the lion alludes to silver. Silver is a pure, white metal possessing a

Chapter Four: Origins of Disease

brilliant luster. It excels all other metals as a conductor of heat and electricity. It thus shines as (white) light. This relates to the lion, as the Hebrew word for "lion" (*aryeh*) is cognate to the word for "light" (*or*).[100]

Hassidic teachings explain the rabbinic maxim[101] that the three metals of gold, silver, and copper allude to three levels of health/sickness and to the manner in which the ailing person gives charity, thereby arousing Divine mercy to heal him. The name of each metal is read as an acronym:

- Gold: "This is the healthy giver."
- Silver: "When there is the danger of fear."
- Copper: "The giving of an acutely sick person who said, 'give!'"[102]

We can draw the following correspondences between the three syndromes of fear described above and their rectifications:

Giving "gold" rectifies the triplet of the innate, behavioral properties of the soul (*netzach-hod-yesod*), healing those diseases that relate to the corresponding physiological systems of the body. Giving gold refers in particular to good and charitable deeds, which, in the words of our sages,[103] are man's most essential "progeny" in life (*netzach-hod-yesod* are the soul's "children"), his dearest possession on earth. One's children, both on the physical and spiritual planes, are one's gold. If one is always devoted to give gold, to do all in his power to help others, one's health remains sound: "This is a healthy giver." Giving gold is preventive medicine.

Giving "silver" rectifies the triplet of the emotive attributes of the soul (*chesed-gevurah-tiferet*), healing those diseases that relate to the corresponding physiological systems of the body. Good feelings are "silver"; in Kabbalah, feeling love for another, in particular, is "silver."[104] When ill, but not seriously ill, one's access to gold (his strength to act and give birth in the outside world) becomes limited, and he must now devote himself to giving silver. He must try to arouse in his heart, and express in his prayers, love for others. Our sages teach us that he who prays for others is himself, with regard to his own needs, answered first.[105] One gives silver "when there is danger of fear [of disease]."

Giving "copper" rectifies the triplet of the intellectual properties of the soul (*chochmah-binah-da'at*), healing those diseases that relate to the corresponding physiological systems of the body. Good, sound thoughts are "copper." When acutely ill, lacking even the strength necessary to arouse the emotions of the heart (silver), one must try to concentrate all of his thoughts on God and His Divine providence. In thought, one gives all of himself to God, saying (to all around, i.e., making his sincere intention known to all present, arousing them as well to give themselves totally over to God): "Give [all]!" One focuses all of his attention on the copper snake that Moses made, commanded by God. One looks upward to heaven, perceiving the source of his illness in Divine providence, which, ultimately, is for his good. In pure thought, one elevates and gives all "back" to God. This, more than anything else, arouses God's great, infinite mercy on him, and, miraculously, He heals him.

Chapter Four: Origins of Disease

To summarize:

focus of fear	metal: healing method	properties of soul
snake syndrome	copper: good thoughts	intellectual
lion syndrome	silver: good feelings	emotive
wolf syndrome	gold: good deeds	behavioral

5

Understanding Illness

ALLOSTASIS AND DISEASE

The three physiological systems that most characteristically reflect the interplay between body and soul—the nervous system, the endocrine system, and the immune system—contribute significantly to the general well-being of the individual. The inter-dependent functioning of these systems is described in modern medicine as the neuro-endocrine-immune mechanism. This physiological team helps the body adapt to potentially stressful challenges, a process referred to as allostasis.

Allostasis achieves psychological and physiological stability through change and adaptation. Proper maintenance of allostasis depends on a careful balance of multiple mechanisms. Dysfunction of these mechanisms results in disease.[1]

A common phenomenon is that under acute stress, impending infections may be held at bay, but resistance may collapse when the pressure is relieved. Thus, we see that the whole process of allostasis demands the highest degree of equilibrium and sensitivity to the present state of mind/body.

Stress, a major cause of disease, is still enigmatic and resistant to scientific definition. What is known is that psychological effects of the mind on health are exerted via influences on the immune system. Extended states of stress may well suppress and weaken the immune system to the extent that it becomes unable to properly perform its function to fend off disease.

Of all the physiological systems, the nervous system is most directly associated with the mind itself. Thus, when we say that the mind exerts influence on the immune system, we mean that the nervous system communicates in some way to the immune system. This communication is now known to be bi-directional, and that when stress affects the immune system, the immune system communicates back to the nervous system.

Modern research suggests that the nervous system communicates with the immune system via the endocrine system. A full cycle of communication is thus achieved, from the nervous system to the endocrine system to the immune system and back to the nervous system.

A Kabbalistic model lends insight into this complex physical mechanism.

When we examine the correspondences of the ten *sefirot* and the various physiological systems of the body (as explained above in Chapter 3), we find that *da'at*, *netzach*, and *hod* correspond to the nervous, endocrine, and immune systems, respectively.

```
            ┌─────────────────────┐
            │       da'at         │
            │ posterior of brain  │
            │  **nervous system** │
            └─────────────────────┘

┌──────────────┐                    ┌──────────────┐
│     hod      │                    │   netzach    │
│   left leg   │                    │  right leg   │
│**immune system**│                │**endocrine system**│
└──────────────┘                    └──────────────┘
```

We noted above that allostasis demands the highest degree of equilibrium and sensitivity to the present state of mind/body. Sensitivity is the property of *da'at*, the posterior region of the brain. Equilibrium is controlled by *da'at*,² although its major expression in the body is the balance between *netzach* and *hod*, the loins and the two legs upon which the body stands.³

The arrangement in the above chart forms a triangle. This is no accident. Indeed, these three *sefirot*—*da'at*, *netzach*, and *hod*—form the higher triangle of the Star of David (*Magen David*), while *chesed*, *gevurah*, and *yesod* form the lower triangle (with *tiferet* in the middle).⁴

In Kabbalah, each of the *sefirot* is identified with an archetypal soul. The two companion *sefirot* of *netzach* and *hod* are identified with the souls of the holy brothers Moses and Aaron, of whom it is said, "Behold, how goodly and how pleasant it is for brothers to dwell together."⁵ The origin of these two souls is in the *sefirah* of *da'at*, the power to be together. Thus, the secret of the higher triangle of the Star of David is, in fact, the "birth" of the souls of Moses and Aaron from their common origin.⁶

Acting together, the two brothers, Moses and Aaron, were God's emissaries to take us out of the Egyptian exile. As we saw earlier, disease relates to the spiritual state of exile. Liberation from Egypt is liberation from disease.

After the splitting of the Red Sea, and the song of thanksgiving that Moses and the Jewish people sang to God, God promised:

> *If you will diligently listen*
> *to the voice of GOD, your God,*
> *and will do that which is right in His sight,*
> *and will give ear to His commandments,*
> *and keep all His statutes,*
> *I will not place on you any of the diseases*
> *that I have brought upon the Egyptians;*
> *for I am GOD, your healer.*[7]

At the time of the giving of the Torah to Israel at Mt. Sinai, the culmination of the Exodus from Egypt, we were not only healed of all our ailments, but also liberated from the Angel of Death. Had we not sinned, we would have never more been sick, and never would have died. However, as voiced in the above-quoted verse, our sins brought back upon us the plague of disease and death.

After the Exodus, Moses became the Divine conduit through which God gave the Torah to Israel. Aaron became the High Priest of Israel, representing the apex of our service of God. Thus, Moses and Aaron became the two archetypal healers of Israel: Moses through the power of the Torah and Aaron through the power of the Priestly Blessing. By connecting ourselves to the Torah and devoting our lives to the service of God, we draw down Divine healing power into our souls.

We see Moses' role as healer after the sin of the Golden Calf, the archetypal sin of the Jewish people, equivalent, in Kabbalah, to the primordial sin of Adam and Eve. When God threatens to annihilate the nation of Israel, Moses pleads for pardon. The word in Hebrew for "pardon" (*mechilah*) is related to "disease" (*machalah*). In other words, Moses prayed that God heal the diseased spirit of the people:

> *And Moses beseeched* GOD, *his God, and said:*
> *Why, O God, do you direct Your wrath*
> *against Your people…"*[8]

Here, the word "beseeched" (*vayechal*), a synonym for prayer, is also related to the word for "sickness" (*machalah*). The sages learn from this etymological equivalence that Moses prayed so hard to God to forgive the sin of the people that he became physically sick with fever.[9] From this we may infer that in sickness itself lies the inherent ability to undergo self-transformation from illness to well-being, all through the power of prayer. We will examine the healing power of prayer in detail in Chapter 8.

THE TRANSFORMING POWER OF DISEASE

The relationship of "pardon" (*mechilah*) to "disease" (*machalah*) noted above is but one example of what Hebrew, and its sister language Aramaic, can teach us about disease and healing. We see, for instance, that the two-letter Hebrew sub-root (*ch-l*) of "sick" (*choleh*) possesses variant meanings, among which are apparent opposites. Indeed, this root can mean either "weak" or "strong."

In the Book of Judges, when Samson reveals to Delilah the secret of his strength, he tells that if he were to shave his hair, he would become "weak" (*v'chaliti*):

> *He told her all his heart, and said to her:*
> *"A razor has never come upon my head,*
> *for I have been a nazirite unto God from my mother's womb.*
> *If I be shaven, then my strength will go from me,*
> *and I shall become weak, and be like any other man."*[10]

Hassidic thought derives from this verse that the very concept of sickness is relative in nature. What for any other human being might be a state of good health and well-being, for Samson was a state of illness. For Samson, to lose his strength and "be like any other man" was, relative to him, to lose his male status—to become, physically, as one of the weaker sex. (In a similar vein, what we consider to be woman's natural, healthy, menstrual cycle is seen in the Torah to be an innate state of "illness," which resulted from Eve's eating of the forbidden fruit[11] and which will be healed with the coming of the Messiah. Indeed, the fact that women are becoming stronger and stronger in body and soul is a sign that we are approaching the Messianic Era.)

In contrast, the word *chayil*, cognate to "sick" (*choleh*), means "strength," as the Psalms state with regard to the righteous:

> *They go from strength to strength.*
> *Every one of them shall appear before God in Zion.*[12]

Similarly, a "soldier" is a *chayal*; a "woman of valor" is an *eshet chayil*.

Another pair of opposites from the same root (primarily in its Aramaic usage) is *chala*, in the sense of "bitter" or "tart"[13] and *chala*, in the sense of "sweet."[14]

The relation between bitterness and disease is apparent from the fact that the name of the organ that according to the sages[15] is the major seat of disease—the gall bladder (*marah*)—comes from the word meaning "bitter" (*mar*). The Talmud states that the 83 illnesses that afflict mankind are dependent on the gall bladder; indeed, the numerical value of the Hebrew word for "disease" (*machalah*) is 83.[16]

The bile of the gall bladder was termed by the ancients the yellow or green "humor" in the body. In Kabbalah, it is associated in particular with the body's natural desire to pursue physical pleasure. Bile is further referred to as "the lower waters" of creation, in contrast to "the higher waters," that is, spiritual and Divine pleasure. When the two waters are separated and distanced from one another, the lower waters become bitter (in the negative sense of becoming totally engrossed in physical pleasure, to the extent of becoming addicted to the vanities of this world), and illness ensues.

Even when imprisoned in the clutches of physical pleasure and estranged from its spiritual source, the inner consciousness of the lower waters still cries out bitterly to

God: "We also desire to be in the presence of God, to experience Divine pleasure as do the higher waters!"[17]

Thus, Hassidic thought maintains that disease and its remedy depend upon the rectification or redirection of the "pleasure principle," the transformation of the bitter—the counterfeit sweetness of physical pleasures—to the truly sweet pleasure in the Divine. This sweet pleasure is the experience of the ultimate Divine unity underlying all reality, both physical and spiritual.

Based upon these two phenomena—the etymological relationship of "weakness" to "strength" and "bitterness" to "sweetness," all in conjunction with the word for "sickness"—we are taught in Hassidism that "sickness" is actually an intermediate state of being between "life" and "death." "Life" is a state of holiness (for that which is truly holy lives forever), whereas "death" is a state of profanity (the origin of all impurity; impurity issues from contact with death). The word for "profane" (*chilul*) is the strongest grammatical form of the sub-root of "sick" (*ch-l*). It means "to pierce" or to create a "vacuum" (*chalal*, which also means "corpse"). The profane pierces, as it were, the holy.

The intermediate state between the holy and the profane is the realm of the "mundane" (*chol* or *chulin*, from the sub-root of "sick," *ch-l*). In Kabbalah, it is referred to as "the translucent shell" (*kelipat nogah*), the intermediate between transparency (i.e., holiness, *kedushah*) and opacity (i.e., the three totally impure shells, *kelipot hatemeiot*); that is, between clear revelation of the Divine nature of reality and concealment/non-recognition of the Divine.

Thus, sickness may serve as a bridge in two directions: from life to death or from death to life. To recover from sickness is to be reborn, alive once more. It is to recognize that one actually became sick in order to return stronger and healthier than ever before.

Sometimes, one becomes sick in order to connect to and thereby elevate fallen souls. This is the case with regard to the Messiah who, before his coming (that is, his revelation to mankind), suffers both spiritually and physically in order to raise the people of Israel and all of humanity from the realm of the opaque (the three impure shells), thereby redeeming them. In the words of Isaiah:

> *[The Messiah] is a man of pain,*
> *acquainted with illness....*
> *Truly, he has borne our illness*
> *and he has suffered our pain.*[18]

As taught in Hassidism, each of us possesses a spark of the Messiah. An essential part of the Divine providence at play in a person becoming sick is that he or she comes to identify with all suffering souls, and, in supplication to God, wishes to recover and be redeemed together with them all.

The coming of the Messiah will end the exile of Edom, which began two thousand years ago when the Romans destroyed the Temple in Jerusalem and scattered the Jewish people throughout the world. At that time, the inherent bitterness of disease will become sweetened. In the first period of the messianic age, illness will disappear, although death, at very old age, will remain.[19] Eventually, when "the impure spirit" will vanish from the face of the earth,[20] death as well will be "swallowed up forever."[21]

As we saw earlier, the existence of disease is strongly connected in the Torah to that of exile. People in exile have been banished from their homeland, from their source of life. This estrangement, whether on the spiritual or physical plane, is equivalent to disease. In general, disease is the estrangement of the soul from the body; in the terminology of Kabbalah, the estrangement of the light from the vessels.

In the primordial world of chaos, the inner lights of reality were disassociated and distanced from their vessels, which thereby broke, became sick, and ultimately died. All of our Divine service is aimed to repair this primordial world.

The *Zohar* goes so far as to say that the *Shechinah*—God's Presence in creation, His infinite, immanent light that "fills all worlds"—is "sick" in exile together with the Jewish people. Rabbi Shneur Zalman of Liadi explains this at length in the *Tanya*:[22]

> The statement of the *Tikunim* is well-known: "the *Shechinah* suffers [literally: 'is sick'] in exile."
>
> The *Shechinah*'s sickness is like a bodily disease: the cause of illness or health lies in the spread and flow of the life-force vested in the blood which flows from the heart to all the limbs; and the blood with the spirit of life in it circulates in all the limbs, through the blood vessels in them, and returns to the heart.
>
> When the circulation and flow of this spirit of life is consistently as it should be, in its proper order as arranged for it by the blessed Fountainhead of Life,

the individual man is perfectly healthy. For all the limbs are bound together and receive their proper vitality from the heart through this circulation. But if there is any disorder in whatever place, restraining, hindering, or reducing the circulation of the blood with the spirit of life vested in it, then this bond—which by means of that circulation binds all limbs of the body to the heart—is broken or diminished, and the individual will fall ill and sick (May God have mercy).

Precisely so, metaphorically speaking, all the souls of Israel are regarded as the limbs of the *Shechinah*, which is called the "heart," as it is written: "the Rock of my heart"; and as it is written: "and I shall dwell amongst them." That is, the term *Shechinah* denotes the light of God that dwells in the Worlds of Creation, Formation, and Action [*Beriah*, *Yetzirah*, and *Asiyah*] in order to animate them.

This life-force is drawn [into the world only] after first having been enclothed in the souls of Israel. This is so because none of the created beings are in any approximation to the blessed Creator; for all before Him are as naught. Thus, it is impossible for them to receive life-force from His blessed light and effluence and be created *ex nihilo*, living and subsisting, other than through the souls [of Israel] that arose in His thought and preceded the creation of the worlds by His speech. And so did our sages, of blessed memory, say: "With whom did the Holy One, blessed be He, take counsel? [With the righteous souls of Israel]," as is explained elsewhere.

All life-force and the effluence that flows from the upper to the lower worlds is from them [i.e., the life-force, vested in the blood, first enclothes itself in the souls of Israel, the limbs that receive their life-force from the Divine heart, the *Shechinah*, and by means of the souls, the life-force flows downward and upward throughout the worlds], as is stated in *Sefer Yetzirah*: "their beginning is wedged in their end, and their end is wedged in their beginning." In the writings of Rabbi Yitzchak Luria, of blessed memory, this is referred to as "direct light" (*or yashar*) and "reflected light" (*or chozer*), as it is written: "and the living beings ran forward and backward [*ratzo vashov*]."

Thus, according to these words and this truth—which it is not possible to explain properly in writing—it follows that the *Shechinah* is referred to as the "heart," and the souls as "limbs." This teaches us that when all souls are attached and bound together, the circulation and flow of the life-force and of the effluence circulates properly, and "their end is wedged in their beginning," binding and joining them all to "God [who] is One," to be attached to Him, blessed be He. And thus it is written: "you are standing this day, all of you, before GOD, your God...."

And thereby will be understood the saying of our sages, of blessed memory, that the destruction of the Second Temple and the fall of Israel into exile, and the withdrawal of the *Shechinah* and its descent to Edom, into a state of exile, as it were—all this was because of the sin of causeless hatred and a division of hearts, may the Merciful One save us. And that is why [the *Shechinah*] is referred to as "sick," metaphorically speaking. As to the phrases, "He raises the fallen, and heals the sick"—in plural form, this alludes to all the limbs, etc.

As explained earlier (see Chapter 2), the blood relates to the *sefirah* of *binah*, the mother-principle—"the mother gives her child the red [i.e., the blood]." The final and most extended exile, the exile referred to in the passage of *Tanya* cited above, is the exile of Edom, from the word "red" (*adom*) and "blood" (*dam*).

In Hassidic thought[23] it is explained that the consummate rectification of the mother principle in the soul is accomplished through unbounded love for one's fellow Jew. Here, one experiences the entire Jewish people together, in love and fellowship, under the protective wings of the Divine "mother." Loving all Jews as oneself connects the limbs of the Divine "body"; the love itself is the life-giving blood that unites all of the body's limbs. The word for "blood" (*dam*) is associated with the word for "man" (*adam*), which connotes in the Bible the Jewish people as a whole.[24] Only by undeserved love (*ahavat chinam*) for all of Israel do we rectify the cause of exile, causeless hatred (*sinat chinam*).

The sages teach[25] that all exiles of the Jewish people, including the last, the exile of Edom, reflect the first, archetypal exile, the exile of Egypt. In Kabbalah, Egypt also corresponds, in the realm of impurity, to the womb of the mother. The Exodus from Egypt is the birth of the people of Israel from this impure womb.

The Talmud describes the moment of birth as follows:[26]

> Rabbi Simlai expounded: "What does an embryo resemble in its mother's womb? A folded slate, its hands resting on its two sides, its two elbows

on its two knees, and its two heels on its two buttocks. Its head rests between its knees; its mouth is closed and its navel is open, and it eats what its mother eats and drinks what its mother drinks, and does not excrete lest it kill its mother. Once it exits [the womb] to the outside world, that which was closed opens and that which was open closes, and were this not to occur, it would not be able to live for even a moment...."

As the sages point out here, the transition from life in the womb to life in the outside world depends upon a quick and precisely-timed reversal of physiological states and functions. This is true not only with regard to the digestive system *per se* (the mouth and the navel), but also with regard to many of the physiological systems, which indeed are interdependent, most significantly with regard to the circulatory system and the respiratory system.[27]

The dramatic changes that take place in the body at the moment of birth are in fact among the greatest miracles in God's creation of the universe and living beings.

As is well known to modern medicine, the most critical of the changes that take place at the moment of birth relate in particular to the circulatory system.[28] As redemption from exile is likened to the moment of birth, we may conclude that redemption depends upon a healthy circulatory system.

The malfunctioning of the blood results in the weakening of the immune system. In the terminology of Kabbalah: "*binah* extends until *hod*," as will be explained.

The Torah draws a further comparison to the spiritually diseased state of exile and its connection to the property of *hod*, an immune system property, in the story of Jacob's struggle with the angel of Esau (called the *ish*).[29] Although Jacob won the struggle, he was injured on his left thigh. Though God healed him (by the soothing light of the sun[30]), the injury, or the power by which the angel of Esau was able to injure him, left a deep impression on Jacob's soul and, ultimately, was responsible for sending Jacob and his children into exile. Jacob's injured thigh signifies the nature of the exile of the Jewish people. As a result of this event, the Torah forbids us to eat of the sciatic nerve, this itself symbolizing disease and exile.

As mentioned in Chapter 1, it is the left leg or thigh that is identified with *hod*. Inasmuch as this is where Jacob was injured by Esau's angel, we are taught in Kabbalah that in general, this limb is the one most vulnerable to injury.

This relates as well to the body's system that corresponds to the *sefirah* of *hod*—the immune system. This is the system most susceptible to disorder, confusion, and inability to distinguish between Esau (invading or diseased cells) and Jacob (positive, healthy cells). With Jacob's victory over Esau's angel, it was essential for him to re-establish and reinforce his very identity. He insisted that the angel bless him with his true name, Israel, not known until then.

When we rectify our ability to acknowledge and thank God for everything that we have, to relate to Him above logic and reason, and return to Him in submission (all characteristics of the soul's rectified attribute of *hod*), we will then be healed from the illness of exile and will be able to experience our return to health and redemption.

Thus, we find that *hod* signifies vulnerability to disease (for that is the point at which the angel attacked), as well as the point at which disease is overcome. Our weaknesses are precisely the points at which we can become strong, our illnesses are the points at which we can be healed. Thus, in every illness is embedded the clue to the nature of the cure itself.[31] Indeed, this is one way in which God prepares the cure *before* inflicting the disease, as the sages teach.

ILLNESS AS SPIRITUAL DEFICIENCY

Illness and disease derive from a spiritual state of deficiency, of "lack" or "emptiness" (a spiritual "vacuum," as explained above with regard to the root of the word for "profanity"). In Kabbalah, the word "sick" (*choleh*), whose numerical value is 49, indicates that the sick person lacks the fiftieth gate of understanding, the knowledge of God[32] without which one lives in a spiritual state of "vacuum." Thus, "to heal" is "to fill" or "to complete" one's consciousness with the fiftieth gate of understanding. 50 is the numerical value of the word for "all," *kol*, indicating that less than 50—i.e., 49, illness—is lacking "allness" or wholeness.

In Kabbalah and Hassidism[33] we are taught that there are four levels of spiritual deficiency, which we will now describe.

The first level of deficiency in the soul is the absence of the inner light of the Torah. The soul yearns to fill its consciousness to the brim with the light of the Torah—that light which resolves all of the conflicts of life, which answers all of life's existential questions: Why are we here? Where are we going? Why has the Messiah not yet arrived?

Paradoxically, the very concern or "worry" with regard to life's existential questions is itself half the cure which makes one a vessel to receive the light of Torah, as in the words of the sages:

> The mysteries of the Torah are bestowed only
> to one whose heart is anxious within him.[34]

This level of deficiency corresponds to the *yud* of God's Name, *Havayah*, the level of Divine wisdom and insight into the mysteries of the Torah. Here, one is not actually "sick" but only "concerned" or "anxious."[35]

The next level of deficiency in the soul is the longing to return to one's beloved from whom one has become estranged. The Torah calls this spiritual state "lovesickness." This is the state described in the Song of Songs:

> *Support me with cups of wine, revive me with apples,*
> *for I am lovesick.*[36]

Lovesickness is the experience of spiritual exile, the source of disease, as was explained above.[37]

This state of sickness reflects the spiritual blemish of *binah*, corresponding to the first *hei* of God's Name. It is here in particular that the sick person lacks the fiftieth gate of understanding, associated in Kabbalah with the consummate experience of love described in the Song of Songs:

> *How beautiful and pleasant are you,*
> *O love that experiences delights!*[38]

The first two levels of spiritual deficiency correspond to the first two letters of God's Name (the *yud* and the first *hei*) and are referred to in Kabbalah as "the concealed things [that] belong to GOD, our God."[39] Here, although constantly conscious of Divinity, one lacks Divine revelation. In contrast, the next two levels of deficiency, which correspond to the two final letters of God's Name (the *vav* and the final *hei*), are referred to in Kabbalah as "the revealed things [that] belong to us and our children."[40] These states of lacking are the lack of Divine consciousness itself. As will now be explained, to the extent that we long for worldly pleasures, so do we lose Divine consciousness.

On the physical plane (the two final letters of God's Name are relatively physical, in contrast to the first two letters, which are relatively spiritual) there exist two states of illness or disease. In the words of the sages: "a sick person who is not in mortal danger" and "a sick person who is in mortal danger."[41] Both states issue from our animal soul's craving for physical pleasure, which draws us away from consciously clinging to the Divine by dulling our Divine soul's innate sensitivity to Godliness. Hassidism explains the difference between these two states of illness, in their origin:

"A sick person who is not in mortal danger" is one who longs for worldly pleasures that, in principle, are permissible according to the Torah. Although the Torah does not forbid us to partake of these pleasures, the element of desire entailed in their conscious pursuit distances our minds and hearts from God. God wants us, His children, to partake of and enjoy all of the pleasures He has created for us in His world, within the parameters defined by His Torah.[42] But at the same time, He wants us to always retain full consciousness of His presence in everything and experience (and express) heartfelt gratitude to Him for His benevolence. Physical desire draws us down and away from God. In particular, it blemishes the emotions of our hearts—the "six attributes" known as *midot* (from *chesed* to *yesod*)—which correspond to the *vav* of God's Name.

"A sick person who is in mortal danger" is one who longs for worldly pleasures forbidden by the Torah. For such a person the commandments of the Torah are like a doctor's prescription. That which the Torah forbids is mortally dangerous for the soul and the body. Mortal danger exists at the level of *malchut* ("kingdom"). In the Torah it is written of kings who followed the lusts of their hearts, without regard to the precepts of the Torah: "and he reigned and he died."[43] By craving for and partaking of those worldly pleasures that are forbidden by the Torah, we blemish our innate attribute of *malchut*, which is defined in Kabbalah and Hassidism as our very ego or sense of self as a living soul vested in a physical body. We thereby endanger our lives. The blemish of *malchut* is that of the final *hei* of God's Name.

In summary:

Name of God		sefirah	experience of spiritual deficiency
concealed levels	י *yud*	*chochmah* "wisdom"	anxiety
	ה *hei*	*binah* "understanding"	lovesickness
revealed levels	ו *vav*	*midot* six "emotions"	sickness
	ה *hei*	*malchut* "kingdom"	mortal danger

ILLNESS AS SPIRITUAL ESTRANGEMENT

As noted above, the phenomenon of disease is one of separation or estrangement. Estrangement reflects a blemished state of *hod*—the *sefirah* that correlates with the body's immune system and which represents the soul's power to acknowledge that which is true and good and to express thanks to others for their kind gifts. A blemished attribute of *hod*—insensitivity to others and inability to perceive and acknowledge the truth in the words of others and to thank them for their acts of goodness—results in confusion. This is the inability to distinguish between ally and foe (as mentioned above) or between self and non-self (as will be explained). Confusion leads to spiritual blindness, *total* insensitivity to others. A blemished attribute of *hod* thus brings a person to total estrangement from (benevolent) others and from God.

In particular, disease is the estrangement of the *sefirot* of the left axis from those of the right:

The blood carries the cells of the immune system that fight off disease. The blood relates to the *sefirah* of *binah* ("understanding"), the blood vessels to the *sefirah* of *gevurah* ("might"), and the immune system to the *sefirah* of *hod* ("thanksgiving"). These are the three *sefirot* located on the left axis of the Tree of Life. When the *sefirot* of the left become estranged from *chesed* ("loving-kindness") and its companion *sefirot* of the right, then disease is manifest through the malfunction of the immune system.

This estrangement is expressed in the Book of Psalms:

And I said:
"It is my infirmity
that the right hand of the Most High has changed."[44]

The "changing" of "the right hand of the Most High" refers, in Kabbalah, to the concealment of the Divine principle of "right," due to the estrangement of the left from the right. Exile is the concealment of the right, the concealment of God's loving-kindness from the souls of His people, Israel. This state is here referred to as infirmity or sickness.

In Hassidic thought,[45] the Hebrew for "my infirmity" (*chaloti*, from the two-letter sub-root of "sickness," *ch-l*) is interpreted in four related senses:

1. "in my trembling"—a symptom of weakness and disease,[46]
2. "in my sickness,"[47]

3. "in my prayer" (as above, with regard to Moses' prayer after the sin of the Golden Calf),[48] and
4. "in my ability to sweeten the bitter" (the inner purpose of illness, as above).[49]

"The right of the Most High" refers not only to the right axis of the *sefirot*, but also to the supernal crown, *keter*, of which is said, "There is no left in that Ancient One [an appellation of the supernal crown]; all is right."[50]

In Kabbalah, *keter* is also referred to as *Arich Anpin*, literally, "the long [or 'infinitely extended'] face." The word for "long" (*arich*) is cognate to the word for "healing" or "cure" (*arukah*). The right axis of the *sefirot* is referred to in the *Zohar* as "the long axis."[51] The word *arich* is seen as an acronym formed by the initial letters of the verse from Exodus: "For I am God Who heals you."[52] (It is also seen as an acronym formed by the initial letters of the conclusion of all prayers to God: "Amen, so may it be His will."[53])

The apparent redundancy in the above quotation from the *Zohar*—"There is no left in that Ancient One; all is right"—is interpreted in Kabbalah to mean that the spiritual origin of the left is indeed present in *keter*, but that at that level, it too is "right"—"*all* is right." Thus, the super-conscious *keter* is what inspires all of the *sefirot* on the left to recognize the goodness of the right and to desire to identify with it.

The beginning of the union of right and left, the union of two different *sefirot*, one to the right and one to the left, occurs at the level of the mind. This is the union of *chochmah* and *binah*, the union of the father and the mother, and in the soul, it is the union of the experiences of selflessness and joy.

With regard to the one disease whose onset and cure are explicitly described in the Torah—*tzara'at* ("leprosy"[54])—we are taught in Kabbalah and Hassidism[55] that the root of this disease is the disassociation of *chochmah* from *binah*.

In accordance with the physiological correspondences described above, this means that the bone marrow is not continually producing new blood cells. The cure depends upon the powers of *keter*—faith, pleasure, and will—to reunite the "two companions" of *chochmah* and *binah*.[56]

Physiologically, *keter* corresponds to the respiratory system. As *keter* serves to reunite *chochmah* and *binah* (the bone marrow and the blood), we may infer that in addition to the functioning of a healthy respiratory system to oxygenate healthy blood, to be supplied to the body and all its organ systems, a healthy respiratory system affects, in particular, the process of the bone marrow becoming new blood cells. The new, reinforced blood will then continue to descend down the left axis of the *sefirot*, until reaching and strengthening the immune system to overcome disease.

As *tzara'at* is the archetypal disease of the Torah, its source applies to all disease. As explained in Kabbalah and Hassidism, all disease results from the disassociation of *chochmah* from *binah*, selflessness from joy.

In particular, with regard to tumors (undesired "growth" or "inflation" in the body), the Lubavitcher Rebbe, Rabbi Menachem Mendel Schneerson, taught that the spiritual source of their cure was given to the world with the revelation of Hassidism, whose light cultivates in the soul the attribute of selflessness (deflation of the ego).⁵⁷ In accordance with the analysis of the physiological systems and their correspondence to the *sefirot* presented here, this would seem to suggest that a cure for such diseases should relate to the proper functioning of the bone marrow.

In contrast, the cure of other diseases—which manifest themselves in the opposite way, as a lack or "deflation" within the body in need of "filling" (a power ultimately deriving from the fiftieth gate of understanding, as noted earlier)—is dependent upon the faculty of *binah* and the soul's experience of being filled with joy. In accordance with our analysis, their cure should relate to the healthy functioning and circulation of the blood.

Thus, the cure of all disease may be seen as dependent upon the proper functioning and balance of these two origins of cure, *chochmah* and *binah*, the flow from *chochmah* to *binah*, and the inclusion of *binah* (the left) in *chochmah* (the right).

The proper flow and inter-inclusion of *chochmah*—selflessness—and *binah*—joy—energizes the mind to strengthen the body's immune system, corresponding to *hod*, sincerity and acknowledgement. In Hassidism, we learn that the *chochmah-binah-hod* cycle (the marrow-blood-immune cycle)—from wisdom to understanding to acknowledgement to a higher level of insight/wisdom—raises our level of consciousness to recognize and acknowledge elusive truths that otherwise would have remained outside our grasp. Our faith in God's transcendent, healing light becomes reinforced in our consciousness, the light permeates our being, and we so obtain the power to overcome (and prevent) disease.⁵⁸

MALFUNCTIONS OF THE IMMUNE SYSTEM

As we have seen, it is the immune system that acts as the body's natural defense mechanism against disease. By monitoring the internal status of the body to determine what properly belongs and is healthy, the immune system sounds the alarm upon detecting the presence of foreign, non-compatible, or even threatening substances. Upon sensing the invasion of some foreign substance, the immune system then determines if its presence is a threat, that is, if it is damaging to healthy cells. The presence of such a substance, such as a virus, signals an alert and demands a response. At this point, the immune system creates antibodies—compounds designed to either neutralize or destroy the foreign substance within the body.

The immune system—our sensitivity to foreign matter—can be understood on a broader spiritual plane to refer to our innate sense of self and non-self. We are at home with ourselves, with that which we perceive to be part of us. We naturally recoil from what we sense to be non-self, some type of foreign invasion, be it on a biological level in the form of a disease or on a psychological level in the sense of strange and undesired influences.

A problem of the immune system is a problem related to the defense mechanism of the body. An extreme example of such a problem is autoimmune disease (such as Lupus or AIDS), which attacks the root of the body's defense mechanism, rendering it unable to distinguish between healthy and unhealthy elements. The immune system may then experience such internal confusion that it mistakenly perceives the person's own healthy body as the threat. In response, it actually creates antibodies to fight against the healthy cells and organs of the body itself.

In the words of the prophet Isaiah:

Woe unto them that call evil good and good evil;
that put darkness for light
and light for darkness;
that put bitter for sweet
and sweet for bitter![59]

In all of the three psychological misinterpretations that characterize the nature of sickness, as depicted here by the prophet (evil vs. good, darkness vs. light, bitter vs. sweet), the person who suffers from disease first sees the negative to be positive, and only thereafter sees the positive to be negative. And so it is with regard to the body: in autoimmune disease, the body first misinterprets the invading, unhealthy matter to be healthy, and only then begins to fight against its own healthy cells, as if they were foreign invaders.[60]

In Kabbalah, we are taught that the word "woe" (*hoi*) as used by Isaiah refers to a state in which spiritual light and life-force disappear from the body. In particular, the life-force that normally extends to all parts of the body, by means of the blood,[61] disappears from the body and returns to its source in the unconscious realm of the mind. The mind is no longer able to affect the limbs, to permeate the body with the innate ability to understand what is good for it and what is bad for it.

As we saw above, disease relates to the well-being of the blood and the circulatory system. It is the function of the blood to bring "understanding"—*binah*—to all the cells of the body. "Woe" to the malfunction of the blood as reflected in the misunderstanding of the immune system.

This "misunderstanding" plays itself out in the *sefirah* of *hod* in the following manner.

Hod means "acknowledgement"—particularly of that which is true and good. In Hassidic thought, this is the power of one's soul to commit itself to pursuing a life of truth and goodness.

Commitment to an ideal implies acknowledging that which transcends our normal realm of understanding; a true ideal is not one that is formed and developed in the rational mind but rather one that reflects the deepest intuitive sense of the soul as to what is ultimately true and good. *Hod* takes hold of the ultimate ideal and pursues its fulfillment. However, here, more so than with regard to any other *sefirah*—specifically because *hod* relates to the transcendent, yet undefined realm of the soul and reality—one is liable to misconstrue, in this case, to misidentify the true ideal. Instead of committing ourselves to serving God and dedicating our lives to His Divine plan, we may veer off course and end up making a commitment to the very opposite.

With regard to the body, the Book of Daniel[62] describes the sick body's inability to properly acknowledge what is true and good, what is self and non-self:

My pleasant appearance was horribly altered.

The Hebrew word used for "pleasant appearance" is *hod*. When *hod* is spelled backwards, it reads *davah*, which means "to be ill." Kabbalah explains that the quality of *hod* during a time of exile—a dysfunctional state where normal conditions disappear and confusion sets in—is that of illness or infirmity, of *davah*.[63]

When discussing Samson and Delilah above, we referred to the state of "illness" inherent in the feminine menstrual cycle. In the Torah, the period of menstruation is described as "the separation of her infirmity" (*nidat devotah*).[64] This relates *hod* to a feminine tendency—in the words of the Zohar, "*she* is in *hod*"[65]—as will be explained later.

The immune system is thus understood to be feminine in nature, a feminine physiological system which, metaphorically, either recognizes her true soul-mate and loyally commits herself to fulfilling their mutual life's purpose, or strays away, disloyal to her soul-mate, unable to recognize him as the complementary side of her true being, without whom she cannot fulfill herself.[66]

We will now examine how this plays out in a particular autoimmune disease, as we take up a study of Lupus.

6

Lupus

THE DIMENSIONS OF THE DISEASE

An example of a disease that originates in the immune system and can be linked to the primordial fear of the wolf, the fear of rape, is Lupus.[1] Indeed, "lupus" is Latin for "wolf." The French physician Pierre Louis Alphe Cazenave[2] gave the disease this name in 1851 because he thought that the rash that often develops in this disease resembled a wolf's bite.

In the spirit of Kabbalah and Hassidism, the very fact that, by Divine Providence, the name "wolf" was attributed to this disease can be seen as evidence of its relation to a problem originating in the immune system, which, as we saw above, relates to the "wolf syndrome." The problem with Lupus, or any autoimmune disease, arises from a misconstrued fear—the body reacts as if a healthy element is a foreign intruder. As explained above, the fear of intrusion is in essence the fear of rape, the fear of the wolf.

Approximately 90% of Lupus cases are found in women, a clear indication that Lupus is primarily a feminine disease. In Kabbalah, femininity in general is related to the *sefirah* of *hod* (the *sefirah* associated with the immune[3] system)—as the *Zohar* (quoted above) states, "*she* is in *hod*."

A further indication of the relation of Lupus to the rape syndrome is seen in the medical findings that note that for many Lupus patients, the sun will either spark an episode of the disease (if it is in remission) or intensify an existing manifestation. Psychologically, Lupus patients often have an aversion to sunlight and tanning; they prefer being in the dark, in order to remain hidden or private. Lupus patients feel that the sun is their "enemy." The spiritual root of this condition is an underlying fear that exposure to the sun allows the sun to touch and enter one's body. This psychophysical aversion to sunlight, similar to the fear of rape, places the sun in the position of the wolf.[4]

As an autoimmune disease, Lupus creates a situation in the immune system where it is unable to distinguish the healthy cells of a person's own body from harmful invading particles. The result is that the body produces "self-reacting antibodies," antibodies that fight against the healthy cells of the body.

The property of *hod* normally serves to acknowledge or identify the presence of a foreign substance in the body. In Lupus patients, this ability becomes corrupted to the point that their immune system can no longer properly identify anything. Even the disease itself evades identification, as will be discussed presently. We can say, therefore, that Lupus is a disease of mistaken identity, which emerges at a number of levels.

For the Jewish people, this phenomenon can be likened to our generation, whose major dilemma is mistaken identity, where a Jew does not know what it means to be Jewish. The crisis of our time is that not only do Jews *not* know who we are as a people, but also we have come to regard ourselves as what we are not. Consequently, in a situation such as this, we can even come to regard our true selves as something foreign, to be rejected and fought off. This can find expression in the phenomenon of the self-hating Jew.

The phenomenon of mistaken identity can cause Lupus to be misdiagnosed. Lupus often resembles other diseases, and it can disguise itself within their symptoms. For example, Lupus may begin abruptly with a fever simulating an acute infection. Often, Lupus will disguise itself as syphilis, another link of Lupus, an autoimmune (*hod*) disease, to sexuality and the fear of rape.

In Kabbalah, symptoms are considered to be the clothing of a disease, acting as garments through which the disease puts itself on display. This aspect of "dressing up" is also a feminine quality, further strengthening the connection of this disease to women.

Significantly, Lupus strikes women during the years of fertility—from puberty until menopause—thus relating it to the feminine reproductive system, which, according to Kabbalah, is *yesod* tending toward *hod*, as explained above.

COLLAGEN DISEASE

Conventional medical research has classified Lupus as a collagen disease. Collagens are the basic structural proteins of connective tissue. When Lupus afflicts the connective tissue in the body, the result can be sore joints, a symptom of arthritis. This also parallels problems of the psyche, as in psychological disorders relating to disconnection, of feeling disconnected (or alienated) from God or from other people.[5]

In the terminology of Kabbalah, the root of the problem lies in how one understands the doctrine of the *tzimtzum*, or Divine self-contraction in the creative process. *Tzimtzum* refers to God's apparent withdrawal of His infinite light in order to create finite reality. If one understands this to be literal—that God is not to be found in reality—then one will feel disconnected from God. In Lupus, this phenomenon shows up in the body as empty space between cells and tissue that are lacking connection. When the body interprets this emptiness as "literal," experiencing the distance between the disparate joints of the body, pain and soreness will ensue.

On the psychological level, clearly, if we feel disconnected psychologically and socially from other people, we will not be able to form comfortable bonds with others. Ultimately, the psychological weakness of feeling disconnected from others results from spiritual disconnectedness from God, and may well find physical expression as a collagen disease.

The spiritual treatment of a collagen disease begins with understanding and experiencing the *tzimtzum* in accordance with the teachings of the Ba'al Shem Tov. Perceiving the contraction as non-literal preserves the sense of connection. We awaken to a consciousness that God is present on every level of reality, and that our sense of disconnection is only a matter of perception. The connection has always been there and now is only temporarily concealed. With this understanding, we will discover that the pain of disconnection will disappear and so will its physical manifestations.

The feeling of disconnection can be seen in the symptoms of Lupus. Lupus causes the cell core of the individual's DNA to be pushed to the side. This microcosmic phenomenon can be seen to parallel a person's feeling of being disconnected from others, of being pushed out of society. Likewise, Lupus is described as a disease in which the patient becomes "allergic" to himself or herself; psychologically, this would correlate to one's not liking oneself, being constantly dissatisfied with one's self-image, and being disconnected from oneself.

FATIGUE AND PERSEVERANCE

A most common symptom of Lupus is fatigue. Fatigue, incidentally, is a symptom of any dysfunction of the immune system; such dysfunction may result in chronic viral infection, which in turn gives rise to chronic fatigue syndrome (CFS).

Fatigue is, not surprisingly, an affliction of *hod*. *Hod*, "acknowledgement"—corresponding, in Kabbalah, to the left leg that controls the sense of walking—connotes "perseverance." Perseverance evokes the image of a person who is continuously walking toward a goal, always "acknowledging" his goal, without becoming tired.⁶ This aspect of *hod* refers to our ability to go through life and see things through to the end.

On a spiritual level, the decision to continue and persevere to the end, without giving up in the middle, is the essence of our process of returning to God. The spiritual service of returning to God (*teshuvah*) begins at the level of *binah* ("understanding") and concludes with the healing of *hod*. Here, *hod*, "acknowledgement" (*hodayah*), takes on the meaning of "confession" (*vidui*), the verbal expression of returning to God. This reflects the principle in Kabbalah that "*binah* extends until *hod*." As the prophet Isaiah says: "And his heart shall understand [*yavin*, from *binah*] and he shall return and be healed."⁷

The fatigue that comes with Lupus is seen particularly in pregnant women with the disease. A pregnant woman (a symbol of *binah*, a mother-to-be) with Lupus has a high risk of miscarriage, an inability to see a pregnancy through to the end. Once more, we see the relation of Lupus and its symptoms to the female.

TREATMENTS OF LUPUS

The immune system insures that antibodies are produced when needed and in the right quantity. When too many antibodies are produced, instead of warding off illness, they start fighting among themselves.

Psychologically, this can be likened to a person who is over-concerned and over-worried about disease; his hypersensitivity makes him more likely to feel ill, and often to actually become ill.

In Kabbalah, rectified *hod* is characterized by "walking simply"[8] with God. To walk simply with God implies that we focus all our efforts and thoughts on accomplishing our mission in life, trusting God to care for the well-being of our body and soul. A person who embodies this attitude does not worry about disease; rather, he is always conscious of God as the "healer of all flesh and doer of wonders."[9]

The innate wisdom[10] of the immune system lies in its adaptability—its ability to experiment through trial and error to detect and ward off threats to the body. To do this, it creates antibodies, which come in contact with foreign substances and eradicate them. The expression of the sages that, "There is none so wise as one who possesses experience"[11] reflects this learning ability in the immune system.[12] When something invades the body, the immune system senses it and learns to respond.[13]

The problem with Lupus is that the person's immune system seems not to know how to respond to it, as if it has lost its ability to learn by trial and error, cannot learn from experience, and is unable to "walk" straight without stumbling. Stumbling relates to the left leg (the leg of Jacob[14] injured in his wrestle with the angel of Esau, as discussed above), the limb of the body identified with the *sefirah* of *hod*, which controls walking.[15]

An Ancient Remedy

Recent developments in the medical world for the treatment of Lupus have seemingly taken us back to our distant past. Plasmapheresis, which is a variation on one of the oldest medical practices known as "bloodletting," has reemerged as a viable option for dealing with Lupus. Plasmapheresis involves removing blood from the body and centrifuging it in order to separate the cellular elements from the plasma. In the Talmud we find numerous references to the practice of bloodletting and to the circumstances under which it is advisable for health.

In a sense, bloodletting is similar to menstruation, which removes the "bad" blood from the body. Both bloodletting and menstruation—two manifestations of ridding the body of negative energies (in this case, blood, the vital fluid of the body that originates in *binah* and extends to *hod*)—relate to *hod*.

(Since the period when Lupus strikes the female is during the years of her fertility, it would be of interest to study whether women whose cycles are regular are less likely to contract Lupus.[16])

As we saw above, when *hod* is spelled backwards it forms the word *davah*, "illness." In the Torah,[17] the illness referred to as *davah* is, in fact, the state of weakness experienced by the woman during her period of menstruation. Here we see that this natural "illness"—menstruation—is nature's (that is, God's) remedy for a much more real and severe illness, that of Lupus.

Remission

In many cases, Lupus may go into remission, that is, the symptoms of the disease may disappear either temporarily or permanently. This phenomenon is not necessarily the result of treatment or medication.

In Hebrew, the word for "remission" is *hafugah*. It is interesting to note that the numerical value of the two-letter sub-root of *hafugah*, *p-g*, is 83. As noted above, the number 83 is identified by the sages as the number of diseases that afflict mankind.[18] We may understand this numerical equivalence to signify that every disease has the potential of going into remission. Every disease can appear and disappear, which, in the terminology of Kabbalah, means that every disease can vary between the "revealed world," where it is active, and the "concealed world," where it is passive or dormant. Moreover, in the "concealed world," disease becomes "sweetened [i.e., healed] at its source."

In his Code of Law, Maimonides (who, in addition to being one of the greatest of the medieval sages was also one of the greatest physicians of his time) arranges all the laws of the Torah into 83 sections or categories. He states explicitly in the introduction to his work that he has divided it into 83 sections (he does not mention that the Code comprises exactly 1000 chapters!). The great doctor may thus be seen to imply that the devoted study of the Torah—study for the sake of fulfilling all of its commandments—possesses the power to cause all the diseases that afflict mankind to go into remission, to disappear, and, ultimately, to be cured. Torah study in itself, even the study of the revealed "body" of Torah law, lifts the soul to the level of the "concealed world," where affliction is "sweetened at its source."[19]

In Kabbalah, the link or turning point between the "revealed world" (corresponding to the *sefirah* of *malchut*) and the "concealed world" (corresponding to the *sefirah* of *binah*) is *hod*. The "revealed world" (*malchut*, the lower *hei* of the Name *Havayah*) ascends to *hod* while the "concealed world" (*binah*, the higher *hei* of the Name *Havayah*) descends to *hod*. When rectified, *hod* is the power of the soul that causes negative phenomena to disappear while simultaneously causing positive phenomena to appear.

The very recognition that at any moment disease may disappear greatly reinforces the *hod*-characteristic described above of "walking simply with God." By placing all of one's trust in the Almighty, knowing that He created nature such that disease can go as easily as it came, one arouses His grace to command nature that the disease disappear.

Meditation, Positive Thinking, and Support

Among the key methods of Kabbalah to heal body and soul is active engagement in meditation. Proper meditation, focused on God and His providence over all, will enable a person to transcend his psychological enslavement to his own condition, thus creating a sense of self-nullification (*bitul*) that will help either totally rid the body of disease or at least produce a state of remission.

The practice of meditation entails as well in-depth contemplation directed at understanding the spiritual roots of one's disease. Understanding the disease will further its recovery. Particularly, when a person gains a Kabbalistic understanding (*binah*) of his or her disease, that understanding will positively affect the immune system (*hod*), enabling it to overcome the disease, for "*binah* extends until *hod*."

Daily meditation enhances one's ability to think positively the entire day. Regarding positive thinking, the Hassidic dictum states: "Think good and it will be good!"[20]

From time immemorial, the interrelationship and interdependence of mind and body—the holistic nature of the human condition—was known intuitively and taken for granted. Today, science fully recognizes, and by experiment has established, this fundamental truth. In the medical world, the interest in psycho-neuro-immunology fueled by the widespread perception that the way one thinks has significant effects on the health of the individual, is continuously rising.

Other suggestions that will work to rectify the attribute of *hod* in a person include strengthening the support system of family and friends. Encouragement of this kind has been shown to make dramatic improvements in the conditions of patients with Lupus. A good bedside manner is called the healing of the "mouth"—the power of words of encouragement, which we will discuss in the next chapter. It also reflects the power of positive thinking.[21]

PART THREE

Kabbalistic Understanding of Healing

ברוך אתה ה׳ רופא כל בשר ומפליא לעשות

Blessed be You, GOD, who heals all flesh and works wonders

Morning Blessings

7

Methods of Healing

THE POWER OF THE PHYSICIAN

The process of healing, according to Kabbalah, is accomplished through the inter-involvement of the physician's eyes, hands, and mouth.

The Physician's Eyes

The model physician in the Torah is the priest (*kohen*), who diagnoses (and heals) by sight.[1] In Kabbalah, the innate power of the priest's soul derives from the *sefirah* of *chochmah* ("wisdom"), which, as mentioned above, is associated with the sense of sight.

In Kabbalah, the consciousness of the *sefirah* of *chochmah* transcends death, as it is written in the Book of Job: "They shall die, but not with wisdom."[2] This is interpreted to mean that wisdom cannot coexist with death; only when wisdom departs may death ensue. Furthermore, the priest is not permitted to come in physical contact with death. For this very reason, he is the ideal physician: a physician who believes only in life, and is unwilling to sanction death. This is supported by the famous statement of Rabbi Menachem

Mendel of Lubavitch³ that the Torah allows the physician to heal, but not to pronounce, in despair, a terminal prognosis.⁴

Of course, all mortals die. Even of the Messianic Age, it is written, "the youth of a hundred years will die,"⁵ that is, even though longevity will be such that a person a hundred years old will be considered a "youth," death will nonetheless persist. But it is concomitantly clear to one who believes in God and the Torah that our Divine soul, "an actual part of God," is not subject to death. The soul lives on after the death of the body, and, when so judged, returns to this world in another body. In the End of Days, the soul will once more descend to earth and live forever in the resurrected body in which it lived in this world.⁶

In Kabbalah, the 45th of the 72 three-letter mystical Names of God⁷ (which is spelled *samech alef lamed*) is read as an acronym for the Talmudic phrase, "the end of man is to die" (*sof **a**dam **l**amut*).⁸ Human mortality is indeed a Divine phenomenon. The phrase "the end of man is to die" alludes to the verse at the end of Ecclesiastes: "The *end* [*sof*] of the matter, all having been heard: Fear God and keep His commandments, for this is the whole *man* [*adam*]."⁹ From meditation on "the end of man," we come to fear God and keep His commandments, and thereby to merit eternal life (this being "the *whole* man").

Often, it is indeed the moral responsibility of the physician to prepare a patient for the passage of his or her soul from this world to the next. In this situation, the physician takes on the task of a rabbi, a priest of old, as seen in the Torah where the priest serves the function both of the doctor and the rabbi or teacher. Here, his connection to God and belief in the eternal life of the soul come to their peak. Here becomes manifest the paradox characteristic of Jewish faith: to concentrate on life alone, never to lose hope and despair, while simultaneously knowing that God is one, equally present with us in either of the two worlds, this or the next.

This is the simple faith that the eyes of the physician radiate to his patient in the most difficult moments of his care for him. In the words of King David, "Even though I walk through the valley of the shadow of death, I shall not fear evil, for You are with me. Your rod and your staff comfort me."[10]

It is explained in Kabbalah and Hassidism, as has been noted above, that disease results from a lack of selflessness (*bitul*), the inner experience of *chochmah*. When our body is healthy, we are not aware of it—it is merely an intrinsic part of our overall selves. Only when the body is ill do we become aware of it as something possessing a distinct existence. Thus, overt self-awareness is an indication of disease, whether latent or potential.

The emotive correlate of *chochmah* is *chesed* ("loving-kindness").[11] In Kabbalah, the priest is identified with *chesed*.[12] The physician/priest observes his patient, and reflects upon his ailment, with love. The physician's energies of selflessness (*chochmah*) and love (*chesed*), projected from his eyes toward the patient, join to begin the healing process. The physician's visual diagnosis—based on and permeated by selflessness and love—effectively transmits the healing power of selflessness and love to the ailing person.[13]

In particular, it is the physician's selflessness that endows him with the wisdom and insight to properly diagnose his patient, whom he loves. It is his love that transmits the healing power of selflessness to his patient.

Traditional medical diagnosis begins with *observation* of the patient prior to examination, alluding to the power of the eyes as the gateways of healing.

In this context, we may suppose that the various diagnostic examinations available to the modern physician as technological extensions of his physical eyesight—x-rays, CAT scans, etc.—serve to compensate for the weakening of his spiritual eyesight over the generations. Nevertheless, while they may well aid in diagnosing a condition, they certainly do not project the healing power of love that do the eyes of the physician.

The Physician's Hands

In the Five Books of Moses, the Hebrew root of "healing" (*refuah*, *r-p-h*) appears fourteen times, the numerical value of the word for "hand" (*yad*). These fourteen appearances divide naturally into two groups of ten and four: ten appear in various thematic contexts,[14] while the remaining four all appear in the context of the disease of *tzara'at* (and are all in the past tense and the passive form—"was healed"[15]).[16] This natural division into ten and four further alludes to the relationship between the root of "healing" and the word for "hand," inasmuch as the numerical values of the two letters that spell the word for "hand" (*yud* and *dalet*) are 10 and 4, respectively.[17]

The first of these fourteen appearances is in the verse, "And God healed Abimelech."[18] We are taught that "everything follows [the lead of] the beginning,"[19] which implies that every phenomenon in the Torah is defined by its first appearance in the Torah. Indeed, the numerical value of the subject of this verse (the word for "God," *Elokim*), in reduced numbering, is 14, the value of the first four letters being 10 and the value of the fifth, final letter being 4.[20]

As the word for "hand" (*yad*) also signifies "strength" and "ability," all this suggests that there is healing power in the hand of the physician.

In particular, the word for "hand" is used idiomatically five ways in the Torah. These can be seen to correspond to the four letters of the Name *Havayah* and the upper tip of the *yud*, as follows:[21]

the Name Havayah	sefirah	meaning of "hand"	example
י upper tip of *yud*	*keter*	prophetic inspiration	"…and the hand of God was upon him."[22]
י *yud*	*chochmah*	point [of wisdom]	"You open Your hands…":[23] "do not read 'Your hands' but 'Your *yud*'s.'"[24]
ה *hei*	*binah*	intellectual grasp	"…as far as the hand of his intellect can grasp…"[25]
ו *vav*	*midot*	manifestation of emotion, strength, and ability	"…the great hand [*chesed*]…,"[26] "…the mighty hand [*gevurah*]…,"[27] "…the uplifted hand [*tiferet*]…"[28]
ה *hei*	*malchut*	place	"…you shall have a place [lit., 'a hand'] outside the camp…"[29]

In Kabbalah, the verse, "With wisdom [*chochmah*] GOD [*Havayah*] founded the earth"[30] is seen to imply that all four levels inherent in the Name *Havayah*, corresponding to its four letters, are included in *chochmah*, which corresponds in particular to the first letter, the *yud* of the Name *Havayah*. The name of the letter *yud*, the tenth letter of the Hebrew alphabet, itself is cognate with "hand" (*yad*). And so, all of the four/five idiomatic usages of "hand" are derived ultimately from the soul's faculty of wisdom, the healing power of the soul, as explained above.

To manifest healing power in his hand, the physician must imbue his hand with the consciousness of the Name *Havayah*, which refers in particular to God's attribute of mercy or compassion.[31] Mercy originates in *keter*, corresponding to the upper tip of the *yud*, which possesses thirteen individual attributes or channels of mercy, channeling God's infinite mercy from the unfathomable, unconscious depths of *keter* to the beginning of consciousness in *chochmah*.

The conscious expression of mercy begins with opening the hand to give, opening the concealed point of wisdom (whose origin is in the "concealed [unconscious] mind"—*mocha stima'ah*—of *keter*) to shine its light to the patient. In Kabbalah, the verse "You open Your hands…"[32] is interpreted, "do not read 'Your hands' but 'Your *yud*'s'"[33]—a direct allusion to the *yud* of the Name *Havayah*. This is similar to the x-ray power of the eyes mentioned above.

The hand continues to grasp, intellectually, the origin of the disease, thereby lifting it out, as it were, from the patient. This process of spiritual surgery corresponds to the higher *hei* of the Name *Havayah*.

Next, manifesting the heart's emotion of love, the hand sutures and soothes the wound. This corresponds to the *vav* of the Name *Havayah*.

Finally, the hand concludes the cure, restoring the affected area to its primal state of health, smoothing the skin. This last stage corresponds to *malchut*, the final *hei* of the Name *Havayah* (as explained above), until the place of the wound becomes unknown.

In the Bible,[34] we find an explicit reference to the power of the hand to heal. Na'aman, the commander of the army of the king of Aram, was a leper. The king, having heard of the wonders wrought by the prophet Elisha, sent Na'aman to Israel to be healed. Elisha told him to immerse seven times in the Jordan river. In anger, Na'aman walked away, saying,

> *"I thought he would come out to me,*
> *and would stand and invoke* GOD, *his God, by Name,*
> *wave his hand toward the place,*
> *and cure the affected part."*

Na'aman's servants calmed him and convinced him to try the simple advice the prophet had given him. Upon immersing seven times in the Jordan, he was cured; his skin returned to that of a babe.

From this story, we see that it was customary among nations of old to heal by the power of the hand. The prophet was surely not an ordinary "healer," and in order to sanctify

God's Name, instructed Na'aman simply to bathe in the Jordan, just as he was accustomed to bathe in the rivers of Damascus.

Nonetheless, there is a deep relationship between the Jordan River and the healing power of the hands. The name *Jordan*, as written in Hebrew (*yardein*), is an intertwining of two two-letter words: "hand" (*yad*) and "sing" (*ran*). The "singing hand" is the hand of the musician playing an instrument. When desiring to arouse the prophetic spirit, it was the prophet Elisha who called upon a musician to play music, and then, "the *hand* of God was upon him."[35]

Thus, we may infer that listening to the music of the Jordan River, immersing in it, and integrating it into one's soul confers healing power upon the hands of the physician. The song of the Jordan River is that the Land of Israel was given by the hand of God to the people of Israel.

Above, in the first part of this book, while describing the Kabbalistic models pertaining to the hands and the fingers, we began discussing the properties of sensitivity and balance, the cornerstones of rectification in the worldview of Kabbalah. These properties are of greatest importance to the physician in diagnosing and treating his patients.

By means of the sensitive touch of the fingers, communication is established between the physician and the patient. Traditionally, the laying on of hands was an intrinsic part of medical diagnosis and treatment. This is especially the case with regard to surgical therapy.[36]

While modern diagnostic and surgical technology, requiring much less physical contact between doctor and patient, is certainly helpful to the modern physician, the price of the physical distancing of patient from doctor is the decrease in doctor-patient interaction. It is commonly said that technology has impeded the development of the *art* of medicine in modern times. It is generally felt that the physician of the past had better-developed diagnostic acumen than that of today's physician.

As we have seen, the proper balance of "touching and not touching" is an innate characteristic or sense that relates to the hands. In the practice of modern medicine, proper balance must be maintained between diagnostic and therapeutic technology and hands-on contact between doctor and patient. In diagnosis and treatment, the physician must learn to rectify the sense of balance innate to his spiritual and physical hands.

In abstraction, not only the balance of physical "touching and not touching" relates to the hands, but the deep sense of balance, with regard to the physician's expression of empathy with the condition and suffering of his patient, pertains to the spiritual hands of the physician as well. In order to practice medicine objectively, the physician must often consciously distance himself from his patient, lest his emotional involvement in the patient's plight overwhelm him and incapacitate him.

In Kabbalah, the inner sense of balance, with regard to one's expression of empathy with another, is seen as a property of the third, hidden "hand" (vested in the torso, or heart, and reaching upward to the head), the hand of *tiferet*, between the two revealed hands of *chesed* (the right hand) and *gevurah* (the left hand). *Tiferet* is the *sefirah* most identified with the discipline of medicine.[37] Its inner experience is compassion (*rachamim*), or empathy with another. The essence of balance is a property of *da'at*, the inner soul of *tiferet*. By the power of *da'at*, one knows when and how to extend the expression of his third hand, outwardly, to the other, and when to contract it, inwardly, to himself.

In the physician's third, hidden hand, lies his "sixth sense," a sense that cannot be learned from the textbooks, but comes only with experience and practice to a soul gifted with an innate affinity toward healing. Indeed, medicine is an art as well as a science.

In medical practice, there is often a dichotomy between the textbook solution to problems and the "practical" solution, between what is learned and what is applied. Surgeons are fond of saying, "we could train a monkey to be a surgeon," meaning that the technical aspect of surgery is not overly complex. Far more crucial and difficult is the physician's judgment—his *da'at*—regarding whether to operate or not and when to stop or proceed in a surgery; when to extend his hand and when to contract it.

The Physician's Mouth

The letters of the Hebrew word for "healing" (*refuah*) permute to spell the phrase, "the light of the mouth" (*or peh*). The physician's sympathetic advice and reassurance to his patient radiate healing light and energy.

The Torah begins with the account of creation: "In the beginning, God created...." In Hebrew, the verb "to create" is cognate to the verb "to be or make healthy."

Chapter Seven: Methods of Healing

According to Kabbalah, there are indeed two stages of creation: first, creation *ex nihilo*, and then, a "healing" of the ailments inherent in the initial state of creation.

God created/healed the world with ten utterances of His mouth. The first explicit utterance[38] is recorded in the third verse of the Torah, "And God said, 'Let there be light,' and there was light." God's very words, "Let there be light," became light. Light was the first "sound" state of reality to emerge from the mouth of God, healing the previous "ill" state of reality: "The earth was unformed and void, and darkness was on the face of the abyss…."[39] With the goodly light of His mouth, God healed all of reality. And so is every man, and the physician in particular, instructed, "Open your mouth, and let your words shine light."[40]

Seven different Hebrew letters are used in the twenty-three-letter verse: "And God said, 'Let there be light,' and there was light"; three (*alef*, *vav*, and *reish*) spell the word for "light" (*or*) and the remaining four (*mem*, *yud*, *lamed*, and *hei*) are numerically equal to the word for "mouth" (*peh*).[41] Thus, the entire verse is, in essence, the healing power (*refuah*) of "the light of the mouth" of God.

In Kabbalah, the origin of the mouth in *keter*—the origin of the soul's power of expression in its super-conscious will—is the twelfth of the thirteen attributes of Divine mercy, all of which are rooted in *keter*, as noted above. Of this supernal "mouth," it is said, "knowledge is concealed [*ganiz*] within the mouth."[42] This concealed knowledge—*da'at*—is itself the concealed light (*or haganuz*) of creation. *Da'at* is the power to connect, as in marital union.[43] By the power of *da'at* concealed in his mouth, the physician connects to his patient.

While instructing the patient what to do and what not to do, the words of the physician calm, reassure, and encourage the patient to follow his instructions with the implicit promise that surely, with the help of God, he will be well. The positive words spoken by the mouth of the physician become positive thoughts in the mind of the patient. As we have seen, positive thinking creates positive reality.

King Solomon, the wisest of all men, said, "If there be anxiety in a man's heart, let him suppress it, and a good word will turn it into joy."[44] According to the sages of the Talmud, the Hebrew word for "let him suppress it" has two additional meanings: "let him ignore it" and "let him articulate it."[45] According to the reading, "let him articulate it," this verse portrays, in particular, the dialogue between a patient and his physician. First, the patient articulates to the physician the anxiety within his heart, the symptoms of his illness. The physician responds with "a good word," which, in itself, has the power to heal by turning the anxiety in the heart of the patient into joy.

Eyes, Hands, and Mouth

Each one of these three members of the physician's body—his eyes, his hands, and his mouth—projects spiritual, healing light and energy. The physician must devote himself to Divine service in order to refine these three members of his body, so that they become conduits to transmit healing powers. Each must be refined independently and they must learn to function together, in harmony.

As explained above, we refine our eyes by guarding them to see only good and positive facets of reality, to envision God before us constantly. We refine our hands by emulating God by opening our hands to give charity.[46] We refine our mouths by guarding them from evil words and by speaking words of Torah, which are a source of life[47].

In most general terms, the relation between the eyes, the hands, and the mouth of the physician is that the eyes see the disease, the hands treat the disease, and the mouth calms and reassures the patient.

The spiritual light projected from the eyes, as explained above, is one of pure love; the spiritual energy in the hands expresses compassion; the light of the mouth projects trust.[48] In Hassidic thought, love (*ahavah*), compassion (*rachamim*), and trust (*bitachon*) are the lights and inner experiences of the three *sefirot*—*chesed*, *tiferet*, and *netzach*.

The Ba'al Shem Tov teaches, as noted earlier, that any complete process of spiritual growth or, indeed, any complete act of rectification, must proceed through three stages: submission, separation, and sweetening. Since true healing is a spiritual as well as a physical process, the consciousness of a true healer must also proceed through these three stages.[49]

3.	sweetening	mouth	reassuring, healing words
2.	separation	hands	treating illness
1.	submission	eyes	diagnosing illness

We have seen above that the two extreme stages of submission and sweetening correspond to the two states of *chash* ("silence") and *mal* ("speaking"). *Chash* characterizes *chochmah* (as our sages say, "silence is a fence for *wisdom*"⁵⁰), the source of the sight of the eye. (*Chash* also means "sense," the foremost sense of external reality being the sense of sight, as explained in Hassidism.) Thus, *chash*, "submission" (here in the sense of true selflessness, the inner experience of *chochmah*), refers, in particular, to the eyes of the physician. *Mal* refers to the mouth of the physician. The intermediate stage of *mal* ("severance"), characterizing the rectified *brit*, relates to the sense of touch in the hands of the physician. In Kabbalah, the sense of touch is identified with the sense of marital relations, the function of the *brit*. (In the terminology of our sages, the male *brit* itself is referred to as a "finger."⁵¹)

The eyes of the physician project a selfless feeling of love for his patient. In compassion, the charitable hands of the physician provide the patient with what he needs, separating the "poor man" from his state of poverty. Finally, the good and reassuring words of the physician (the "light" of his mouth) "sweeten" the consciousness of the patient, filling him or her with hope and confidence.

All three energies—from the eyes, the hands, and the mouth of the physician—apply, whichever method of healing the physician employs, as we shall see next.

CONTEMPORARY MEDICAL PRACTICE

Contemporary medical practice may be seen to employ four general methods of healing: homeopathy, allopathy, osteopathy, and naturopathy.

1. Homeopathy

The underlying principle of this healing system is known as the "law of similars," where one paradoxically uses either the disease itself or something similar to the disease as the cure. This principle, long known to mankind, finds its explicit expression in the idiom of the sages as healing "like by like."[52] Furthermore, the sages teach that this is the method employed by God Himself, who "sweetens [that is, heals] bitterness with bitterness."[53] "Like by like" implies that the cure lies within the disease itself, meaning that the disease is merely a foreign "shell" of evil containing within it a kernel of good.

2. Allopathy (conventional medicine)

This healing system is based upon the logic that the way to fight off disease is by using an opposing force that confronts the illness head on. Human intelligence then proceeds to employ scientific methods to extract from nature chemicals whose properties are intended to counteract the symptoms and overt physical manifestations of a given disease. The disease is considered to be no more than its physical manifestations, which are seen to be negative in essence and must be fought off in their entirety. (Only in most recent years is conventional medicine beginning to recognize the relation of the psyche to the body and that there is more to disease than that which meets the eye.)

3. Osteopathy

According to this healing system, which includes Western chiropractic and Chinese acupuncture and acupressure, the body is rectified without any medicinal intervention, but only by the hands (or needles) of the physician balancing body energies and realigning the body to its proper state. Osteopathy treats the muscles and penetrates to the nervous system by treating the spinal cord.

4. Naturopathy

This system of healing through herbs and other resources taken directly from nature reflects the belief that God, the Creator, surely provided a cure, in the natural realm—the creation of His hands (as noted above, "to create" in Hebrew is cognate with "to heal")—before He made possible a disease.[54] This system presupposes that there must be something in our world that can serve as a natural cure for every disease, something that does not require human manipulation to alter its state. This sense, which reflects a deep appreciation of the great, latent potential inherent in the earth, is alluded to in the verse in Psalms that states, "Truth will sprout out of the earth."[55]

"Truth" in Kabbalah is the ultimate healing power, applying even to the revival of the dead. The word for "truth," *emet*, is read, "*alef* [the first letter of the alphabet, alluding to God, revives] *meit* ['the dead']."

Furthermore, the effectiveness of the natural method of healing is suggested by another verse found in Deuteronomy that, "man is a tree of the field,"[56] implying our essential connection to nature and nature's power to heal our ailments. In addition to herbal remedies, naturopathy, more than the other methods of healing, emphasizes the importance of proper diet and nutrition, physical exercise and healthy lifestyles in general.

Of these four methods of healing, the three—allopathy, osteopathy, naturopathy—are all under the direction of mortal reason. Only homeopathy transcends mortal reason, with the paradox of healing bitterness with bitterness, and is the bridge between the other levels and the fifth level—pure spiritual healing, employing Torah-inspired methods—that we will discuss in the next section.

The various systems of healing can be seen as corresponding to the letters of God's essential Name *Havayah*, as follows:

׳ upper tip of *yud*	pure spiritual healing	employing Torah-inspired methods
י *yud*	homeopathy	applying the law of similars
ה *hei*	allopathy	fighting disease "head on"
ו *vav*	osteopathy	aligning the body
ה *hei*	naturopathy	tapping the resources of nature

The implication of homeopathy that cure lies within the disease itself and that the disease is merely a foreign "shell" of evil concealing within it a kernel of good is a Divinely-inspired insight into the nature of reality in general and the human condition in particular. This insight corresponds to the wisdom embodied in the point of the *yud* of God's Name.

Allopathy, that is, conventional Western medical practice, is based on the pattern of mortal reason (in contrast with Divinely-inspired insight) that corresponds in Kabbalah to the first *hei* of God's Name.

Osteopathy, as noted above, treats the muscles (the physiological system that corresponds to the *sefirah* of *tiferet*) and even deeper, penetrates to the nervous system (the system that corresponds to the *sefirah* of *da'at*, the inner "soul" of *tiferet*) by treating the spinal cord. *Tiferet*—the torso, which corresponds to the *vav* of God's Name—means "beauty," referring in particular to a beautiful body. In the words of the *Zohar*, "beauty [*tiferet*] is the body."[57] A "straight" or "upright" body (the work of the chiropractor) is a beautiful one.[58]

Naturopathy, with its emphasis on finding the cure in nature, corresponds to the final *hei* of God's Name, which refers to the level of Divinity inherent in nature itself, that is, the healing power contained within every created being, to heal both itself and others.

Four Methods as One

As the four methods described above correspond to the four letters of God's essential Name, *Havayah*, and as "God is one," the ideal physician is one who knows how to employ all four methods of healing, recognizing their common Divine source, the healing power of God.

In general, in less severe instances of disease, it is wise to begin with natural means, and if not sufficient, to proceed up the ladder of the four methods. Of course, the accomplished physician will know from experience which method is best for which disease.

As the letters of the Name *Havayah* correspond to the *sefirot*, which in turn correlate to the physiological systems, it would appear from our above analysis that:

- Diseases related to the respiratory system (associated with *keter*, the upper tip of the *yud* of the Name *Havayah*) or to the bone marrow (associated with *chochmah*, the *yud* of the Name *Havayah*) might well be treated by homeopathy.

- Diseases related to the blood (associated with *binah*, the first *hei* of the Name *Havayah*) might best be treated by conventional medicine.

- Diseases related to one of the physiological systems that correspond to the emotive attributes of the soul, in particular those related to the muscular system (associated with *tiferet*, the central attribute amongst the emotions, the *vav* of the Name *Havayah*) would best be treated by osteopathy.

- Diseases of the digestive system (associated with *malchut*, the final *hei* of the Name *Havayah*) most certainly should be treated, initially, by natural methods, beginning with diet.

To summarize:

God's Name	sefirah	method of healing	diseases related to
י *yud*	*chochmah*	homeopathy	respiration and the bone-marrow
ה *hei*	*binah*	allopathy	the blood
ו *vav*	*midot*	osteopathy	the muscular system
ה *hei*	*malchut*	naturopathy	the digestive system

HEALING AND THE SOUL

In a Hassidic discourse, one of the great Kabbalists of the 19th century, Rabbi Yitzchak Isaac HaLevi Epstein of Homil, outlines six levels of healing, which can be can be understood to correspond to the five levels of the soul, plus the soul's very essence. These levels of soul are named and experienced as follows:

Chapter Seven: Methods of Healing

	level of soul		experience
6.	*etzem haneshamah*	essence of the soul	"an actual part of God"
5.	*yechidah*	"single one"	unity with God
4.	*chayah*	"living one"	awareness of God
3.	*neshamah*	"breath" of life	intelligence
2.	*ruach*	"spirit"	emotion
1.	*nefesh*	innate life-force	physicality

We will now describe how these levels of soul correspond to six levels of healing.

1. Healing at the level of *Nefesh*

The first level of healing, lowest yet most fundamental in the six-rung ladder of healing, is that employed by an expert physician, whether that physician is a conventional practitioner or a homeopath, osteopath, or naturopath. The skilled and accomplished practitioner (especially the one that knows how to use and unite all of the four methods of healing described above) knows the proper way to treat any specific ailment of the body.[59]

The physician's expertise relates to the natural level of the body, the physical level on which the body "lives," meaning, the life-force of the soul as it clothes itself within the body.

The correct treatment for a given disease possesses the power to contact this lowest level of the soul—the *nefesh*—and draw it into the body. At this level, however, the consciousness of the physician is primarily, if not solely, directed to the body and its ailments; he or she is not necessarily consciously aware of the connection of body to soul.

The soul—the *nefesh*—is connected to the body through the blood. In the Torah[60] we find it explicitly stated that "the blood is the soul [*nefesh*]." The Hebrew word for "blood," (*dam*) is related to the word for "likeness" (*demut*) as used by the Torah in describing the creation of the first human being:

> *God said:*
> *"Let us make man [Adam] in our image,*
> *as our likeness [kidmuteinu]."*[61]

The very name of the first human, *Adam*, is cognate to the word for "blood" (*dam*). The name *Adam* can be read "I shall become blood," alluding to the power to draw the *nefesh* into the body by means of the blood, the function accomplished by the expert physician. (While in the phrase, "I shall become blood," "I" refers to the *nefesh*, implying that the focus of consciousness is that of the *nefesh* entering the blood to animate the body, the physician focuses primarily on the body, drawing into it, whether consciously or unconsciously, the life-force of the *nefesh* by its entry into the blood.)

To continue: If Adam is seen to allude to the expert physician, we may envision the three principal characters in the story of the Garden of Eden—Adam, Eve, and the snake—as alluding, allegorically, to the doctor, the patient, and the disease, respectively.

The name Eve (*Chavah*) is cognate in Aramaic to the word for "snake" (*chiviah*), implying that having been seduced to sin, or bitten by the snake, she became infected with the disease represented by the snake; she is thus the patient figure. From the snake itself, the essence of the disease, may be extracted the remedy or medicine to heal the disease, in accordance with the homeopathic "law of similars." For this reason, the snake has universally become the symbol of medicine, as in the episode of the "copper snake," which Moses placed on a pole to heal those who were bitten by snakes, as explained earlier.[62]

2. Healing at the level of *Ruach*

The second level of healing acts through the power of "charms," called in Hebrew, *segulot*.[63] Although in its origins this was a most authentic science, over the generations it has degenerated to a large extent and has become identified with various superstitious practices.

Rabbi Yitzchak Isaac of Homil describes in his discourse how this works. For example, by drawing the form of a man on a wall, the master of charms may spiritually influence and physically affect the pictured man by manipulating or altering the picture. In this way, a good master can heal a diseased patient.

The wisdom employed at this level is "suggestive" in nature. An act done *here* "suggests" that a similar act will happen *there*. The power of suggestion relates in Kabbalah and Hassidic thought to the emotive attributes of the soul, the level of *ruach* ("spirit").

While at the first level of healing, the body was affected directly by the soul (at the level of *nefesh*) by means of the blood, here, the body is affected indirectly. The charm touches the level of *ruach*, which thereafter affects the body indirectly.

The master of charms is a true "spiritualist," addressing the human spirit. The process of healing is indeed a spiritual happening; it impinges on the self-conscious emotions of the soul. In Kabbalah, this level of consciousness is identified with the Tree of Knowledge of Good and Evil. Here, good and evil are mixed together, for which reason this level of healing is most susceptible to misuse, albeit often unintentional.

When the emotions are aroused constructively—by Torah-inspired associations (charms) projected from the physician to the patient[64]—the *ruach* becomes sufficiently energized to affect and heal from above the body to which it relates.

All methods of healing that seek to employ vital energies projected from healer to patient belong to this level of healing. The intellectual basis for such methodology and techniques is referred to in Kabbalah as "the [intellectual] power of association," more literally: "the power of imagination." From this it is clear why so many so-called "healers" nowadays play solely on the imagination of the patient.[65]

3. Healing at the level of *Neshamah*

The third level of healing acts through the power of the Names of God that are inscribed within an amulet (*kameia*) carried on the body or retained in another conspicuous place.

The Names of God have the power to draw Divine influx to the super-rational aspects of the soul, producing a supernal, Divine experience that strengthens the soul and provides it with sufficient power to heal the body.

In particular, this method of healing relates to the third level of the soul, the *neshamah*, the pure intelligence of the Divine soul of man, that is, the soul's ability to perceive God's presence directly in the world and to sense the Divine breath of life entering its being.

The level of *neshamah* is initially super-conscious in the psyche of the human being, for the initial, innate state of consciousness is solely that of *nefesh* (physical consciousness) and *ruach* (spiritual consciousness). The Divine life-force or vitality of the soul's pure intelligence infinitely exceeds its innate spiritual state of consciousness, for to be conscious of the spiritual dimension of reality is still far from being aware of its Divine inner core.

The Divine Names address the *neshamah* and bring it into a state of conscious awareness and experience. The person feels that God is always with him or her. King David in Psalms says, "God is your shadow, on your right-hand side,"[66] meaning that God is always there to protect the individual and heal all of his spiritual and physical ailments.

The master healer who makes use of Divine Names must be an expert Kabbalist. He must know the exact nuance and power of each Divine Name, and when writing an amulet, must, in a state of sincere humility and selflessness, meditate on all the intentions prescribed by Kabbalah with regard to the specific Divine Name, together with the name of the patient, praying all the while to God that his remedy be effective.

We are told that in an amulet written to heal an ailing patient the Ba'al Shem Tov would inscribe his own proper name alone. By this he affected the patient's consciousness at the level of the *neshamah*. The patient became aware that his or her soul was connected to the soul of a *tzadik*, a true holy man. The *tzadik* draws into the consciousness of all souls connected to him an awareness of God's absolute unity and goodness which can heal all flesh.

4. Healing at the level of *Chayah*

The sages in the Talmud describe the fourth level of healing:

> If one's head aches, he should delve into the study of Torah...if one's body aches, he should delve into the study of the Torah...[67]

and:

Whoever delves into the light of the Torah, the light of the Torah enlivens him.[68]

To draw physical vitality from the light of the Torah, one's soul must be bound to the Torah, the word of God. The light of the Torah is God's transcendent light, the infinite light that "encompasses all worlds."[69] At this level, the soul experiences itself as one within the presence of God. This is so, for "the Torah and God are one."[70]

This consciousness is at the level of the *chayah*, "the living one," the awareness of the light of the Torah as "our life and the length of our days."[71] The power of the reinforced bond of the soul to the Torah suffices to draw healing force into the body.

This level of healing is analogous to the law that an impure (sick) body of water instantly becomes purified (healed) when brought to "kiss" (that is, to contact) the waters of a pure *mikveh*.[72] In the same way, when the soul touches—"kisses"—the pure waters of the Torah, it receives sufficient life-force to heal the body.[73]

However, in the above-quoted saying of the sages, the reference is to a relatively minor condition such as a headache ("if one's head aches..."), implying that the ailment referred to here is not one that has mortally impaired one of the vital, inner organs, but only an "ache" (even if the whole body may be affected by it: "if one's body aches...").[74] This suggests that when the vital, inner parts of the body have been mortally impaired, the "kiss" of the light of the Torah is not sufficient to miraculously heal them (that is, return them to their previously complete state of being).

5. Healing at the level of *Yechidah*

Although it may be physically impossible to heal a mortally ill body, even by the Divine light of the Torah, nevertheless, it is possible for one's own soul to assume the role of the body and to "replace" it by enacting all of its physical functions in its stead. The body remains mortally ill as before, but somehow the person continues to live.

This is healing from the fifth level of the soul, the *yechidah*, "the single one." Of this level it is said, "as though the Holy One dwells within him."[75] This phenomenon makes the body appear to be functioning normally although it is virtually dead. The transcendent sanctity of God is separate from the physical body; thus, the body is in no way affected by the presence of God dwelling within it and "living" for it.

The soul-level called *yechidah*—"the single one"— implies "singularity," as reflected by its ability to function independently in the body.[76] In Hassidic thought, this is the level referred to as "essential life" (*chai be-etzem*) in contrast to "bestowing life" (*chaim lehachayot*), which describes the level of *chayah*. Rather than bestowing life to the body (when this is physically possible), the *yechidah* "lives," in its essential state of life, for the body.

6. Healing at the level of *Etzem HaNeshamah*

The sixth level of healing is the one for which we reserve the word "miracle" in its truest sense. Though many of the above levels of healing appear to be supernatural, it is at *this* level that the mortally ill body itself undergoes a miraculous, existential metamorphosis; the physical body becomes reborn.

Almost every physician in clinical practice has witnessed miraculous cures that defy all known laws of medicine. These experiences serve to humble the practitioner and remind him or her that all healing is truly supernatural, an act of God. Such experiences reinforce the physician's awareness that his or her principal role is that of God's emissary to heal the sick.

The resurrection of the dead is the ultimate healing process.[77] We are taught that at the time of the resurrection, bodies will rise from the grave in exactly the same state of being and physical condition as at the moment of death. Then, instantaneously, they will be healed.

The state of the first moment of resurrection, alive though ill as at the moment of death, corresponds to the fifth level of *yechidah* described above. The state of the second moment of resurrection, the rebirth of the body itself, corresponds to the sixth level, the revelation of the essence of the soul.

At this level, all manifestations of soul (i.e., the five previous levels from *nefesh* to *yechidah*) and body are one. The essential life of the soul and the eternal life of the body are the same.

An example of this sixth level of healing is the miracle of Hananiah, Mishael, and Azariah, as related in the Book of Daniel.[78] When they were thrown into the furnace by order of the Babylonian king, the fire did not burn their bodies, though it did burn those of others around. The state of the body in fire is a physical analog to that of mortal, terminal disease. For the body to survive and emerge unaffected exemplifies the power of spontaneous rebirth.

This is the revelation of the Divine "Holy of Holies" of the soul, above the level described above with regard to the *yechidah*—"as though the Holy One dwells within him." The Divine "Holy of Holies" imbues the soul of the would-be martyr (the consciousness of Hananiah, Mishael, and Azariah) with the power to metamorphose the physical body.

This level corresponds to the "actual spark of God" within the *yechidah* of the Jewish soul. This spark derives from the essence of the infinite light that preceded the primordial contraction (*tzimtzum*). The primordial contraction conceals the essence of God's infinite light, thereby excluding, from the perspective of creation, the possibility of an absolute miracle such as that described above. Nonetheless, the "actual spark of God" vested within each Jewish soul allows for the manifestation of such a miracle. This manifestation is the ultimate secret and purpose of the presence of the Jewish soul in creation.

In summary:

	level of soul		level of healing
6.	*etzem haneshamah*	essence of the soul	miraculous Divine power
5.	*yechidah*	"single one"	presence of God
4.	*chayah*	"living one"	light of Torah
3.	*neshamah*	"breath" of life	Names of God
2.	*ruach*	"spirit"	charms
1.	*nefesh*	innate life-force	contemporary medicine

8

The Healing Power of Prayer

DRAWING DOWN HEALING POWER

During the time when the Kingdom of Judea was in flower, one of its exemplary kings, King Hezekiah, became deathly ill. And the prophet Isaiah came to tell him that his illness was terminal:

> *"Thus said God:*
> *'Instruct your household, for you are going to die,*
> *you will not get well.'"*[1]

But rather than despair at this verdict, Hezekiah began to pray from the depths of his heart.[2] Almost instantly came God's reply:

> *"I have heard your prayer,*
> *I have seen your tears; behold, I will heal you.*
> *On the third day you shall go up to the House of God,*
> *and I will add to your days fifteen years.*
> *And I will save you and this city from the hand of the*
>   *king of Assyria;*
> *and I will defend this city for My own sake,*
> *and for My servant David's sake."*[3]

The sages teach that King Hezekiah learned to pray even after the decree of death was pronounced against him by the word of God from the example of his ancestor, King David, the author of the Book of Psalms, "the sweet singer of Israel."[4] King David articulated his absolute faith in the power of prayer to elicit God's mercy even in seemingly hopeless situations, saying: "Even if a sharpened sword is placed on one's throat, one should not despair of praying for God's mercy."[5]

Modern, scientific research has verified that which has been long known to mankind—prayer to God is potent; it possesses the power to heal. Or, expressed in words of faith, heartfelt prayer draws down healing power from above.

In Kabbalah, we are taught that there are five levels of prayer for the sick, which correspond to the four letters of God's essential Name *Havayah* and to a fifth, transcendent point represented by the upper tip of the *yud*.

We shall now examine how these levels of prayer draw down healing power. Our examination will begin at the lowest level.

The Prayer of the Sick Person

The sages teach that "a sick person's prayer for himself is more potent than that of others for him."[6] Who more than the patient himself can experience and identify with his suffering and trepidation? His own prayer issues from the depths of his heart. With all of his soul, he turns to God as his only hope for recovery.

In Kabbalah, we are taught that the suffering, afflicted soul—the soul in a spiritual state of exile—corresponds to the *sefirah* of *malchut*, which in turn corresponds to the final *hei* of the Name *Havayah*.[7] The more connected a person is with the attribute of *malchut*, the more potent is his prayer for himself. To connect with *malchut*, the sick person identifies his own personal suffering with that of the *Shechinah*, the Divine Presence, and the entire "congregation of Israel," both of which are appellations of *malchut*.

In Kabbalah, the *sefirah* of *malchut* represents God's immanent light in creation, the *Shechinah*, as well as the Divine "womb" or "body"[8] from which all souls of Israel are born into reality. At the level of *malchut*, one's "I" becomes identified with the collective "I" of all Israel ("the congregation of Israel," *keneset Yisrael*) and with that of the *Shechinah* itself. When one's "I" suffers, one experiences the suffering of "the *Shechinah* in exile."

The Prayer of a Wise Man

Elsewhere, the sages teach that "if there is a sick person in one's home, one should go to a wise man and ask him to beseech [God] for mercy."[9] Here we see that the prayer of a wise man (*talmud chacham*) possesses the power to arouse God's mercy for the sick more than the prayer of others, including the sick person and those closest to him or her. (Of course, every individual's prayer for another is potent, as acknowledged even by modern science, and the closer one is to the sick person, in heart and soul, the more potent is one's prayer.)[10]

The ability to arouse compassion for another depends upon one's connection to the *sefirah* of *tiferet*, whose inner experience is one of compassion for the other. The *sefirah* of *tiferet* corresponds to the *vav* of the Name *Havayah*. The archetypal soul who corresponds in Kabbalah to the *sefirah* of *tiferet* is that of Jacob. It is he who arouses mercy on "the congregation of Israel," as personified by his wife Rachel, the archetypal soul who corresponds to the *sefirah* of *malchut*. (Upon first meeting Rachel, Jacob lifts up his voice and cries, thereby arousing great mercy on "the congregation of Israel."[11]) Jacob is also the archetype of a wise man, the Torah-sage.[12]

From the higher perspective of *tiferet*, the suffering of *malchut* is seen in a different, deeper light. This perspective gives *tiferet* the ability to arouse mercy on *malchut*. Nonetheless, even this higher perspective on reality and the prayer it inspires are considered part of the "revealed" levels of Divinity (corresponding to the letters *vav* and final *hei* of the Name *Havayah*) in contrast to the "concealed" levels of Divinity (corresponding to the letters *yud* and first *hei* of the Name *Havayah*), which we will examine next.

The Thought of a *Tzadik*

Hassidism teaches[13] that a true *tzadik*, a holy man, as opposed to a wise man, by the power of his thought alone—without necessarily expressing his thoughts and emotions in prayer—is able to miraculously heal the sick by Divine grace.

In his concentrated thought on the suffering soul of others, the true *tzadik* connects his own soul to them, extends his hand to them, and lifts them out of their pain, redeeming them from illness.[14]

Thought (in contrast to speech) corresponds to the "concealed world" of *binah*, which in turn corresponds to the first *hei* of the Name *Havayah*. Thus, the *tzadik*'s power of thought is effective at this concealed level.

Every Jew has the inner potential to become a *tzadik*, as the prophet Isaiah states of the future: "Your people are all *tzadikim*."[15] Therefore, in a certain sense, this level pertains to each and every Jew. Especially important is the Hassidic teaching with regard to the power of thought in relation to oneself (or in relation to those for whom one is deeply concerned) mentioned above: "Think good and it will be good."

The Priestly Blessing

Above this level is the power of the Priestly Blessing as uttered by the priests (*kohanim*), which was explored in Chapter 2 in our discussion of the hands:

> *May God bless you and guard you.*
> *May God shine His countenance upon you and be*
>   *gracious to you.*
> *May God turn His countenance toward you and grant*
>   *you peace.*

Here, the intention and verbalization of the priests draw down Divine energy and healing power from an even higher level than that inherent in the *tzadik*'s thought.

God's will, as expressed in the Torah's precepts—including the commandment[16] that the priests lovingly bless the people by uttering the Priestly Blessing—derives from the level of *chochmah*, the *yud* of the Name *Havayah*. In the *Zohar*, we find the statement, "The Torah issues from *chochmah*."[17] The inner experience of *chochmah* is one of true and absolute selflessness. This state of selflessness is indeed the seminal essence of the love which the Children of Israel experience towards each other, with which the priests bless the people.

The Priestly Blessing begins with the letter *yud*. Of its fifteen words, each of the first thirteen possesses the letter *yud*. These thirteen *yud*'s of the Priestly Blessing are understood in Kabbalah to correspond to the thirteen attributes of Divine mercy. These attributes originate in the *sefirah* of *keter*, but are revealed to the world by the faculty of *chochmah*, the first letter of God's Name, the *yud*.

When blessing the people in the Holy Temple, the priests would utter God's ineffable Name *Havayah* as it is written. (In any other place and context this is strictly forbidden.) The Divine power thus elicited derives from the level of *chochmah*—as stated in Proverbs, "*Havayah* is in *chochmah*"[18]—the level of the "World of Emanation" (*Atzilut*), which is God's "private domain" (the Holy Temple above), and which is called in Kabbalah, "the secret of the Name."[19]

Outside the Holy Temple, where the Name *Havayah* may not be pronounced as it is written, and especially in the time of exile when, due to our sins, the Temple has been destroyed and the souls of Israel have been dispersed to the four corners of the earth, the potency of the Priestly Blessing to heal is surely less than it was (and will be) in the time and place of the Temple. Nonetheless, even now it is an explicit commandment of the Torah for the priests to bless the people by uttering the words of the Priestly Blessing at given times of the year. These times depend on whether one is in the Land of Israel or the Diaspora and vary with the customs of the different Jewish communities.

In essence, even now, the potency of the Priestly Blessing to heal depends upon the degree of faith (in the infinite power inherent in God's commandment to utter the Priestly Blessing) and love with which the priests bless the people, and on the degree of faith and love with which the people turn to the priests to be blessed.

Before performing the commandment to bless the people, the priests pronounce the following blessing:

> Blessed are You, GOD, our God, King of the universe, who has sanctified us with the sanctity of Aaron and has commanded us to bless His people Israel with love.

From this we see clearly that the most essential spiritual component of the blessing is love. The numerical value of the word for "love," *ahavah*, is 13, alluding to the 13 appearances of the letter *yud* in the blessing—the power inherent in the blessing to arouse the 13 attributes of Divine mercy, as explained above.

Infinite Patience

Above the two concealed levels and the two revealed levels, there exists a fifth, transcendent level. This is the level of "infinite, Divine patience," corresponding to *keter* and the upper tip of the *yud* of the Name *Havayah*.

Here, one simply waits, with the power of infinite patience, for God's salvation. One neither prays with audible words nor thinks conscious thoughts. One simply trusts that all of God's ways are good. Such complete faith in Divine providence transforms one's general state of consciousness into one of joy—"joyful in suffering."[20] In complete silence, one is drawn upward to reach the level of absolute oneness with the Eternal. Paradoxically, while at this level of perfect faith there is no end to one's patience and perseverance, this is also when "the salvation of God comes in the blink of an eye."[21]

In summary:

	Name of God	sefirah	level of prayer
transcendent level	י upper tip of *yud*	*keter* "crown"	silence and patience
concealed levels	י *yud*	*chochmah* "wisdom"	blessing of the priest
	ה *hei*	*binah* "understanding"	thought of the holy man
revealed levels	ו *vav*	*midot* "six emotive attributes"	prayer of the wise man
	ה *hei*	*malchut* "kingdom"	prayer of the sick person

FORMS OF PRAYER

Although we have referred to all of the levels of connecting with the Divine as "prayer," only the first two, which correspond to the two revealed levels of the Name *Havayah*, are indeed explicit prayer to God. In a broader sense, however, any spiritual state that arouses Divine mercy to heal the sick, or fill any other human lack, is regarded as a form of prayer.[22]

Indeed, we see from the above description of the levels of prayer that these include not only explicit prayer, but also thought, blessing, and silence. In Hassidic thought, the basic difference between prayer and blessing is that prayer is an "ascending" service (reaching upward toward God) whereas blessing is a "descending" service (God's grace descending to earth).

At the first, lowest level—the prayer of the sick person—one's eyes and heart turn upward to God, beseeching His salvation. Standing in prayer before God, one feels oneself situated "below," striving to reach upward to heaven.

At the second level, the prayer of the wise man for the sick person, the prayer ascends to God while, simultaneously, the wise man (who is situated "above" the sick person) intends to draw down healing power from above. Thus, relative to the first level of ascent alone, the second level is "ascent for the sake of descent," that is, for the sake of drawing down healing power.

At the first level, one prays to God that He effect the descent. The sick person is only able to humbly beseech, not to pull the necessary strings. At the second level, the wise man, in his heartfelt prayer, joins together with God to draw down the healing power.

At the third level, the power of thought is an intermediate state between explicit prayer from below and blessing from above (the fourth level). It is the "telepathic" linking of souls as equals, because "all Israel are friends."[23] In Hebrew, the root of the word for "friends," *chaver*, means "connected" or "bound together."

At the fourth level, the spiritual act of blessing, in contrast to prayer, obeys a dynamic of "descent" from on high. Here, the priest "stands," so to speak, at the spiritual origin from whence the blessing's Divine energy derives. He "commands" the blessing to descend from on high to the soul that he blesses. In the Holy Temple, when blessing the people, the priests would actually stand higher than them, on the dais.

At the fifth level, silence is yet a higher state of equality. In silence, one neither ascends nor descends. This, paradoxically, is the ultimate origin of all blessing and healing power. For this reason, God's essential Name, *Havayah*—of which it is written in the Book of Malachi:[24] "I, God do not change"—is referred to as "the Name of mercy."[25]

To summarize:

5.	silence	at one with God	neither ascent nor descent
4.	blessing	above, at spiritual origin of Divine energy	descent from on high
3.	power of thought	telepathy between equals	"horizontal" influence
2.	prayer of the wise man	prayer ascends to God while healing power descends	ascent for the sake of descent
1.	prayer of the sick person	below, reaching up	ascent

THE HEALING POWER OF *TESHUVAH*

The sages teach: "Great is repentance [*teshuvah*], for it brings healing to the world."[26]

Above, we saw that the apex of prayer to God is reaching a state of inner silence—when one's eyes are turned upward to God and His impending salvation, which "comes in the blink of an eye," and one's heart is full of joy, "being joyful in suffering."[27]

The apex of prayer is the origin of the soul's service of true and complete repentance, *teshuvah*. Literally, *teshuvah* means "returning" to God. Illness is the physical symptom of one's being distanced, estranged from God. *Teshuvah* is coming home. And so, *teshuvah* is the ultimate healing power of the soul.

As we saw above, illness and disease derive from a spiritual state of deficiency or emptiness, and since the Hebrew word meaning "sick" (*choleh*) has the numerical value of 49, this indicates that the sick person lacks the fiftieth gate of understanding. We can thus conclude that "to heal" is "to fill" or "to complete" one's consciousness by reaching the fiftieth gate of understanding.

The power in the soul to fill all states of spiritual and physical emptiness must derive from a place of consummate "satiation," a place in the soul where all is present, nothing lacks. This is the super-conscious level known as the higher "crown" (*keter elyon*), which, upon entering the consciousness, is known as the fiftieth gate of understanding. The soul's conscious aspiration to reach this level is the spiritual service of *teshuvah*.

The truly understanding heart is the heart that knows and desires to return to God,[28] and thereby to be healed. In the words of Isaiah:

> *And his heart shall understand,*
> *and he shall return and be healed.*[29]

As with regard to all that happens to us in life, illness is a *gift* of God. While relating to a spiritual lack, and resulting from the soul's having blemished one of the four letters of God's essential Name, *Havayah*, illness, in and of itself, cleanses our souls, thereby arousing us to return to God. We fill our lack by sincere *teshuvah*, committing ourselves, with love and awe of God in our hearts, to abide in full by all of the commandments of the Torah and to devote every moment of our lives to shining God's light and bringing God's teachings to the world. We thereby draw down healing light and energy from the higher *keter* (corresponding to the upper tip of the *yud* of the Name *Havayah*) to fill all of the deficiencies within the four letters of the Name *Havayah*, and thus to rectify all of the blemishes and illnesses of our bodies and souls.

This healing power derives from the soul's *keter*, that level of the soul that always remains whole, that never lacks and is never blemished. As we return to God, healing the blemishes that we have caused in the four letters of His holy Name, so does He return to us, to heal all of our spiritual and physical illnesses.

In the words of Isaiah:[30]

> *I create the speech of the lips:*
> *"Peace, peace, to the distant and to the near," says God,*
> *"and I will heal him."*

The root "to create" in Hebrew (*b-r-a*) means, as well, "sound health." And so, "I create the speech of the lips" may be read, "I make healthy by the speech of the lips." The "speech of the lips" refers both to the sincere words of confession of the returnee (*ba'al teshuvah*) as well as to the healing power present in the speech of the healer, the "light of the mouth" described above.

The sages interpret God's words—"Peace, peace, to the distant and to the near"—as addressing the *ba'al teshuvah*, one who was distant and has become near.[31] He has returned to God, and so will God return to him and heal him: "says God, 'and I will heal him.'"

Supplementary Essays

1
Right and Left[1]

The left hemisphere of the brain (*binah*) is seen in Kabbalah to oversee and give life-force to the heart, which tends toward the left side of the torso. (Physiologically, both the circulatory system, centered around the heart, and the respiratory system, centered around the lungs, are controlled by the brainstem. The relationship of *binah* to the heart and *chochmah* to the lungs is thus not meant to be confused with this. Here, we are referring to a more spiritual influx of energy and life-force than the physiological control of the vital organs by the nervous system.)

Binah is identified with the body's blood and *gevurah*, the "branch" of *binah* on the left axis of the *sefirot*, with its circulatory system. The heart is part of the circulatory system but also part of the muscular system, which is identified with *tiferet*, on the middle axis of the *sefirot*. From this it becomes clear why the heart is positioned in the middle of the torso (*tiferet*) tending to the left (*gevurah*, the "branch" of *binah*).

Similarly, the right hemisphere of the brain (*chochmah*) is seen to oversee and give life-force to the lungs. Of the two lungs, on the right and left of the torso, the right lung is larger, comprising three lobes, while the left lung is smaller, comprising only two lobes. The life-force that descends from

---

[1] See p. 25.

the right hemisphere of the brain (*chochmah*) to the torso extends to both its right and left sides, for *chochmah* is a more all-inclusive source of life-force than is *binah*. In the imagery of Kabbalah, this life-force is referred to as spiritual "moisture" that descends by way of the trachea from the right hemisphere of the brain to the lungs. "Water" is the spiritual element associated with *chochmah*, the right hemisphere of the brain, while "fire" is the spiritual element associated with *binah*, the left hemisphere of the brain. In the body's physiological systems, this corresponds to the "hot" blood, as noted above. (The life-force from the left hemisphere of the brain [*binah*] descends to the heart via the circulatory system [*gevurah*] in general and the jugular vein in particular.)

We will see that the lungs, the major organ of the respiratory system, relate to the soul's superconscious, the *sefirah* of *keter*. And so, *chochmah*, while overseeing the workings of the lungs, thereby connects to its own source, the *sefirah* above it, *keter*. *Chochmah* corresponds to the *yud*, the first letter of God's essential Name, while *keter* corresponds to the upper tip of the *yud*, essentially one with the *yud* itself.

Generally, we see the right hemisphere of the brain in control of the left side of the body and the left hemisphere of the brain in control of the right side of the body. This phenomenon is explained in Kabbalah to reflect the principle of "inversion" (*achlifu duchtaihu*), pictured as two hands crossing, the right hand placed on the left leg and the left hand placed on the right leg. The body possesses different energy levels. At higher energy levels, this phenomenon becomes manifest, while at lower energy levels, the right controls the right and the left, the left.

2

Three Planes[1]

Another way in which we can visualize the basic division of the powers of the soul into three, and three into three, as mirrored in the human body, is to see the body as made up of spheres. Here, we first envision the human stature as being divided into two primary components, head and body: in the sefirotic terminology of the Kabbalah, "the higher three"—*keter*, *chochmah*, and *binah*—and "the lower seven"—*chesed* to *malchut*. The last of the seven, *malchut*, the mouth, ascends in the human stature to serve as a third, intermediate level between the head and the body.

In the sphere of the head, three great circles are apparent, each defining a circular plane of the sphere. The eyes define the horizontal plane; the ears define the vertical plane from right to left; and the nose (and the mouth) defines the vertical plane from front to back.

These three planes correspond to the three *sefirot* of the intellect: *chochmah* ("wisdom"), *binah* ("understanding"), and *da'at* ("knowledge"):

The eyes, through which the sense of sight is manifest, correspond to *chochmah*: the inner wisdom of the soul is spiritual sight. The ears, through which the sense of hearing is manifest, correspond to *binah*: the inner understanding of the

---

[1] See p. 27.

soul is spiritual hearing. The nose and the mouth, through which the senses of smell and taste are manifest, correspond to *da'at*: the inner knowledge of the soul is spiritual smell and taste.

In the mouth itself (the intermediate level between the head and the body), the teeth define the horizontal plane, the plane of wisdom; the lips (visualize the circle formed by open lips) define the vertical plane from right to left, the plane of understanding; the tongue (visualize the circle formed by the turn of the tongue into the throat) defines the vertical plane from front to back, the plane of knowledge.

In the body, the torso (rotating around its axis) defines the horizontal plane, the plane of wisdom; the arms (raised up and down) define the vertical plane from right to left, the plane of understanding; the legs (walking or bicycling) define the vertical plane from front to back, the plane of knowledge. (In the idiom of the Bible,[2] we find the tongue "walking," for, as we see here, the motion of the tongue and the motion of the legs define the same coordinate.)

As the three planes descend in the body—from the eyes, which define the first and highest of the three planes of the head, to the plane of the legs, the last and lowest of the three planes of the body—physical motion, which is life's most basic dynamic, becomes more pronounced. Physical motion begins, albeit most subtly, in the eyes (in Hebrew, the two-letter sub-root of "eye," *ayin-nun*, inverts to spell "motion," *nun-ayin*), yet reaches its manifest *height* in the legs.

---

[2] Leviticus 19:16, *et al.*

3

Six[1]

The three basic models of Kabbalah—the model of four, the model of ten, and the model of twenty two—possess a clear, abstract mathematical interpretation which we will observe by analyzing them as a sequence, a progressive quadratic series "led" by the number 6 (arrived at by the mathematical process of taking "finite differences").

$$
\begin{array}{ccccc}
4 & & 10 & & 22 \\
 & 6 & & 12 & \\
 & & 6 & &
\end{array}
$$

This series is symmetric (symmetry being one of the most fundamental phenomena of nature), i.e., the three numbers 4, 10, 22 mirror-image themselves as the three previous numbers of the series:

$$
\begin{array}{ccccccc}
22 & 10 & 4 & 4 & 10 & 22 \\
-12 & -6 & 0 & 6 & 12 & \\
6 & 6 & 6 & 6 & &
\end{array}
$$

The sum of 4, 10, and 22 is $36 = 6^2$. The original 36 (the 4, 10, and 22 to the right in the above array) correspond to the 36 righteous individuals in every generation. But in

---

[1] See p. 28.

Kabbalah, we learn that just as there are 36 revealed righteous ones, so are there 36 hidden righteous ones, each set of 36 reflecting, in perfect symmetry, the light of the other.

One of the most basic teachings of Kabbalah is that every rectified set of objects possesses the property of "inter-inclusion," appearing as a hologram where each element of the set reflects and manifests in itself all of the others. Thus, the inter-inclusive, perfected reality of 4 is $16 = 4^2$; that of 10 is $100 = 10^2$; and that of 22 is $484 = 22^2$. Together, these three numbers total 600, or 6 times 10^2. We again observe the role of 6, here in relation to the inter-inclusion of the ten *sefirot*, our beginning point.

In mathematics, 6 is the first "perfect number," i.e., a number that equals the sum of all its divisors, not including itself: 6 equals the sum of its three divisors, 1, 2, and 3. (The next such number is 28, followed by 496, 8128, 33550336....) 6 is the number of directions or vector forces in three-dimensional space, the number of sides of a cube. In the Torah, the world was created in 6 days, the first word of the Torah, *breishit*, possesses 6 letters, and of the 28 letters of the first verse of the Torah, the letter *alef* appears 6 times. Of the 613 commandments of the Torah, there are 6 constant commandments, the "duties of the heart."[2]

---

[2] As explained at length in *Living in Divine Space: Kabbalah and Meditation*.

4
Basic Colors[1]

The fact that yellow appears between blue and red on the color wheel and green is the midpoint between blue and red on the spectrum lends support to the conception that yellow-green is the fundamental color.

The three primary colors plus the three secondary colors plus the six intermediate colors between them give a total of twelve hues. As explained elsewhere, these may be seen to correspond to the twelve months of the year:

Nisan	yellow-green
Iyar	yellow
Sivan	orange-yellow
Tamuz	orange
Menachem Av	red-orange
Elul	red
Tishrei	violet-red
Marcheshvan	violet
Kislev	blue-violet
Tevet	blue
Shevat	green-blue
Adar	green

---

[1] See p. 36, and endnote 12, p. 268.

Nisan begins the Jewish year, as it is written, "This month shall be for you the head of the months; it is the first for you of the months of the year."[2] Its color is yellow-green.

Elsewhere, it is explained that *red* is the most basic, all-inclusive color (both in the Torah and in common parlance, as when referring to the fact that someone's face has color, for example). The explanation of this is that the three colors white, red, and yellow-green are three stages in the development of color: White is the abstract totality of all colors together, as can be seen from the fact that if we spin the color wheel quickly enough we see white. Red is the first, generic manifestation of the phenomenon of actual color; if there were only one color, it would be red. Yellow-green is the beginning (and source) of the differentiation of discrete colors. Red is thus the simple, uncompounded (*pashut*) color, while yellow-green is the fundament of compounded (*murkav*) colors.

This threefold development (abstract through simple to compound) is an exquisite example of the meaning of the division of the sefirotic tree into right, left, and central axes, each of which expresses its respective phase of this development.

Moreover, these three stages reflect the three stages of the maturation of consciousness, referred to in Kabbalah as "pregnancy" (*ibur*), "nursing" (*yenikah*), and "intellect" (*mochin*). Pregnancy is an abstract state of infinite possibility; birth, childhood, and youth are characterized by simplistic,

---

[2] Exodus 12:2.

one-dimensional thinking; maturity is the ability to appreciate and blend divergent opinions and views.

5

Sight and Shabbat[1]

The power of sight corresponds to the life-giving spirit of the body and to the fifth, transcendent level of God's Name—the upper tip of the *yud*. But here, the upper tip of the *yud* is seen in the inner point of the second *hei*. As *Sefer Yetzirah*[2] reveals, "the end is wedged in the beginning, and the beginning in the end."

In the *Zohar*, the eye, the power of sight, relates to Shabbat.[3] In Hebrew, the word for Shabbat is composed of three letters: *shin*, *beit*, and *tav*. The letter *shin* is formed of three lines (three *vavs*, each with a head, a *yud*, at its top) rising out of a common base. These three lines allude to the three patriarchs, Abraham, Isaac, and Jacob, and so the letter *shin* is referred to as "the letter of the patriarchs."[4] The two remaining letters of the word *Shabbat*, the *beit* and the *tav*, spell the word *bat*, "daughter," which also means the "pupil" of the eye.[5]

The *shin* of Shabbat thus alludes to the three colors of the eye around the pupil, while the *beit* and *tav* of Shabbat allude to the pupil itself. On Shabbat, the day that alludes to

---

[1] See p. 38.

[2] 1:7.

[3] 2:204a. See also *The Mystery of Marriage*, p. 31.

[4] *Zohar* 1:2b; *Tikunei Zohar* 51 (86b); see also *The Hebrew Letters*, p. 314.

[5] As in Psalms 17:8.

the revelation of the World to Come, the rectified eye of man—which reflects all three patriarchs together with King David—envisions the Divine light of this holy day, alluded to in the word Shabbat, which in the *Zohar* is taken to be a Name of God. Shabbat, when seen as a whole, manifests a light that infinitely transcends that of its component letters.

To summarize:

Shabbat	God's light	power of sight	*keter*
shin	Abraham	white of the eye	*chochmah*
	Isaac	red of the eye	*binah*
	Jacob	colors of iris	*midot* (and *da'at*)
bat	David	black pupil	*malchut*

6

Implications of Nakedness[1]

The term used at the beginning of *Sefer Yetzirah* for "the *brit*," *maor*, derives from the root in Hebrew whose primary meaning is "nakedness." The first act of Adam and Eve following the primordial sin was to cover their nakedness. So, too, did Shem and Japhet cover the nakedness of their father, Noah.

The *mitzvah* of circumcision given to Abraham is, paradoxically, to remove the covering of the foreskin from the *brit*, thereby stripping off its foreign clothing and rendering it "naked." This "awakens" in the super-conscious of the Jewish soul the "memory" of the bliss of man in the Garden of Eden, before his fall, when he lived "naked, without shame." Only then can the Jew begin to "walk humbly with God." As God said to Abraham upon commanding him to circumcise himself: "Walk before Me and be perfect."

Regarding King David, the sages relate[2] that when naked he came to realize that then he possessed only one *mitzvah*—the "sign of God" inscribed on his very flesh—his circumcision. Thus, the *mitzvah* of circumcision renders a Jew "naked" yet "covered" by the Divine clothing of God's will—the essence of every *mitzvah*.

---

[1] See p. 41.
[2] *Menachot* 43b.

The root of *maor* also implies an "awakening" or "arousal." Before circumcision, the Divine soul is dormant in the body, in such deep slumber that it is unable to awaken itself.

God made Adam fall into a state of deep slumber in order to sever from him the body of Eve. The sages teach us that during the dialog between Eve and the snake, Adam was asleep.[3] In sleep, an impure spirit may take hold of the extremities of the body, the fingertips, and the *brit*. Adam's sleep was actually the beginning of a spiritual process that ultimately resulted, on the physical plane, in the "stretching" of the impure foreskin over the holy organ of procreation.

The commentaries on *Sefer Yetzirah* relate the word *maor* to the verse: "as the embrace [*kema'ar*] of man and companion."[4] This idiom refers to the forms of the cherubim in the Temple constructed by King Solomon. The image is one of husband embracing wife, as is said in relation to Adam and Eve (and all of humanity to follow) upon their creation, before their sin: "...and he shall cleave to his wife and they shall become one flesh."

The root of *maor* also means "to pour." The commentaries on *Sefer Yetzirah* understand this to allude to the pouring forth of creative life-force and sustenance from *yesod* into *malchut*, as in the union of husband and wife.

The more general meaning of the word *maor*, as used in this sense, is "to be involved" (or more literally, "to be tied into"). Thus, we can understand that the effect of

---

[3] *Bereishit Rabbah* 19:3.
[4] 1 Kings 7:36.

circumcision on the Jewish soul is to evoke its power to "involve" itself with its task to rectify physical reality. In each true involvement inheres a procreative act.

This is further supported by the fact that the Hebrew word *brit* meaning "covenant [of circumcision]" is related to the words *barah*, "to clarify" or "to rectify," and *bara*, "to create."

In Psalms[5] we find that the sub-root of *maor* (*ayin-reish*) means "to destroy a foundation [*yesod*]." It also appears throughout the Bible in the sense of "desolate" and "barren" (without children). As is common to Hebrew roots, this root also possesses the opposite sense, "[to construct or found] a city." Just as we shall see with respect to the "word of the tongue," that "death and life are in the hand of the tongue," so do we see with respect to the "circumcision of the *brit*" that destruction and construction, of *yesod* in particular, depend upon it.

---

[5] 137:7.

7

The Thirty-two Pathways[1]

Sefer Yetzirah opens with three statements, *mishnayot*:

- With thirty-two wondrous pathways of wisdom, God...created His world with three books: "scribe," "book," and "story."
- [There are] ten ineffable *sefirot* and twenty-two letters of foundation...three mothers, seven doublets and twelve simple units.
- [There are] ten ineffable *sefirot*, corresponding to the ten fingers, five opposite five, and the single covenant is placed in the middle, in the word of the tongue and the circumcision of the *brit*.

The first *mishnah* of *Sefer Yetzirah* introduces the 32 pathways of wisdom; the second *mishnah* divides the 32 pathways into two groups of 10 *sefirot* and 22 letters, which further subdivide into three groups of 3, 7, and 12 letters. In the third *mishnah*, the text begins to deal with the ten *sefirot* explicitly, and continues to do so throughout the rest of the first chapter.

These first three *mishnayot* themselves follow the order of the three *sefirot* of the intellect: *chochmah* ("wisdom"), *binah* ("understanding") and *da'at* ("knowledge"). The first *mishnah*

---

[1] See p. 41.

opens with the 32 pathways of *chochmah*, the right hemisphere of the brain. The second *mishnah* analyzes and divides these 32 into subgroups, a process dependent upon the intellectual faculty of *binah*, the left hemisphere of the brain. The third *mishnah* presents a concrete, physical model for the ten *sefirot*, thus employing the faculty of *da'at*, the middle, posterior region of the brain, which serves to concretize the abstract intellectual cognition of *chochmah* and *binah*.

It will have been noted that the process of division into subgroups takes place in two stages: first the 32 pathways of wisdom are divided into 10 *sefirot* and 22 letters, and then the second category or division of 22 letters is further subdivided into three sub-categories of 3, 7, and 12. We thereby arrive at the final division of the original 32 into four subgroups of 10, 3, 7, and 12.

This process of division alludes to the process whereby the four letters of God's essential Name, *Havayah* (the first of the three basic models of Kabbalah described above[2]), become manifest. It is written: "For by God [*yud-hei*], GOD [*yud-hei-vav-hei*] formed worlds."[3] The sages interpret this to mean that the World to Come was created with the *yud*, the first letter of the first Name of God appearing in this verse (*Kah*) and this world was created with its second letter, *hei*. The creative process God followed in creating this world is depicted in detail in the second Name of God in this verse by the three letters *hei-vav-hei* in place of the original one *hei*. (The meaning of *hei-vav-hei* as a word is "the present," i.e., this

---

[2] pp. 1-32.

[3] Isaiah 26:4; see *Tosafot, Berachot* 51a, *s.v. Zocheh*.

world.) Thus, we see that God's Name was first divided into two components/letters *yud-hei*, and then further subdivided as *yud-hei-vav-hei*.

The four subdivisions of the original 32 pathways of wisdom (all levels are initially contained, in potential, at the level of wisdom) correspond to the four letters of God's Name in order: the ten *sefirot* to the *yud* (*chochmah*), whose numerical value is 10; the three mother-letters to the first *hei* (*binah*, the mother-figure); the seven double-letters to the *vav* (the emotions), which means "a hook," to link two parallel aspects of reality (thus creating an impression of "duality" or "double-ness"); and the twelve single letters to the final *hei* (*malchut*, symbolized by the moon and its twelve months).

8

The Five Fingers[1]

The five names of the five fingers (*agudal*, *etzba*, *amah*, *kemitzah*, and *zeret*) when added together equal (numerically) 1105 = 13 · 85. 85 = *milah*, "circumcision." 13 = *milah* in "reduced numbering" (where 40, the normative value of the letter *mem*, reduces to 4, and so on). Upon fulfilling the *mitzvah* of circumcision, God's 13 Attributes of Mercy reveal themselves, as mentioned above. This very secret we see to be reflected in the fingers themselves which the circumcision serves to balance.

The number 1105 = 5 · 221. Thus, the average value of each one of the names for the five fingers is 221. 221 = *ya'ir*, "he shall shine light." We are taught in Kabbalah that when one points one's finger, he actually radiates light. The word *etzba* (the word for "finger" in general, and the name of the pointing finger, in particular) is an acronym for *or-tzeva-behirut-otzma* ("light" that radiates the three dimensions of color: "hue," "brilliance," and "saturation"). (The word *tzeva*, the root word of *etzba*, which means "color," is itself the acronym for the three dimensions of color: "hue," "brilliance," and "saturation.") 221 = *etzba* (163) plus *chen* (58), "grace." In Kabbalah, 163 is the value of the full spelling of the Divine Name of *da'at* (*alef-hei-vav-hei*, pronounced *Akvah*); 58 is the average value of the four primary spellings

---

[1] See p. 50.

of God's essential Name *Havayah* (whose individual values are 72, 63, 45, and 52).

All five numbers 1105, 13, 85, 5 and 221 share in common their being "inspirational" numbers, i.e., the sums of two successive square numbers. 1105 is the 24th inspirational number ($1105 = 24^2 + 23^2$). Similarly, 13 is the 3rd inspirational number, 85 is the 7th, 5 is the 2nd and 221 is the 11th! Inspirational numbers convey the consciousness of connection to God by means of His *mitzvot* (the full number of *mitzvot* in the Torah is 613, the 18th inspirational number; the number of negative *mitzvot* is 365, the 14th inspirational number), beginning with the *mitzvah* of *milah*. *Milah* = 85, which is the 7th—and hence the most "beloved"—inspirational number, as mentioned above. Each inspirational number is the middle-point of a square number. 85 is the middle-point of $169 = 13^2$, the secret of the 13 Divine Principles of Mercy revealed upon circumcision.

The value of the names of the five fingers, 1105, equals that of the first five words of the *Shema*. The sixth word, *echad* ("one"), thus signifies "the single covenant" which appears "in the middle" of the fingers in order to balance them and unite them.

The word for "hand," *yad*, equals 5 in "reduced numbering," signifying the five fingers of the hand, where the thumb is separate from the remaining four fingers. In the normative numbering system, *yad* = 14, corresponding to the 14 joints of the five fingers. In two hands there are 28 = *koach* ("strength") joints, corresponding to the 28 letters, inscribed in the hands, from *alef* to *alef*, from 1 to 1000 (the 22 letters from *alef* to *tav*, from 1 to 400; the five final letters—*kaf, mem*, *nun*, *pei*, *tzadik*—from 500 to 900, and return to *alef*, which, as a word, means "one thousand").

In the most commonly cited reflective alphabetic transformation of *atbash*—whereby the first letter of the alphabet, *alef*, is paired with or exchanged by the last letter, *tav*, and the second letter, *beit*, is paired with the second last letter, *shin*, and so on—each of the first four pairs of letters (*at bash gar dak*), when calculated in "reduced numbering," = 5. *At bash* thus allude to the ten fingers of the hands, while *gar dak* allude to the ten toes of the feet.

Each of the next five pairs (*hatz vap za chas tan*) = 14 (*yad*, "hand"). The Torah speaks of "five hands" with reference to Joseph's allocation of the produce of Egypt as viceroy of Pharaoh. Each of the two remaining pairs (*yam kol*) once more = 5.

The entire alphabet of 22 letters in "reduced numbering" = 100 (10^2), where the six pairs that equal 5 add to 30 and the 5 pairs that equal 14 add to 70. The division of 100 into 30 and 70 corresponds to the division of the 10 *sefirot* into the 3 higher *sefirot* of the mind and the 7 lower *sefirot* of the heart.

9

Partzufim and Contact Points[1]

Each self-contained state of reality, including each human being, possesses five personas (*partzufim*), which develop from the five initial points of *keter*, *chochmah*, *binah*, the *midot*, and *malchut*, corresponding to the tip of the *yud* and the four letters of God's essential Name, *Havayah*:

- *Arich Anpin* ("the Long Face"),
- *Abba* ("the Father"),
- *Ima* ("the Mother"),
- *Z'eir Anpin* ("the Small Face," the son or groom), and
- *Nukva diZ'eir Anpin* ("the Female of *Z'eir Anpin*," the daughter or bride).

Each of these possesses all three energy centers/contact points running down their middle line, giving fifteen energy centers or contact points.

Indeed, every one of us, created in the image of God, reflects, in body and soul, all five Divine personas, for which reason every one of us is considered to be a "complete world."[2] And so, we may identify fifteen energy centers or contact points running down the middle line of our bodies.

---

[1] See p. 53.
[2] *Sanhedrin* 37a.

In Kabbalah, every meditative state and spiritual endeavor to arouse energies and create unions relates to a specific prayer to God. The meditation on the fifteen contact points is an "intention" (*kavanah*) of the blessing that follows the recital of the *Shema* every morning. The text of this blessing—confirming the absolute truth of Judaism, which finds its expression in the recital of the *Shema*—begins with the word *emet* ("true") followed by fifteen synonyms or variations of the concept "true," each of which is prefaced with the letter *vav* ("and," implying connective energy; as a word, *vav* means "a hook").

The middle line of the body or the middle axis of the supernal *sefirot* is referred to in general as *emet*. In particular, the three letters of *emet*—*alef*, *mem*, and *tav*—the "beginning, middle, and end of the alphabet,"[3] correspond to the three contact points of the inner dimension of *Atik Yomin* ("the Ancient of Days"), which permeate and give life-force to all of the five general personas of each world. Ultimate truth is neither right nor left; it is the power that unites the right and the left to become one. It derives from the origin of the "middle" that transcends both antithetical states of right and left. It possesses a full spectrum of fifteen "hues," reflected in the body as fifteen contact-points running down its middle line.

The fifteen contact-points divide into five groups of three, each group corresponding to one of the five primary personas of the complete human "world." The first group of three are: (1) the point at the top of the skull, (2) the point

---

[3] *Y. Sanhedrin* 2a.

where the hair meets the forehead (the place above which the head-*tefilin* are placed), and (3) the point of the middle of the forehead (referred to as the essential point of the "forehead of will"). All three of these points embody super-rational energy; they are all above the eyes, the beginning of conscious perception. They correspond to the three points (figuratively: mouth, chest, and *brit*) of *Arich Anpin* (above *Abba* and *Ima*, the Father and Mother—*chochmah* and *binah*, the rational mind).

The next group of three are: (1) the point between the eyes (the "mouth" of wisdom), (2) the point of the nose, and (3) the indent above the upper lip (the point that the angel strikes before birth to cause us to forget all the Torah we learned in the womb). These are the three points (mouth, chest, and *brit*) of *Abba*.

Next come (1) the tip of the tongue in the mouth, (2) the point of the chin, and (3) the middle point of the throat. These are the three points (mouth, chest, and *brit*) of *Ima*.

Then come (1) the point between the shoulders, (2) the middle point of the upper chest (referred to as the "bird of the soul"), and (3) the middle point of the (lower) chest (the essential point of the chest, the point of embrace described above). These are the three points (mouth, chest, and *brit*) of *Z'eir Anpin*.

Finally come (1) the point of the navel (the "mouth" during pregnancy), (2) the point of the lower abdomen (the point of the female womb), and (3) the point of the (male) *brit*. These are the three points (mouth, chest, and *brit*) of *Nukva diZ'eir Anpin*.

The words in the blessing following the *Shema* correlated to these fifteen points are: (1) *veyatziv* ("and firm"), (2) *venachon* ("and established"), (3) *vekayam* ("and enduring"), (4) *veyashar* ("and straight"), (5) *vene'eman* ("and faithful"), (6) *ve'ahuv* ("and beloved"), (7) *vechaviv* ("and cherished"), (8) *venechmad* ("and precious"), (9) *vena'im* ("and pleasant"), (10) *venora* ("and awesome"), (11) *ve'adir* ("and mighty"), (12) *umetukan* ("and corrected"), (13) *umekubal* ("and acceptable"), (14) *vetov* ("and good"), and (15) *veyafeh* ("and beautiful"). The sentence concludes: "…is this upon us forever," referring, as we said, to the *Shema*, Judaism's essential statement of faith.

word from the blessing		partzuf		body
veyatziv	firm	Arich Anpin "The Long Face"	mouth	top of skull
venachon	established		chest	where hair meets forehead
vekayam	enduring		brit	middle of forehead
veyashar	straight	Abba "Father"	mouth	between the eyes
vene'eman	faithful		chest	nose
ve'ahuv	beloved		brit	indent above upper lip
vechaviv	cherished	Ima "Mother"	mouth	tip of tongue
venechmad	precious		chest	chin
vena'im	pleasant		brit	midpoint of throat
venora	awesome	Z'eir Anpin "The Small Face"	mouth	between the shoulders
ve'adir	mighty		chest	midpoint of upper chest
umetukan	corrected		brit	midpoint of lower chest
umekubal	acceptable	Nukva diZ'eir Anpin Female of Z'eir Anpin"	mouth	navel
vetov	good		chest	lower abdomen (womb)
veyafeh	beautiful		brit	male *brit*

10

Contraction and Relaxation[1]

In Hebrew, the word for "blood vessel" (*gid*) is related to the word for "opposition" (*nigud*). In *Tanya*,[2] we are taught that while the root *n-g-d* means "against" or "opposed to," it implies as well "removed" or "distanced from." The removal of the opposing force allows for relaxation between successive contractions. In the *sefirah* of *gevurah* itself, the *gevurah* within *gevurah* contracts while the *chesed* within *gevurah* relaxes (in preparation for the subsequent contraction).

The dynamic of contraction and relaxation characterizes the class of angels whose spiritual abode (the "heaven" known as *Ma'on*[3]) is in the realm of the *sefirah* of *gevurah*. These angels are referred to as *chashmalim*, which means that they are "at times silent, at times speaking."[4] The time of silence is the time of contraction; the time of speaking is the time of relaxation. As it is written, "The words of the wise spoken in a state of tranquility, are heard."[5]

The dynamic of contraction and relaxation is found throughout the body. For example, in the circulatory system, it is evident in the vascular contraction and relaxation of the

---

[1] See p. 79.
[2] *Igeret HaTeshuvah* 11.
[3] *Chagigah* 12b.
[4] *Ibid.* 13b.
[5] Ecclesiastes 9:17.

heart, arteries, and veins. Varicose veins result from turbulent blood flow due to damage to valves, resulting in secondary contraction/relaxation dysfunction. In the muscular system, the variation of the slow and rapid twitch of the muscles is a function of the contraction and relaxation of the muscular tissue. In the gastrointestinal system, the peristalsis of the intestines is a contraction/relaxation dynamic. The recovery time of various organs differs, varying with their cycles of contraction and relaxation. Nausea and vomiting result from imbalances in the contraction/relaxation equilibrium of the intestines. Pressure changes in the brain (a contraction/relaxation phenomenon) depend on the balance of water and minerals in the body.

11

Light, Water, Firmament[1]

Clearly, the innate capacity to recreate one's own self derives from the very essence of one's soul—the *etzem haneshamah*, in the terminology of Hassidism. The essence of one's soul is one with God's infinite light. Thus, the power to reproduce is one's innate "power of the infinite" (*koach haein sof*); it originates in infinity and extends, from generation to generation, to infinity.

In Kabbalah, we are taught that reproduction begins with the manifestation, in the mind, of the essence of one's self as pure "light" (*or*). The light then becomes "seed," or "water" (*mayim*), in the idiom of Kabbalah. When the male seed fertilizes the female seed, the newly-formed embryo is called the "firmament" (*rakia*).

In Hassidism, the triplet of "light," "water," "firmament"—*or, mayim, rakia*—parallels another basic triplet of concepts, "light," "life-force," "energy"—*or, chayut, ko'ach*. First, there is the revelation of transcendent "light," which hovers above the body. Then, the transcendent light enters the body to become immanent "life-force." Finally, the relatively spiritual life-force is converted into physical "energy," which actualizes, in the development and functioning of the body, the latent potential of the spiritual life-force. (In many so-called "healing" systems these three

---

[1] See p. 82.

concepts are greatly confused. Both triplets begin with "light." "Water" corresponds to "life-force," as we find in the idiom of the Torah, "living waters." Indeed, the living human body is 60-70% water. "Firmament" corresponds to "energy," for it is the energy of the mother that defines and develops the relatively spiritual seed of the father, just as the firmament defines the water, separating the higher, spiritual waters from the lower, material waters.

Indeed, light-water-firmament (*or-mayim-rakia*) is the process by which God created the world. On the first day of creation, the word for "light" [*or*] appears five times; on the second day of creation, the words for "water" [*mayim*] and "firmament" [*rakia*] each appear five times.

The initial letters of *or-mayim-rakia* spell *omer* ("saying"), the root of the word used in the Torah for the ten *sayings* of creation. With each creative utterance God created a facet of reality, each in a manner similar to physical reproduction.

Before our present-day understanding of the physiology of reproduction, the idea that the male seed originates in the brain seemed to materialists like another fantasy of pre-scientific imagination. Today, the tables have turned. In terms of modern medicine, the physiology of arousal occurs along the neurohypophysial axis. The emotion of love (in the heart) stimulates the hypothalamus (in the brain), which in turn stimulates the adrenal gland to secrete adrenal hormones (ACTH) that act on the seminiferous tubules to produce male seed.

In Hassidism, we are taught that the essence of the soul, the unconscious source of all light, dwells in the innermost point of the heart, where true love is born. The initial conscious manifestation of light, *or*, is the moment at which a new insight—a bolt of lightning—flashes across the mind. The *or* stimulates the endocrine system to secrete hormones that ultimately produce male seed, *mayim*. In the female womb, *mayim* becomes *rakia*.

The root *omer* is closely related to the word for "truth" (*emet*). The first two letters of the two words (*alef-mem*, the initial letters of *or mayim*) are identical; the third letter of *omer*, *reish* (= 200), doubles itself numerically to become the third letter of *emet*, *tav* (= 400). And so we find the idiom in the Book of Proverbs:[2] "sayings of truth" (*imrei emet*).

Emet ("truth") is the inner experience of *yesod* ("foundation"), the *sefirah* corresponding to the reproductive system in human physiology. In Kabbalah, we are taught that *yesod*, while being the sixth and concluding emotive attribute of the soul, possesses a special affinity to the mind that the other emotive attributes do not possess. We are told that *yesod* ascends to the mind to draw down the seed into the reproductive organ. The description presented above greatly enhances our understanding of the functioning of the reproductive system as corresponding to the *sefirah* of *yesod*.

---

[2] 22:21.

12

Spirituality and Reproduction[1]

The lower triangle of the *Magen David* is constructed of three *sefirot*, namely, *chesed*, *gevurah*, and *yesod*, corresponding to the skeleton, the blood vessels, and the reproductive system, respectively. The 248 bones of the skeleton correspond to the 248 positive commandments of the Torah (the do's) and the 365 major blood vessels correspond to the 365 prohibitive commandments of the Torah (the don'ts). The healthy functioning of the reproductive system may thus be understood to depend on the sound health, on the physical plane, of one's bones and blood vessels and, on the more spiritual plane, on one's commitment to the Torah's commandments, both positive and prohibitive.

God chose Abraham, the numerical value of whose name equals 248, to be the first Jew, "for he will instruct his children and household to guard the way of God [i.e., perform all of His commandments]."[2] Because of his devotion to perform the commandments, he was blessed with progeny. Initially, his reproductive system did not function; he was barren, physically unable to bear children. When commanded by God to circumcise himself, at the age of 99, he was given an additional letter to his name—Abram/Abraham—bringing its numerical value of his name

---

[1] See p. 125.
[2] Genesis 18:19.

to 248. Only then did he receive, together with his wife Sarah, full potency to bear Isaac, the son who would inherit him and continue the lineage of the Jewish people.

The sages further explain that to rectify one's reproductive system, one must know how to properly balance the functions of one's right and left hands. These correspond to the two *sefirot* of *chesed* and *gevurah*; in the body, to the skeleton and the blood vessels. The right hand "draws near" while the left hand "rejects."[3] The positive commandments of the Torah give full expression to the force of the right hand to "bring near," while the prohibitive commandments give expression to the force of the left hand to "push off.") This balance is especially necessary with regard to the sexual drive—in the terminology of the sages, the *yetzer*, the base "inclination" of the soul—the power that drives the funtioning of the reproductive system.

---

[3] *Sotah* 47a.

13

Regularity and Health[1]

In the blessing recited after discharging digestive waste, we bless God for creating us "with many orifices and cavities. It is revealed and known before Your Throne of Glory that even if one of them were to be closed or one of them to be opened, it would be impossible to endure for even a moment." This blessing refers to the orifices and conduits of all the physiological systems, even though the context in which the blessing is recited is that of the proper functioning of the digestive system.[2]

The reason we bless God for the proper functioning of all our physiological systems in the context of that of the digestive system is that the digestive system is associated with the *sefirah* of *malchut*, the spiritual channel through which all the *sefirot* above it flow into the next level ("world") of reality. "All the rivers flow unto the sea,"[3] the "sea" being a Kabbalistic metaphor for *malchut*, and the "rivers" are a metaphor for the *sefirot* above *malchut*.

This blessing is one of the two blessings found in our prayers that praise and bless God as the Healer *par excellence*. The other is the eighth blessing of the *Amidah*, "…Who heals the sick of His people, Israel." In the latter blessing, we

---

[1] See p. 136.
[2] Rashi on *Berachot* 60b.
[3] Ecclesiastes 1:7.

entreat God to heal us; in the former blessing, we thank Him for healing us and express our amazement at the wondrous workings of our physiology. In particular, we note the miraculous way in which that which is meant to be open does not close and that which is meant to be closed does not open. This alludes to the passage of the Talmud quoted above, that at the moment of birth "that which was closed opens and that which was open closes." And so the blessing concludes: "Blessed are You, GOD, who heals all flesh *and works wonders*."

The first, seminal description of healing in the Torah is the account of how Abraham prayed to God to open the orifices of the Philistines and their king, Abimelech.[4] God had closed these orifices because Abimelech sought to defile Sarah.

Thus, the essence of healing, as described in the first instance of healing in the Torah, is opening orifices that should be open but have been closed.

The expression the Torah uses to describe the Philistines' relief at being healed is "…and they gave birth," alluding to the association between healing and giving birth—via the common element of opening and closing the proper orifices—that we saw in the passage quoted from the Talmud.

The highest form of cure is that effected through prayer. In the story of Abraham and Abimelech, Abraham heals Abimelech through prayer.[5]

---

[4] Genesis 20:17-18; see p. 169.
[5] See p. 195.

Immediately following this episode, the Torah describes how God granted Abraham and Sarah a child after many years of barrenness. From this juxtaposition, the sages point out that when someone is suffering from a certain problem and he prays on behalf of someone else suffering from the same problem, the one who prays is answered first.[6] Inasmuch as this episode is the prime example of healing in the Torah, we see that the most effective prayer for healing is the patient's prayer for another patient!

The priest is the quintessential physician in the Torah.[7] The Torah refers to Abraham as a priest in the verse, "You are a priest forever."[8]

Specifically, the Philistines suffered from the closing of five orifices: the seminal orifice, the anus, the urethral orifice, the ears, and the nostrils.[9] We may understand the fact that five specific orifices were affected as an allusion to the fact that through their sin, the Philistines caused an aberration in the flow of the Divine beneficence that is channeled through the five states of Divine judgement (*gevurah*). This is reflected in Abraham's explanation of their affliction: "There simply is no fear of God [*Elokim*] in this place"[10]; the Name *Elokim* indicates the attribute of Divine judgment and fear is the inner experience of *gevurah*. Also, when describing how God healed the Philistines, the Torah

---

[6] *Bava Kama* 92a.

[7] p. 165.

[8] Psalms 110:4, Rashi *ad loc.*

[9] Rashi, *loc. cit.*

[10] Genesis 20:11.

uses the Name *Elokim* rather than the Name *Havayah,* which we would have expected since it indicates the attribute of Divine mercy: "And God [*Elokim*] healed Abimelech, his wife, and his maidservants...."[11]

The Torah uses the term "stoppage" to describe this disease. The root of this word (*ayin-tzadik-reish*) permutes to spell the root of the words for *tzara'at* (*tzadik-reish-ayin*), the archetypal disease, and "pain" (*tzadik-ayin-reish*). Clearly, this root and its permutations are primary linguistic referents to disease.

Indeed, the great medieval sage and physician, Maimonides, asserts that the first objective in the maintenance of proper health is regularity and that the first sign of incipient disease is constipation.[12]

Abimelech described the sickness he and his people suffered from as "an occurrence that does not occur,"[13] i.e., a supernatural phenomenon. This is echoed in the blessing recited over the proper functioning of the body, in which we refer to the appropriate opening and closing of the orifices as a manifestation of God's supernatural power within nature—"...who heals all flesh and works *wonders*."

This blessing consists of 45 words (according to the version of the Arizal), the numerical value of the word for

---

[11] *Ibid.,* v. 17.

[12] *Mishneh Torah, Dei'ot* 4:13. In the preceding paragraphs, Maimonides describes the principles of proper eating, but he later states that regularity and exercise are so important that their proper maintenance can override the effects of an unhealthy diet.

[13] Genesis 20:9.

"man" (*adam*). The blessing begins, "Blessed are You, GOD, our God, king of the universe, who formed man with wisdom...." In Kabbalah, "wisdom" (*chochmah*) is read *koach mah*, "the power of what?"[14] The numerical value of the word for "what?" (*mah*) is 45, the same as that of the word for "man" (*adam*).

The number of words in the eighth blessing of the *Amidah* ("...who heals the sick of His people, Israel") is 28, the numerical value of the word for "power" (*ko'ach*). Thus, these two blessings allude together to the *sefirah* of *chochmah* (the "power" of "what?"). *Chochmah* is the *sefirah* of life, as it is written, "they die, but not with *chochmah*,"[15] and "*chochmah* gives life to those who possess it."[16]

The blessing of the *Amidah* begins: "Heal us, GOD, and we shall be healed...." The numerical value of this phrase is 700 (10 times 70). The full numerical value of the blessing of thanksgiving for God, the healer, healing us, is 9800, 2 times 70^2, or 14 times 700. The three Hebrew words for "Heal us, GOD, and we shall be healed" comprise 14 letters; the average value of each letter is 50. This number represents the 50 gates of healing the sick, who possesses only 49.[17] 9800 = 14 times 700 (or 50 times 14^2). 14 signifies the secret of the healing "hand" (*yad* = 14) of God.

---

[14] See *Tanya*, ch. 3.

[15] Job 4:21.

[16] Ecclesiastes 7:12.

[17] See p. 138.

14

Six Permutations[1]

The root of the Hebrew word *tiferet (p-a-r)* is a permutation of the root meaning "healing" *(r-p-a)*. Also, in Kabbalah we find that the angel of healing, Raphael, is the angel that corresponds to the *sefirah* of *tiferet*.

According to Kabbalah, each of the "six extremities"—the six emotive attributes of the heart from *chesed* to *yesod*—corresponds to one of the six permutations of the three first letters of God's essential Name, *Havayah*. (God's four-letter Name, *Havayah*, is indeed composed of three distinct letters, i.e., its first three letters, for its second and fourth letters are identical, the letter *hei*.) In the permutations that correspond to the higher three of these six—*chesed (yud-hei-vav)*, *gevurah (hei-vav-yud)*, and *tiferet (vav-yud-hei)*—the letters of God's Name appear in direct order; in the permutations that correspond to the lower three of these six— *netzach (yud-vav-hei)*, *hod (hei-yud-vav)*, and *yesod (vav-hei-yud)*—the letters of God's Name appear in reverse order. Thus, the "direct lights" of the three higher permutations are reflected in the "reflected lights" of the three lower permutations.

Specifically, *chesed* is reflected in *yesod*—as alluded to in the verses: "The world is built upon kindness [*chesed*]"[2] and

---

[1] See p. 138.
[2] Psalms 89:3.

"The righteous one is the foundation [*yesod*] of the world."³ *Gevurah* is reflected in *netzach*—meaning that strength is reflected in victory and conquest—a strong person (*gevurah*) will overcome, succeed, and be victorious (*netzach*). Finally, what is most interesting to us here is that the direct light of *tiferet* is reflected in the returning light of *hod*. This implies that medicine derives from *tiferet* but disease and the power of the body to overcome it relate to *hod*.⁴

All the above will become clear by visualizing the six permutations as they correspond to the six attributes of the heart:

gevurah		*chesed*
הוי		יהו
	tiferet	
	ויה	
hod		*netzach*
היו		יוה
	yesod	
	והי	

---

³ Proverbs 10:25.
⁴ See *Sod Hashem Lireiav*, pp. 102-104.

15

Death and Life[1]

The 72 three-letter mystical Names of God are derived from three consecutive verses in the Torah,[2] each of which contains 72 letters. The first of the 72 Names is formed by combining the first letter of the first verse, the last letter of the second verse, and the first letter of the third verse; the second is formed by combining the second letter of the first verse, the second to the last letter of the second verse, and the second letter of the third verse; and so on. The full array of these 72 Names is as follows:

כהת	אכא	ללה	מהש	עלם	סיט	ילי	והו
הקם	הרי	מבה	יזל	ההע	לאו	אלד	הזי
ההו	מלה	ייי	נלך	פהל	לוו	כלי	לאו
ושר	לכב	אום	ריי	שאה	ירת	האא	נתה
ייז	רהע	חעם	אני	מגד	כוק	להח	יחו
מיה	אשל	ערי	סאל	ילה	וול	מיכ	ההה
פוי	מבה	נית	ננא	עמם	החש	דני	והו
מחי	ענו	יהה	ומב	מצר	הרח	ייל	נמם
מום	היי	יבמ	ראה	חבו	איע	מנק	דמב

---

[1] See p. 166.
[2] Exodus 14:19-21.

Significantly, the Name *samech-alef-lamed* is the 45th of these 72 Holy Names. 45 is the numerical value of the word for "man," *adam*, in the Talmudic phrase, "the end of *man* is to die." It is also the numerical value of the word for "what?" (*mah*), the word that Moses used to express his (and his brother, Aaron's) state of selflessness (*venachnu mah*, "and we are what?"[3]). From this we learn that true selflessness, the inner experience of *chochmah*, above death in essence (the level of Moses, of whom it is said, "Moses did not die"[4]), comes from the very meditation on the Name of the Living God: "the end of man is to die"!

In addition, the Arizal teaches that when, three times a day, we say the verse, "You open Your hand and satisfy the needs of every living being,"[5] we are to bear in mind that the final letters of the first three words in this verse (*poteia**ch** et yade**ch**a*) spell the holy mystical Name *chet-tav-chaf*, "the Name of Livelihood," which, when transformed in *atbash* reads *samech-alef-lamed*, which are the initial letters of the phrase, "the end of man is to die." And so we see again that an awareness that human mortality is indeed a Divine phenomenon connects us to the Source of Life and the Source of Livelihood.

In addition, the very Name *chet-tav-chaf* means "to cut," as in the phrase, "[God] *cuts* [i.e., apportions] life for all the living."[6]

---

[3] Exodus 16:7-8.
[4] *Sotah* 13b.
[5] Psalms 145:16.
[6] Liturgical poem for the High Holy Days.

16

Expert Healing[1]

Sometimes, the expert physician must use a miniscule dosage of poison in order to cure the body. Only a most expert physician is allowed to do so. The Ba'al Shem Tov takes this as an analogy for spiritual healing by an expert "physician" (a great *tzadik*[2]). In modern medicine, vaccination exemplifies this principle. A vaccine is a radically weakened strain of the disease that is administered in order to immunize the body against it.[3] Indeed, as seen above, the healing system of homeopathy is based upon the principle of "the law of similars," healing disease by a minute dose of the disease itself.

We find a beautiful allusion to this in the Book of Ecclesiastes. There, King Solomon enumerates 28 changing "times," listed in 14 pairs. Each one of the 28 "times" is a phase of human experience and endeavor in this world. These phases correspond, in Kabbalah, to the 28 phases of the moon in its monthly cycle around the earth. The third pair of "times" reads: "There is a time to kill and a time to

---

[1] See p. 185.

[2] See *Keter Shem Tov* 9; this parable is explained by the Lubavitcher Rebbe in *Igrot Kodesh*, vol. 3, p. 145.

[3] See *Igrot Kodesh*, vol. 11, p. 58.

heal."[4] From this we may infer that the power to kill can be transformed into the power to heal.

Of the 28 "times," "a time to heal" is surely the time of the physician. The letters that spell the phrase, "and a time to heal" (*ve-eit lirpo*) permute to spell the phrase, "an act of light" (*pe'ulat or*). We have seen[5] that the word for "healing" (*refuah*) permutes to spell "the light of the mouth" (*or peh*) and that the healing power of the physician begins in his eyes, which project comforting and healing light to his patient, just as God began to heal the shattered initial world of Chaos by the creation of goodly light. Indeed, of the 28 times, "a time to heal" is the 6th from the beginning and the 23rd from the end, alluding to the third verse of the Torah—"And God said, 'Let there be light,' and there was light"—which is composed of 6 words and 23 letters. Moreover, as we have seen, the seven different letters of this verse spell *or milah*, "the light of circumcision," which equals numerically *or peh*, "the light of the mouth"—*refuah* ("healing").

---

[4] Ecclesiastes 3:3.
[5] p. 174.

17

Healing and the Torah[1]

Rabbi Yehoshua ben Levi said: "If someone is travelling without an escort, he should delve into the study of the Torah, as it is said, 'for they [the words of Torah] are a gracious escort.'[2] If one's head aches, he should delve into the study of the Torah, as it is said, 'for they are a gracious escort [accessory, i.e., ornament] for your head.'[3] If one's throat aches, he should delve into the study of the Torah, as it is said, '...and a necklace for your neck.'[4] If one's stomach aches, he should delve into the study of the Torah, as it is said, 'it is healing for your navel.'[5] If one's bones ache, he should delve into the study of the Torah, as it is said, '...and drink for your bones.'[6] If one's whole body aches, he should delve into

---

[1] See p. 190.
[2] Proverbs 1:19.
[3] *Ibid.*
[4] *Ibid.*, end of verse.
[5] *Ibid.* 3:8.
[6] *Ibid.*, end of verse.

the study of the Torah, as it is said,[7] '...and healing for all his flesh.'"[8]

Rabbi Yehoshua ben Levi's teaching begins with the thought that the Torah is one's life's "escort" or "companion." This supports our present explanation that the healing power of the Torah derives from the soul-level termed *chayah*, the "living one." In Kabbalah, we are taught that had Eve (*Chavah*), the Torah-archetype of man's marital companion, not sinned, her name would have been *Chayah*. All of life on earth, ever since the primordial sin, is analogous to a traveler walking a dangerous path, in need of a protective escort.

This is because Adam and Eve were expelled from their natural *milieu* of the Garden of Eden. The Hebrew word for "garden" [*gan*] is cognate to "protected" [*mugan*], but outside the garden, one is no longer protected.) At the level of *chayah*, one "touches" or "kisses" the infinite light of the Torah as do waters to waters, like two companions walking together.[9]

Elsewhere,[10] Rabbi Yehoshua ben Levi himself states that "it is forbidden to use the words of Torah to heal." There, the Talmud differentiates between reciting Biblical verses in order to be protected, i.e., to prevent an illness from striking, which is permissible (Rabbi Yehoshua ben Levi

---

[7] *Ibid.*, 4:22
[8] *Eruvin* 54a.
[9] See p. 191.
[10] *Shavuot* 15b.

himself would recite Biblical verses before going to sleep in order to be protected during sleep), and reciting or whispering verses over an infection or disease in order to cure it, which is forbidden.

The commentaries resolve the apparent contradiction between the two statements of Rabbi Yehoshua ben Levi in several manners:[11]

- When Rabbi Yehoshua ben Levi said that "if one's head aches, he should delve into the study of the Torah," he meant that one should study Torah for its own sake, delving so deeply into it that he forgets his own physical ailments. This is certainly permissible and a great *mitzvah* in its own right. The healing of the body will follow spontaneously.

- Since all physical illness derives from spiritual illness, the healing power of the Torah is directed to the soul of man, not to his body. When the soul is healed, the body becomes healed in turn. Thus, if one primarily intends to heal his soul with words of Torah, even though he knows that this will be advantageous for his body, this is permissible, whereas if one intends directly to heal his physical illness with words of Torah, this is forbidden.

- It is only forbidden to recite Biblical verses for the sake of healing physical ailments when one is not in mortal danger. In cases of mortal danger, it is permissible.

- When Rabbi Yehoshua ben Levi said that "if one's head aches, he should delve into the study of the

---

[11] See *Tosafot, Shevuot* ad. loc., s.v. *Assur Lehitrapot*; *Tosafot, Pesachim* 111a, s.v. *Niftach beKel*; *Maharsha, Shabbat* 67a; *Torat Chaim, Shevuot* ad loc.

Torah," he meant that the Torah may be used as "preventive medicine." As we saw above, he himself would recite Biblical verses in order to be protected during sleep. According to this interpretation, the word for "ache" (*chash*) indicates that the person has a premonition that an illness is imminent.

These four interpretations themselves can be seen to correspond to the four letters of God's Name, whose full manifestation, as taught in Kabbalah, is at the level of *chochmah*, the *chayah* of the soul. Studying Torah for its own sake corresponds to the *yud* of God's Name. Understanding that the healing power of the Torah is primarily spiritual corresponds to the first *hei* of God's Name. The apparent "condescension" of the Torah to allow itself to be used to heal physical ailments in cases of mortal danger corresponds to the *vav* of God's Name. (This is where the primordial kings of Edom, the origin of physicality, ruled and died; their "resurrection" comes about by the healing power of the Torah.) The Torah as "preventive medicine" corresponds to the final *hei* of God' Name. Here, one fears the onset of disease and is conscious to take all means to prevent it.

In summary:

י *yud*	studying Torah for its own sake heals spontaneously
ה *hei*	the Torah's healing power is primarily spiritual
ו *vav*	the Torah descends to heal dangerous physical ailments
ה *hei*	the Torah acts as preventive medicine

18

The Indestructible Bone[1]

The sages teach us that there exists an indestructible bone at the top (or, according to certain opinions, at the base) of the spine, from which the body will be resurrected at the End of Days. This is called either *etzem ha-luz* ("*luz* bone") or *luz shel shidrah* ("*luz* of the spine").[2]

The numerical value of *etzem ha-luz* is 248, the number of limbs, according to the sages, in the human body, corresponding to the 248 positive commandments of the Torah. Thus, this one, eternal bone encapsulates all the limbs of the body.

In modern terminology, we may say that this eternal, most essential "bone" (in Hebrew, the word for "bone" [*etzem*] is the same as the word for "self" or "essence") is the fully-encoded description of man in one DNA molecule. From this essential molecule, the whole man will, in the time of resurrection, spring back to life. Indeed, the most potent site of DNA in the body is the bone marrow, corresponding to the *sefirah* of *chochmah*, of which is said, "they will die, but not with *chochmah*."[3] Even upon physical death, not only does the *luz* bone not die, but it ensures the future reconstitution of the entire body.

---

[1] See p. 193.
[2] *Vayikra Rabbah* 18:1.
[3] Job 4:21.

The numerical value of *luz shel shidrah*, 882, equals 2 times *emet* ("truth," 441 or 21^2). In Kabbalah and Hassidism, truth implies eternal life, for to be "true" is never to cease. Of Jacob, "the man of truth,"[4] it is said, "Jacob did not die."[5] 2 times *emet* implies resurrection and eternal life on two simultaneous planes, the physical plane and the spiritual plane. This accords with the opinion of Nachmanides (and that of Kabbalah and Hassidism) that with the Resurrection of the Dead, not only the soul but the physical body as well will live on forever.

---

[4] See Micah 7:20.

[5] *Ta'anit* 5b.

Endnotes

Preface

[1] Rabbi Dov Ber, the Maggid of Mezritch (1710-1772), succeeded the Ba'al Shem as leader of the Hassidic movement.

[2] Quoted in *HaTamim*, #7, p. 28 [vol. 2, p. 664 in archive edition].

[3] A "saying of the wise," quoted by the Lubavitcher Rebbe in *Igrot Kodesh*, vol. 14, #5047. Note that here, "understanding an illness" is interpreted as not only knowing that one suffers from a specific illness, but as fully understanding the spiritual roots of the illness.

In Hebrew, half the numerical value of the word for "cure" (*refuah*, 292; half of 292 is 146) equals twice the numerical value of the word for "wisdom" (*chochmah*, 73; twice 73 is 146). To fully understand an illness, one must unite two levels of wisdom, the wisdom of the Torah (in general, and Kabbalah in particular) and the wisdom of medicine as known to science. These two levels of wisdom, when properly inter-related and integrated, merge to provide a full understanding of the illness, which itself is half the cure.

[4] The Ba'al Shem Tov is the popular name of Rabbi Israel ben Eliezer (1698-1760), founder of the Hassidic movement. *Ba'al Shem Tov* means "Master of the Good Name [of God]."

[5] In the past, Rabbi Ginsburgh has consulted with Dr. Kashuk regarding medical questions that arise in the study of Kabbalah and Hassidism. For example, Rabbi Ginsburgh was asked:

While learning *Tanya* [ch. 9], the question arose whether it was physically true that the left ventricle of the heart is filled with blood and the right ventricle "has no blood." Upon a review of anatomy, this statement is difficult to understand. Each ventricle must fill with blood before pumping it out. However, one clear difference is that the blood in the right ventricle is oxygen depleted, while that in the left ventricle is oxygen rich.

Dr. Kashuk composed the following reply:

There are known significant differences between the left and right ventricles of the heart. As you correctly described, there are differences in oxygen saturation from the right and left heart. In addition, in order to ascertain actual amounts of blood in the two chambers, doctors measure the filling pressures in the respective ventricles through various diagnostic maneuvers. Doing so, one may obtain a pressure tracing of the vacillating pressures that exist in the heart through the contraction (systolic) phase and the relaxation (diastolic) phase. Further, the diastolic pressures in the right ventricle may reach zero!

While in actuality the right side of the heart is never completely void of blood, there may temporarily be periods when the content is so low so as to be clinically insignificant.

Therefore, the statement in *Tanya* that the right side of the heart is void of blood is certainly accurate according to clinical reality, although only temporarily.

Recently, Dr. Kashuk has begun to help Rabbi Ginsburgh respond to the numerous email requests he receives for Kabbalistic insights into medical conditions and treatments. After offering his professional medical analysis, Dr. Kashuk suggests possible conceptual links to Kabbalistic principles, based on the ideas presented in this book. Rabbi Ginsburgh then approves or modifies these proposed links as necessary. The following is an example of such a response, to a woman who asked for advice on how to treat Reflex Sympathetic Dystrophy:

Dear...,

Reflex Sympathetic Dystrophy is also commonly referred to as Causalgia in medical literature. The etiology of RSD is related to undeterred sympathetic nervous actions in the extremities. The careful balance between the sympathetic nervous system and the feedback mechanisms from the spinal cord and brain is interrupted. This can occur from multiple sources: trauma, diabetes, post surgery, or as a result of other medical disorders. The underlying theme of this disease is the interruption of the body's ability to effect sensation in the extremities.

Current medical treatments for this condition include: 1. the creation of a sympathetic block by the injection of anesthesia near the spinal cord. 2. Surgical therapy involving excision or interruption of the affected nerve pathway.

Modern medicine has no exact explanation of the etiology of RSD. Kabbalah can help us gain a deeper understanding of this problem.

The interaction of the nervous system, the environment, and the individual's anatomy are well outlined in Kabbalah. The expression of the neurological entity originates from the *mo'ach* ("brain power") of *da'at*. Kabbalah explains that *chesed* corresponds to the right arm of the body, while *gevurah* corresponds to the left. *Netzach* corresponds to the right leg and *hod* to the left leg. A deeper understanding of treatment of the illness would depend on the location of the extremity affected.

For example: *Hod*, corresponding to the left leg, is related to the feedback mechanisms of the immune system. *Hod* is at the root of the word "*hoda'ah*," which means admission, or self-recognition. This self-recognition is the basis of the immune system.

Netzach, corresponding to the right leg, represents victory. In medical terms, this corresponds to the emotional overplay of the physiological system, or the fight/flight response. The hormonal system corresponds to *netzach*.

The touch sensation, modulated by the sympathetic nervous system, represents the communication between the outside world and one's *mochin* (plural of *mo'ach*). Proper homeostasis (balance) in this system requires uninterrupted communication from the nerve endings in the skin of the affected extremity to the central nervous system. When this system is dysfunctional, such a balance cannot be achieved, and RSD, which manifests as pain, wound formation, and infection, may develop.

This fine balance between the nerve sensation and transmission may be compared to the Kabbalistic concept of *chashmal* ("electric radiance," implying, in Hebrew, the fine balance between "[silent] sensation," *chash*, and "[audible] transmission," *mal*). In fact, neurological discharge and function is a mini-electrical system. It is based on the principle of synaptic discharge and rest. This concept of electrical control exists in many places in the body:

1. in the maintenance of proper vascular control in the blood vessels;
2. in cardiac contraction and relaxation;
3. in proper peristalsis of the intestinal tract.

Rectification of RSD would first require the proper anatomical identification and isolation of the problem. Its treatment could potentially be determined by location of the problem according to the Kabbalistic model, as above.

Refuah shlemah (complete recovery)!

Chapter 1

[1] Genesis 1:26. On the physical plane, one most beautiful reflection of the Divine craftsmanship by which God formed the human body—whose full description is beyond the scope of the present work—is that more than with regard to any other created being the human body possesses a plentitude of "golden proportions" between its limbs. The most pronounced of these—explicitly appearing in Kabbalah—is the division of the body, by the navel, into a higher, relatively spiritual "half" and lower, relatively physical "half."

[2] *Ibid.* 1:27.

[3] *Ibid.* 1:1.

[4] When speaking of our perception of Divinity, the manner in which Godliness—God's self-expression—is perceived, the ten *sefirot* are understood as ten manifestations of Divinity. We find this phenomenon reflected in ten Names for God, each of which corresponds to a given *sefirah*. When reflecting on how this display of Divinity is projected into the living experience of a human being, the *sefirot* become intelligible as the ten powers of the soul. Finally, one finds that the *sefirot* are also cast as the basic structural forces orchestrated in forming our outer reality.

These three modalities of the *sefirot* are called "Worlds, Souls, and Divinity" in the terminology of the Ba'al Shem Tov (*Keter Shem Tov*, p. 3). For a further elaboration of these concepts, see the introduction to *The Hebrew Letters: Channels of Creative Consciousness*; for more on the ten individual *sefirot*, see *The Anatomy of the Soul*. A great deal of further information on these and other topics in Kabbalah can be found on the Gal Einai web-site at www.inner.org.

[5] See *Sod HaShem Lireiav*, pp. 33 ff, 118 ff.

[6] In Hebrew, "to create" and "to heal" possess the same root (*b-r-a*).

[7] Daily Blessings.

[8] Isaiah 6:10.

[9] *Da'at*, however, is often not counted as an independent *sefirah*, but rather is regarded as the conscious counterpart of *keter* (as mentioned in the text above). Therefore, there are said to be only ten *sefirot*, and, according to the Kabbalistic dictum, "when we count *keter* we don't count *da'at* and when we count *da'at* we don't count *keter*," for they are considered to be two expressions of the same spiritual entity.

[10] The *tzadik* relates to his own body as an "other" (see *Tanya*, ch. 29).

[11] In the words of Maimonides, "physical health is part of the way of Divine service…" (*Mishneh Torah, Dei'ot* 4:1).

[12] As a "simple, believing Jew," the "ideal" figure so beloved by the Ba'al Shem Tov.

[13] Proverbs 3:12.

[14] 2 Samuel 6:22.

[15] See *Sha'ar HaYichud VeHaEmunah*, ch. 4. Appropriately, the appellation of this Name of God, *Havayah*, formed by rearranging its letters, means, as a word, "existence."

[16] Significantly, the letter *vav* has the numerical value of six.

[17] See above, endnote 6.

[18] Genesis 1:27.

[19] The primary description of how the powers of the soul are clothed in, or paralleled to, the limbs of the body is found in the introduction to *Tikunei Zohar*, s.v. *Patach Eliahu* (17a).

[20] See Supplementary Essay #1, "Right and Left" (p. 211).

[21] Song of Songs 2:6.

[22] *Sotah* 47a.

²³ This is indicated in *Tikunei Zohar* (Introduction, 17a) by the phrase: "beauty is the body," for it integrates and blends all of the limbs and organs.

²⁴ *Tikunei Zohar* (Introduction, 17a).

²⁵ Ecclesiastes 8:4.

²⁶ Intellect is understood as referring to any direct perception of reality, in contrast to the emotions, which are subjective reactions to reality or experiences of it. All of the levels inherent to *keter* are super-rational levels of intellect, which, by Divine service, may be drawn into the direct perception of the soul's consciousness as Divine inspiration. Often, in Kabbalah, the intellectual triplet itself—connoted "the initial three"—is considered as composed of *keter*, *chochmah*, and *binah*, not including *da'at*.

²⁷ The behavioral characteristics are often counted as four: *netzach*, *hod*, *yesod*, and *malchut*. As a behavioral characteristic, *malchut* is one's natural manner or style of speech. By one's speech, one relates to and "leads" the behavior of others. Thus, *malchut* serves as a bridge between one's own manner of behavior and that of others.

²⁸ See Supplementary Essay #2, "Three Planes" (p. 213).

²⁹ See Supplementary Essay #3, "Six" (p. 215).

³⁰ *Sefer Yetzirah* 1:1.

³¹ *Sefer Yetzirah*, "The Book of Formation," is attributed to Abraham; it was edited in the 1ˢᵗ-2ⁿᵈ century by Rabbi Akiva.

³² In the Hebrew word for "head" (*rosh*, spelled *reish-alef-shin*) is hidden the word for "fire" (*eish*, *alef-shin*).

³³ The thirty-two pathways of wisdom correspond to the four letters of the Name *Havayah*, as follows:

	sefirah	model	thematic connection
י yud	chochmah "wisdom"	ten sefirot	numerical value of yud is ten
ה hei	binah "understanding"	three "mother" letters: alef, mem, shin	binah is "the mother of the children [the emotions]"
ו vav	midot "emotions"	seven "double" letters: beit, gimel, dalet, kaf, pei, reish, tav	the word vav means "hook," a connection between two entities
ה hei	malchut "kingdom"	twelve "simple" letters: hei, vav, zayin, chet, tet, yud, lamed, nun, samech, ayin, tzadik, kuf	malchut is the origin of time, which is manifest in the twelve months of the year

Chapter Two

[1] It is interesting to note that in English "I" and "eye" are homonyms. In Hebrew, "I" (*ani*) and "eye" (*ayin*) are also closely related phonetically.

[2] *Nidah* 31a (see also *Kohelet Rabbah* 5:12). This passage will be quoted in full presently.

[3] *Ta'anit* 24a.

[4] Numbers 15:24; *Ta'anit loc. cit.*

[5] Deuteronomy 32:10.

[6] Ezekiel 1:1-28. As elsewhere in the Torah, the word for "eye" is used in this passage (v. 4) to mean "color." This is why all color theory is based on the anatomy of the eye: the eye not only *sees* color; it *is* the essence of color itself.

[7] In Hebrew, the word for "blood" (*dam*) is related to the word for "red" (*adom*).

[8] Genesis 49:12.

[9] *Ibid.*, v. 11.

[10] Although individuals possess various degrees of *chochmah* and *binah*, these differences are relatively quantitative, in comparison to the qualitative differences between their faculties of *da'at*. This is so because *chochmah* and *binah* relate to "native intelligence," rather than to personality and character. One may possess more or less native intelligence or even "better" or "worse" intellectual faculties, but intelligence alone does not reflect the essence of one's character, which is the nature of one's *da'at*.

[11] The three patriarchs are associated with the three primary emotive attributes—*chesed*, *gevurah*, and *tiferet*—which normally correspond to the three primary colors of blue, red, and yellow-green, respectively. The spiritual sources of these three archetypal souls are the three faculties of the mind that appear above the

three primary emotive attributes, on the right, left, and middle axes of the sefirotic tree—*chochmah*, *binah*, and *da'at*. Often, they are alluded to in Kabbalah and in our prayers as "the God of Abraham," "the God of Isaac," and "the God of Jacob," respectively. In our analysis of the eye and its colors, the patriarchs appear in the place of their spiritual sources. With respect to their normal positions, in the heart, brown replaces red (brown is a derivative of red), for red appears at the level of its own source in the mind, the *sefirah* of *binah* (corresponding to the source of the archetypal soul of Isaac).

[12] This relationship between yellow and green is reflected in the different ways these colors are conceived of in art and science. In art, yellow is seen as a primary color (between blue and red on the color wheel), while green is seen as a secondary color. In science, green is considered the primary color (between blue and red on the spectrum) and yellow the secondary color.

[13] See Supplementary Essay #4, "Basic Colors" (p. 217).

[14] *Vayikra Rabbah* 36:5.

[15] As noted above, the twelve hues correspond to the twelve months of the year, the leading color being yellow-green. Here, in correspondence between the twelve hues to the twelve stones on the breastplate, the leading color is red, the color of the first stone, the ruby (*odem*, from the same root—*a-d-m*—as *adom*, "red"). This is because the order of the stones on the breastplate follows the birth-order of the tribes, while the order of the months (according to the Arizal) follows the order of the tribes as they were arranged in their marching formation in the desert. This latter order signifies mature, developed consciousness.

The root of *adom*, *a-d-m*, is also the root of "man," *adam*. This name applies to a person from birth, whereas the synonym *ish* applies to a person only when he reaches maturity. The first man was named Adam for he was created/born from the "dust of the earth [*adamah*]" (Genesis 2:7). The word for "earth," *adamah*, derives also from the root *a-d-m*.

The word *ish* is used in the passage describing the marching formation: "each man [*ish*] according to his ensign…" (Numbers 1:52). The numerical value of the word *yarok* (310) plus the *kolel* is the same as that of *ish* (311). The *kolel* (1) is identified with the *alef* in the word *ish*—indicating man's spiritual dimension, while the value of *yarok* itself (310) is the value of the remaining two letters, which spell *yeish* ("substantiality")—indicating man's material dimension.

[16] Just as black is the absence of color, so, anatomically, is the pupil itself an "absence." It is really the opening in the iris whose expansion or contraction allows more or less light to pass through the opening to the retina. The powers of expansion and contraction are respectively associated with *chesed* and *gevurah*. The more light (*chesed*) that hits the eye, the greater is the expansion (*chesed*) of the iris and the smaller the opening of the pupil. This mirrors the Kabbalistic concept of *malchut* shrinking into a point beneath *yesod*, a prerequisite to the coupling of these two *sefirot*. The less light (*gevurah*) that hits the eye, the greater is the contraction (*gevurah*) of the iris and the larger the opening of the pupil. Here, the domain of *malchut*—"possessing nothing of its own"—expands in order to "see in the dark" (that is, experience physical reality), in the absence of the intrinsic light (that is, spiritual sense and arousal) of *da'at* and the emotions of the heart.

[17] See *Zohar* 2:215a.

[18] 2 Samuel 6:22.

Let us note, in summary, a general phenomenon with regard to the four colors of the eye. The first and last of the four colors are white and black, two opposite yet complementary states of "all" and "nothing" (white being the presence of all colors and black the absence of color). The two middle colors, red and the remaining hues of the spectrum, include the full spectrum of the colors of the rainbow. As explained above, red is considered to be the "comprehensive color." In many contexts, the very word "color" means "red". All other colors are understood to be derivatives of red, the relation of red to all other colors being that of "mother" to "children." Thus, the *yud* (white) of God's Name relates and connects in particular to the second *hei* (black), whereas the first *hei* (red) relates and connects to the *vav* (all colors). In Kabbalah, this is known as the special relationship of father to daughter and mother to son(s).

[19] According to all of the Torah's classical commentaries (see Ibn Ezra, *Perush HaKatzar* to Exodus 23:21) and the masters of Kabbalah and Hassidism (see Rabbi Hillel of Paritch, *Biur* on *Sha'ar HaYichud* of Rabbi Dovber of Lubavitch, ch. 3).

[20] "Darkness precedes light" (*Shabbat* 77b).

[21] Jeremiah 31:2.

[22] Ezekiel 37:9.

[23] See Supplementary Essay #5, "Sight and Shabbat" (p. 220).

[24] In the description of the formation of man to be quoted in the text, we see that the red of the mother produces the black of the child's eye. Elsewhere, the sages teach that the color black is in effect "defective red" (*Nidah* 19a). Thus, from the intrinsic red of the mother comes the black of the eye in the child: "as mother [the first *hei* of God's Name], so daughter [the second *hei* of God's Name]" (Ezekiel 16:44).

Above, we noted the relation of father to daughter, of white to black. In Kabbalah, every phenomenon possesses two dimensions, referred to as light and vessel. The innate light of the black pupil of the eye, the inner essence of the black of the daughter, derives (spiritually) from the white of the father. The vessel or external reality of the black—"defective red"—derives (physically) from the red of the mother.

[25] *Nidah* 31a (see also *Kohelet Rabbah* 5:12).

[26] *Sefer Yetzirah* 1:7.

[27] See *Kuntres HaAvodah*, ch. 2.
[28] Job 11:11.
[29] Psalms 119:37.
[30] *Ibid.* 16:8.
[31] *Berachot* 8a.
[32] *Migdal Oz*, *Hilchot Ishut* 4:9.
[33] Psalms 8:4.
[34] *Sefer Yetzirah* 1:3.
[35] Literally, "the covenant of the Single One," i.e., the covenant by which God reveals to the Jewish soul His absolute "singleness." In the introduction to *Tikunei Zohar* (17a) we find: "and since You are inside them (the ten *sefirot*)...." Rabbi Chaim Vital (in his commentary on the *Sefer Yetzirah*) explains that God's presence within the ten *sefirot* is the meaning of the "single covenant" between the ten fingers, as first revealed to Abraham (the author of *Sefer Yetzirah*), the first Jew commanded by God to circumcise himself.
[36] See Supplementary Essay #6, "Implications of Nakedness" (p. 222).
[37] See Supplementary Essay #7, "The Thirty-Two Pathways" (p. 225).
[38] The most important model for *tikun* in *Sefer Yetzirah* (see 2:1) is that of a scale. Even more explicitly, in relation to the secret of *tikun*, we find in the beginning of *Sifra diTzeniuta*, the most esoteric section of the *Zohar*, "before there was balance, they were unable to look face to face." Inability to look face to face results in the breaking of the vessels in the primordial world of Chaos.
[39] We are taught that in particular, each one of the ten fingers possesses the sensitivity to detect one of the ten pulses of the body. By the faculty of *da'at*, the origin of the sensitivity innate in the fingers, the fingers of the physician know, by touch, the condition of the patient, which itself is "half the cure." (The relation of the ten fingers to the ten pulses is made by Rabbi

Nachman of Breslov in the story of *The Seven Beggars*, as will be mentioned.)

[40] *Tikunei Zohar*, introduction.

[41] See *Tanya*, ch. 42.

[42] I Chronicles 29:11.

[43] *Yevamot* 53b.

[44] Proverbs 10:25.

[45] Genesis 1:28.

[46] It is said upon the creation of man on the sixth day: "And He breathed into his nostrils the breath of life, and man became a living soul."

[47] See Supplementary Essay #8, "The Five Fingers" (p. 228).

[48] *Ohalot* 1:8.

[49] Numbers 6:22-26.

[50] Moreover, 30 · 30 (the secret of "clapping" together the two hands, thereby revealing the "middle, uplifted hand," as will be explained) = 900 (the value of the final *tzadik*, the righteous one of the World to Come), the last of the 27 letters of the extended alphabet.

[51] As taught by the great Kabbalist of the 13th century, Rabbi Avraham Abulafia.

[52] In the idiom of the sages, the *brit milah* itself is referred to as the *etzba* ("index finger") or *amah* ("middle finger").

[53] Exodus 14:31.

[54] Deuteronomy 7:19, *et al*.

[55] Exodus 14:8, *et al*.

[56] See *The Mystery of Marriage*, pp. 168 ff on speaking vs. kissing.

[57] Modern physics distinguishes between two types of elementary particles: particles of matter (fermions) and particles of force (bosons). The force particles are "messenger" particles or "angels"—in Hebrew, "angel" [*malach*] means "messenger"—whereas the particles of matter are "humans." Electrons, protons, and neutrons are particles of matter, whereas light photons—the

messenger particle of the electromagnetic force—are the primary example of particles of force. Light is spiritual reality relative to matter, as an angel relative to a human. In the Torah, light issues from the mouth: "Open your mouth, that your words may shine" (*Berachot* 22a); "And God said [—the first explicit utterance of creation, Divine creative energy issuing from the 'mouth' of the Creator], 'Let there be light,' and there was light" (Genesis 1:3).

[58] In our Divine service, the "higher union" is our union with God when we are engrossed in the study of His Torah. We fulfill the *mitzvah* of studying the Torah only when we articulate its words; every pronounced word is a "kiss" of God (see *Tanya*, ch. 45). At the giving of the Torah at Mt. Sinai, we are taught that "with every word [that the people heard from God], their souls left their bodies." God resurrected them with the dew He will use to resurrect the dead, the "dew of the Torah" (*Yalkut Shimoni, Devarim* 824). Similarly, in our devoted study of the Torah, we experience at once the "Divine kiss of death" together with the resurrecting "dew of the Torah." (The "Divine kiss of death" is the highest level of death, that experienced by Moses, Aaron, and Miriam, the three siblings through whom the Torah was given to Israel.) And so the sages teach us: "The Torah is only fulfilled in one who dies over it, as it is said, 'This is the [way of the] Torah: a man [must] die in the tent [of its study]'" (Numbers 19:14; *Berachot* 63b).

The "kiss" inherent in every word of the Torah gives birth to an angel. In the physical union of the *maor*, one gives birth to souls (in bodies), thus fulfilling the first, "great" and all-inclusive *mitzvah* of the Torah: "Be fruitful and multiply." In the words of Rabbi Shneur Zalman of Liadi: "One Jew must make another Jew." The two manifestations of the "single covenant" thus correspond to the two general levels of Divine service, the study of the Torah and the performance of *mitzvot*, the "higher union" and the "lower union."

59 See Supplementary Essay #9, "*Partzufim* and Contact Points (p. 231).

60 Genesis 2:24.

61 Deuteronomy 33:1.

62 *Devarim Rabbah* 11:4.

63 See *Zohar* 3:232a, 265a; *Shemot Rabbah* 3:15.

64 Genesis 4:1. Marital relations are referred to as "knowing" only when the *brit* is circumcised, and indeed, we are taught that Adam was created without need for circumcision.

65 See *The Mystery of Marriage*, pp. 377 ff.

66 Ezekiel 1:4.

67 *Ibid.* 1:4, 1:27, 8:2.

68 *Chagigah* 13b.

69 From this it is evident that the Divine "man" depicted in *Sefer Yetzirah* as possessing ten fingers (the ten *sefirot* of *Atzilut*) and ten toes (the ten *sefirot* of *Beriah*) is *Adam Kadmon*, the "primordial man" from (and through) whom God emanates the world of *Atzilut* and creates the world of *Beriah*, as is explained in Kabbalah.

70 1 Samuel 2:3, where the word for "knowledge" appears in the plural.

71 Job 33:33.

72 In the Midrash (*Otiot d'Rabbi Akiva*), the name of the letter *lamed* is seen as an acronym for the words "the heart understands knowledge" (*lev meivin da'at*).

73 Conversely, we find in the Bible the idiom of the tongue "walking," like the feet, as mentioned above (endnote 28). The word for "gossip" (*rachil*) derives from the word "feet." (As explained by Rashi on the Torah, the *chaf* of *rachil* takes the place of the phonetically-related *gimel* of *regel*.) Indeed, the idiom for "telling gossip" is *holeich rachil*—lit., "to walk gossiping."

74 See Tanya, ch. 2. We can now understand why although the order of the two manifestations of the "single covenant" in *Sefer Yetzirah* is first "the word of the tongue" and thereafter "the

circumcision of the *brit*," this order is inverted in the Divine service of *chash-mal-mal* described above. There, it is "the word of the tongue" that follows "the circumcision of the *brit*."

[75] *Sefer Yetzirah* 6:6-7.
[76] *Berachot* 12a.
[77] Genesis 15:7-21.
[78] *Ibid.* 17:1-11.
[79] Psalms 116:9.
[80] See Proverbs 4:22; *Eiruvin* 54a.
[81] *Sefer Yetzirah* 6:5.
[82] The four numbers 1, 3, 7, 12 (the series we have discussed in the text)—the transcendent one above the three above the seven above the twelve of *Sefer Yetzirah*—generate a "three-dimensional" numerical series, which contains an additional 6 positive numbers:

1	3	7	12	17	21	23	22	17	7
2	4	5	5	4	2	-1	-5	-10	
2	1	0	-1	-2	-3	-4	-5		
-1	-1	-1	-1	-1	-1	-1			

These ten numbers, which can be seen to correspond to the ten fingers or ten *sefirot*, add to equal 130 = 10 · 13. Thus, the average value of the ten numbers is 13 (as is the average value of each group of five numbers, skipping from one number to the one after the next; the average value of 1, 7, 17, 23, 17 = the average value of 3, 12, 21, 22, 7 = 13), which equals *echad*, "one." 13 also equals *ahavah*, "love." Sometimes we find that the tongue articulates "one" (as when reciting the *Shema*: "Hear, O Israel, GOD is our God, GOD is *one*," or when speaking the inner mysteries of the Torah) and that the *brit* expresses "love."

Alternately, we find that the normative function and purpose of the tongue is to speak words of love (see *The Mystery of Marriage*, pp. 139 ff), to generate and radiate love to the world around, whereas the function of the *brit* is to create an actual, new state of "one" in reality, as was said upon the creation of Adam and Eve, "and he shall cleave to his wife, and they shall become *one* flesh." This concurs with what has been explained above, that often the higher *da'at* as envisioned by the inner eye of the mind is drawn into reality by the *brit*, whereas the relatively lower *da'at* of the heart finds its outward expression through the words of the tongue.

[83] See Deuteronomy 4:4.

[84] In relation to disease and its cure, our sages teach us that *tzara'at*—the archetypal disease of the Torah—results from the "evil tongue" (*Arachin* 15b; *Vayikra Rabbah* 16:2). This will be discussed further in the next section.

Misuse of the *brit* is also a source of disease, especially of mental disease, as described in Kabbalistic literature. Here again, we see the relation of the mind to the *brit*. The seed, as is explained in Kabbalah, is the condensed essence of mind-substance. All forms of sexual perversion reflect perversion in the psyche (which ultimately takes its toll on the body, as well [*Mishneh Torah, Dei'ot* 4:19]).

[85] Psalms 34:9.

[86] In the words of the *Zohar*: "*chochmah* is the brain...*binah* is the heart" (*Tikunei Zohar*, Introduction [17a]).

[87] Termed "father" and "mother."

[88] *Avot* 3:17.

[89] *Sefer Yetzirah* 1:3.

[90] *Eitz Chaim* 35:4.

[91] In Kabbalah, *netzach* and *hod* are described as "outside the body."

[92] Interestingly, in Hebrew, the word for tongue (*lashon*) also means "language," just as does the word for "lip" (*safah*).

[93] See Rashi on Leviticus 11:2, quoting *Midrash Tanchuma, Shemini* 6.
[94] See endnote 83 above.
[95] Proverbs 18:21.

Chapter Three

[1] Ezekiel 37:1-14.

[2] In certain contexts, the four letters of the Name *Havayah* are seen to correspond to the four *sefirot* of *chesed*, *gevurah*, *tiferet* and *malchut* (and their respective Biblical archetypes: the three patriarchs Abraham, Isaac, Jacob, and King David). This model is referred to as the "four legs of the chariot" (*merkavah*), and is derived by "reducing" the intellectual *sefirot* of *chochmah* and *binah* to their principal emotive derivatives on the right and left axes of the sefirotic tree, *chesed* and *gevurah*, respectively.

This correspondence will shed additional light on the phenomenon to be explained—that in the detailed analysis of the physiological systems, the skeletal system divides into the bone marrow (*chochmah*) and the bones (*chesed*), and the circulatory system divides into the blood (*binah*) and the blood vessels (*gevurah*).

[3] Psalms 104:24.

[4] *Tikunei Zohar*, introduction (17a).

[5] This phrase is borrowed from Psalms 36:10. In particular, the second "super-head" of *keter*, pleasure, is identified as "the source of life."

[6] As with regard to many models, whose components are seen to correspond to the basic frame of reference of Kabbalah, the ten *sefirot*, the ten general soul properties sub-divide further. In this presentation of the basic physiological systems of the body, they are in fact broken into twelve categories. We will further distinguish at the level of *da'at* between two sub-categories of the nervous system, giving us a total of thirteen systems—seven along the middle axis of the sefirotic tree, and three on each of the extreme axes of right and left.

[7] Genesis 2:7.

[8] Psalms 104:24.

[9] *Ibid.* 113:9.

[10] Furthermore, the interrelationship is further seen in that according to the sages, the white blood cells are from the father and the red blood cells from the mother.

[11] Micah 7:20.

[12] This is detailed in the Mishnah (*Ohalot* 1:8).

[13] Isaiah 41:8.

[14] See *Tanya*, ch. 4.

[15] Exodus 3:16.

[16] *Chanah Ariel* 2:20b. See Supplementary Essay #10, "Contraction and Relaxation" (p. 235).

[17] High or low blood pressure results from a misbalance in the contracting power of *gevurah*.

[18] Genesis 31:42.

[19] Deuteronomy 30:19.

[20] Job 31:2; *Tanya*, ch. 2.

[21] As *da'at* is referred to in Kabbalah as the "soul" of *tiferet*, so must the nervous system be understood as the "soul" of the muscular system in particular. In the body, *da'at* corresponds to the posterior region of the brain, in particular, to the cerebellum. With respect to the nervous system, it is the cerebellum that controls the functioning of the muscular system.

[22] See Supplementary Essay #11, "Light, Water, Firmament" (p. 237).

[23] *Kuntres Acharon* 4 (157a).

[24] See *Tur, Even HaEzer* 1.

[25] Genesis 1:28.

[26] When the *brit milah* is pure and rectified, it glows and all one's skin begins to radiate, as was the case with Adam and Eve prior to the primordial sin (*Bereishit Rabbah* 20:12).

[27] The crown on the tip of the *yesod* refers to the relative state of *malchut* within *yesod* itself. Therefore, in the previous description

of the four basic levels of physiological systems, it corresponds to *malchut* in general.

²⁸ In Kabbalah, the king (associated in the body with the digestive system, *malchut*) is the one who descends from his throne (generally by means of word and command) to the lower realms of reality, in order to extract from them their benefits for his people.

²⁹ Proverbs 31:15.

³⁰ See Deuteronomy 8:18.

³¹ In general, education is the discipline that corresponds to *netzach* (see *The Torah Academy*, p. 12).

³² *Kelalei HaChinuch VehaHadrachah* 10.

Chapter Four

[1] *Sefer Yetzirah* 2:4.
[2] *Temurah* 15b.
[3] *Berachot* 12b.
[4] *Tanya*, ch. 14 (19b).
[5] *Sotah* 3a.

[6] The "self" experiences either affinity toward an other (welcoming it with its right hand) or hostility (rejecting it with its left hand).

[7] In contrast, *tiferet*, the heart, when inclined to the right, *chesed* ("loving-kindness"), is also symbolized by the lion. In Ezekiel's vision of the Divine chariot, the lion is "to the right" (Ezekiel 1:10). Love, the right, is the first and most essential emotion of the heart, as implied by the fact that the word "love" (and its cognates in related languages) etymologically relates to the Hebrew word for "heart," *lev*).

The sages teach that the greatest, most intense of all loves between mates in the animal kingdom is that between the lion and the lioness (*Sanhedrin* 106a). One of the seven synonyms for "lion" in Hebrew (*Midrash Mishlei* 20:2), *lavi*, derives from the Hebrew word for "heart," *lev*. In addition, "lion" (*leib*, in Yiddish) in the vernacular relates to *lev*, and appears in the idiom (both in Hebrew and in other languages) "lion-hearted." (See *The Mystery of Marriage*, p. 141.) The lion inclined to the right (the intense love of the heart) is the psychological rectification of the lion inclined to the left (the fear of murder).

[8] Just as we saw in the case of the second fear (in the previous endnote), that the rectification of the lion-syndrome, the fear of murder (*tiferet* tending toward *gevurah*), entails reorienting the heart (*tiferet*) toward the right (*chesed*, love), so is the case with regard to the first and third fears.

The rectification of the wolf-syndrome entails reorienting the sexual power of *yesod* toward the male stance of *netzach*—the confidence of the soul in its "victory" over foreign temptation.

And so, the rectification of the snake-syndrome entails reorienting the mind's power to concentrate and know (*da'at*) toward the right mental faculty of *chochmah*. *Chochmah* is direct insight into the nature of reality (and God's continual recreation of reality) and intuition with regard to cause and effect (recognizing that all is for the good, for all is from God [*Tanya—Igeret Hakodesh* 11 (116a ff)]). It is localized in the right cerebral hemisphere, and is not dependent on the analytical intellectual process of the mind, *binah*, which is localized in the left cerebral hemisphere. The latter's consciousness entails a sense of dependency on the prowess of the mind, a state of consciousness that fears losing control of one's intellectual faculties.

[9] *Sotah* 11b.
[10] *Shir HaShirim Rabbah* 4:12; Rashi on Numbers 26:5.
[11] Leviticus 24:11; Rashi *ad loc.*
[12] *Shemot Rabbah* 1:28; Rashi on Exodus 2:11.
[13] *Vayikra Rabbah* 32:5; Rashi on Leviticus 24:11.
[14] Leviticus 24:11.
[15] Numbers 25:1-9.
[16] The worship of Ba'al Peor involved scatological practices (*Sifri; Sanhedrin* 60b, 64a; Rashi). These practices relate to the digestive system, which corresponds to *malchut*, the culmination of the behavioral properties of the soul (related to the wolf syndrome).
[17] *Sanhedrin* 90a.
[18] *Midrash Tanchuma, Balak* 21. Here, the sages explicitly relate the wolf-image to prostitution.
[19] In Kabbalah, we are taught that the numerical value of the Hebrew word *ze'ev* (10) alludes to the ten plagues of Egypt. This accords with what was explained above—that the punishment for

a sin reflects the nature of the sin. Here, the sinning people of Egypt, symbolized by a wolf, are punished by the wolf, the ten plagues that befell them.

[20] There are several allusions in the Bible (Judges 6-7) to the manner in which Midian persecuted Israel—as a sexual-like/wolf-like invasion into the land and people of Israel. Midian "destroyed" the "seed" of Israel. The Israelites, to protect themselves, made "tunnels in the mountains" and "caves," explicit feminine sexual symbols in Kabbalah. Key words in the story, beginning with the verb that appears first in the account, *vataoz*, allude to the initial letters of the two ministers of Midian, Orev and Ze'ev. Of greatest significance is that both in the words of the prophet and in the prayer of Gideon, the salvation of Israel from Midian is compared to the salvation of Israel from Egypt, salvation from the evil wolf.

[21] Judges 7:25.

[22] This is alluded to in Amos 5:9, where the two words *eiz*, "goat," and *sheid*, "demon," appear in conjunction, albeit with different vocalization. More explicitly, see Leviticus 17:7: "and they shall no longer sacrifice their offerings to the goat-demons after which they go awhoring..." and Isaiah 13:21: "goat-demons shall prance there."

[23] The word "bold," *az*, alludes to yet another animal. The sages teach (and so begins the Code of Jewish Law): "Be as bold as a tiger" (*Avot* 5:20). The commentaries explain that the difference between the boldness of a tiger and the courage of a lion is that whereas the lion senses his innate physical strength and rules over all creatures of the field, the tiger is audaciously brazen, above and beyond the measure of his physical strength. This is what is meant by "boldness." So in the domestic realm, the goat—more than any other domestic animal—exhibits the property of boldness, after which it is named. So too is the rapist bold, while the murderer is strong.

[24] Jeremiah 6:4.
[25] See *The Mystery of Marriage*, pp. 47 ff.
[26] *Bava Metzia* 107b.
[27] Psalms 83:12.
[28] Genesis 49:27.
[29] Judges, chapters 19-21.
[30] *Bereishit Rabbah* 99:3.
[31] *Ibid.*
[32] Genesis 49:27.
[33] *Bereishit Rabbah loc. cit.*
[34] Habakkuk 1:8.
[35] Zephaniah 3:3.
[36] Jeremiah 5:6.
[37] The wolf strikes at *eve*. This is not just an English pun of Eve on eve, for the relationship between "knowing [—a euphemism for sexual relations—] Eve" and the time of evening or night is actually alluded to in Psalms 19:3: "and night unto night expresses [*yechaveh*, cognate to *Chavah*, 'Eve'] knowledge"!
[38] Deuteronomy 22:25-27.
[39] Significantly, the Hebrew word for "rape" (*ones*) is a permutation of the word for "calamity" (*ason*), which refers in particular in the Torah to the death of an assaulted woman (Exodus 21:22).
[40] A further line of thought: We saw above that the wolf relates to the time of "evening" (and "morning"). Similarly, the lion, whose name is cognate to "light," relates to the time of day (as in the beginning of creation: "God called the light day"). The two-letter sub-root of *nachash*, "snake," is *chet-shin*, which is also the two-letter sub-root of *choshech*, "darkness." Thus, the snake alludes to the time of night ("...and the darkness He called night"). Here, we see again how the wolf links the lion to the snake; the two twilight zones of morning and evening link the day to the night.

The fear of the lion, the fear of murder, is a day-like fear. The fear of the snake, the fear of insanity (lunacy, a moon-related phenomenon), is a fear of night. The fear of the wolf, the fear of rape, is a fear of twilight.

[41] Isaiah 11:6-8.

[42] *Midrash Tanchuma, Toldot* 5.

[43] While each gentile nation corresponds to a specific disease, we see here that all the nations are referred to as wolves. From this we may infer that the wolf-syndrome includes all disease.

[44] This is how the Lubavitcher Rebbe reconciles the opinions of Maimonides (*Melachim* 12:1) and Rabbi Avraham ben David (glosses *ad loc.*). According to Rabbi David ben Zimra (*ad loc.*), this prophecy will be fulfilled allegorically in the Diaspora, while in the land of Israel it will be fulfilled literally. Since, at a later stage of the Messianic Era, "the land of Israel will expand to encompass the whole world" (see *Pesikta Rabati, Shabbat veRosh Chodesh* 3), Rabbi David ben Zimra's explanation implies that the literal fulfillment of this prophecy will eventually apply throughout the whole world.

[45] From the Messianic Era we will enter the World to Come, "a day that is entirely Sabbath and the rest of eternal life" (*Tamid* 33b). The ultimate rectified image of the world is the Sabbath. The sages teach us that just as the wolf preys "in front of it and behind it" (*Mechilta, Bachodesh* 7), so does the Sabbath "prey upon" and elevate all the holy sparks of the week, subsequently drawing Divine blessing into all of creation—"in front of it and behind it, i.e., before it and after it."

In the Ten Commandments, the fourth commandment, to keep Shabbat, begins: "*Remember* the Sabbath day, to keep it holy." In the parallel appearance of the Ten Commandments, it begins: "*Guard* the Sabbath day, to keep it holy."

The sages say that "remember" and "guard," which were pronounced by God at the giving of the Ten Commandments simultaneously, refer to the Divine influence of Shabbat on all of reality—"in front of it and behind it." In Kabbalah, we are taught that "remember" refers to the male dimension of Shabbat while "guard" refers to the female dimension of Shabbat. The male dimension is "in front of it" while the female dimension is "behind it." Shabbat is the time of union of male and female, the consummately rectified state of the wolf, the wolf of the World to Come.

[46] Exodus 3:8, 3:17, 13:5, 33:3; Leviticus 20:24; Numbers 13:27, 14:8, 16:13, 16:14; Deuteronomy 6:3, 11:9, 26:9, 26:15, 27:3, 31:20.

[47] On the other hand, the Talmud (*Megilah* 6a; Rashi *ad loc.*) states that the milk with which the Torah praises the land of Israel is *goat* milk. But above, we noted that the two letters that spell "goat" (*eiz*), *ayin* and *zayin*, are the initial letters of the names of the two ministers of Midian, Orev and Ze'ev, and *ze'ev* means "wolf"!

[48] Leviticus 15.

[49] *Bereishit Rabbah* 16:4.

[50] *Machshirin* 6:4.

[51] *Eitz Chaim* 29:8.

[52] Ezekiel 1:14.

[53] *Igeret HaKodesh* 29, which will be quoted and explained at length further on.

[54] As we will note later, one of the meanings of the Hebrew root of *hod* is "echo" (*heid*). In Kabbalah (*Tikunei Zohar* 69 [108a]), we are taught that the pulse carried by the blood echoes the "experiences" of the blood's flow through the body's limbs. From examining the pulse, we can learn much about the body's state of health. In particular, Kabbalah teaches that there are ten basic pulse-rhythms or beats, which correspond to the vowels of the Hebrew language, which themselves correspond to the inner life-force inherent in the supernal *sefirot*. An expert physician is able to feel the particular vowel-beat while taking the pulse of his patient and thereby to correctly diagnose his condition. The great Torah authority and physician, Maimonides, speaks much of the

importance of the pulse in health care. The Chassidic master and storyteller, Rabbi Nachman of Breslov, at the climax of his masterpiece, *The Seven Beggars*, pictures the beggar without hands, a messianic figure, as a physician caring for and healing the princess, the congregation of Israel, by taking her pulse.

[55] *Bechorot* 6b.

[56] *Sha'ar HaKavanot, Chanukah* 1; *Mevo She'arim* 3:1:2, 5:1:1.

[57] Deuteronomy 8:8.

[58] *Mishneh Torah, Deiot* 4:12.

[59] Thus, the numerical values of all four liquids associated with the *sefirot* of *netzach*, *hod*, *yesod*, and *malchut* is 780, twice 390. 780 is the "triangle" of 39, i.e., the sum of all numbers from 1 to 39. 39 is the numerical value of the word for "dew" (*tal*), the liquid associated with *tiferet*, the *sefirah* preceding and directly above these four.

[60] Jeremiah 4:7.

[61] Isaiah 29:1.

[62] Ezekiel, chapter 43.

[63] As we saw above, the altar itself is also referred to as the wolf. The wolf preys upon the sacrifice, elevating its Divine sparks, from below, whereas the heavenly fire in the form of a lion descends to totally consume the sacrifice, to "digest" its very essence. As explained above, the root of the word for "altar" (*mizbeiach*) contains the two letters *zayin-bet*, the two-letter sub-root of the word for "wolf" (*ze'ev*). The middle *alef* of *ze'ev* is the initial letter of the word for "lion" (*aryeh*), alluding to the fire (*eish*) of the lion descending to join the wolf, the altar, to consummately elevate the sacrifice to God's infinite light, as expressed in the *Zohar* (see 2:239a): "the mystery of sacrifices ascends to the mystery of Divine infinity."

[64] Amos 3:8. The initial letters of the phrase "the lion roared" (*aryeh shaag*) spell the word for "fire" (*eish*).

[65] *Pesikta d'Rav Kahana* 13:16.

[66] 1 Chronicles 11:22.

67 See Genesis 36:35: "...who smote Midian in the field of Moab," and Rashi on Numbers 22:4.

68 Although the wolf syndrome pertains to the behavioral properties of the soul and the lion syndrome to the emotive properties, all properties of the soul (and all of the supernal *sefirot*) receive their life-force from the *sefirah* of *chochmah*. The perversion of *chochmah* as reflected in the behavioral properties of the soul is represented by Midian, while the perversion of *chochmah* as reflected in the emotive properties is represented by Moab.

69 *Sefer HaMa'amarim 5659*, pp. 53 ff.

70 Genesis 49:8-12.

71 *Ibid.* 49:16-18.

72 Deuteronomy 33:22. See also Rashi on Genesis 49:16, which equates Dan with Judah.

73 "If he is from among the dead, he is [like] 'Daniel, a man of charisma'" (*Sanhedrin* 98b).

74 *Orach Chaim* 1:1, quoting *Avot* 5:20.

75 Proverbs 22:13.

76 The relationship between the Hebrew words for "wolf" (*ze'ev*) and "flow" (*zov*) is mirrored by the relationship between "lion" (*aryeh*) and *oreh*. This word appears in the Torah in the sense of "gathering" or "harvesting" vegetables, fruit, or fragrant spices (Song of Songs 5:1). As its cognate, "light" (*or*), is also used in the Torah to mean "vegetable" (2 Kings 4:39), *oreh* may thus be seen to allude to the power to gather—"harvest"—potent or viable sparks of light. This relates to the physical process of photosynthesis, whereby light is converted to food—carbohydrates.

The power to gather holy sparks, referred to in Kabbalah as the power to sift and refine reality, is the power of the heart, the power of the lion. The lion pounces on his prey, a symbol in Kabbalah for identifying and redeeming fallen sparks, which the holy lion, consuming his prey, elevates to their source in holiness.

The heart in the body is continuously in a state of war. So we find stated in *Sefer Yetzirah* (6:3): "the heart in the living body is as a king at war." The lion is the king of the animal kingdom. He is continuously in a state of war to capture the sparks entrapped in his prey and elevate them to their source. This is the holy lion. The profane lion, the focus of fear of the lion-syndrome described above, captures human sparks and in consuming them pulls them down to a lower level of reality.

[77] Based on the Tamudic expression, *zerizutei deAvraham* ("the agility of Abraham," *Chulin* 16a), and the fact that Abraham is associated with *chesed*.

[78] *Gitin* 56b. Rabbi Yaakov Emden in *Siddur Beit Yaakov* on *Perek Shirah*, ch. 6, explains that Titus embodied the evil of the primordial snake.

[79] *Shabbat* 77b.

[80] The word for "mosquito" (*yitush*) permutes to spell the word for "[the exaggerated sense of] self-consciousness" (*yeishut*), the evil property of Midian, as explained above. Once more we see a correlation between the wolf and the snake. *Yitush* further permutes to spell *Vashti*, the wife of Ahashuerus, whose death at his hands was a necessary prerequisite for the reign of Esther and the miracle of Purim, of which it is said in the blessing of Benjamin, the wolf, "and in the evening he shall divide the spoil," as explained above.

[81] 1 Samuel 11:2.

[82] Genesis 3:4-6.

[83] *Bereishit Rabbah* 19:6.

[84] Genesis 3.

[85] Deuteronomy 32:10.

[86] Ammon is the paternal brother of Moab. Both are sons of Lot, Abraham's nephew, born to him by his own two daughters after the destruction of Sodom and Gomorrah. In Kabbalah, Moab corresponds to *chochmah* (as explained above), while Ammon

corresponds to *binah*, the seat of rational thought or "sanity." The venom of the snake attacks the rationality of the mind, poisons the mind with doubt (and hence an inability to discern truth rationally), and aims at undermining the soul's innate sanity altogether.

Thus we conclude that the three nations of Midian (descendants of a son of Abraham by his wife Keturah), Moab, and Ammon (both descendants of the two sons of Lot)—the wolf, the lion, and the snake—correspond to the inner dimension of wisdom, the outer manifestation of wisdom, and the faculty of understanding. In apparent paradox, it is the lowest of the three enemies of human health (the wolf) that relates to the highest level of the soul (the inner dimension of wisdom). Sexual perversion begins with the wolf but ends with the snake, an explicit symbol of sex in Kabbalah. The primordial snake raped Eve—as a wolf (*Shabbat* 146a).

[87] A malfunctioning immune system allows for, and gives rise to, most forms of disease. In Kabbalah and Hassidism, it is taught that all disease derives in a certain sense from sexual perversion (see *Likutei Moharan* 29). In the order of the *sefirot*, *yesod* follows *hod* and is seen to be its extension.

According to homeopathy, the archetypal diseases of mankind are gonorrhea and syphilis, conditions that relate to sexual promiscuity.

[88] *Mishneh Torah, Melachim* 12:5.

[89] When Joseph's brothers threw him into the pit, the Torah states (Genesis 37:24) that "the pit was empty, there was no water in it." From the seemingly superfluous phrase, "there was no water in it," the sages infer that "there was no water in it, but there were snakes and scorpions in it" (Rashi *ad loc.*; *Shabbat* 22a). Joseph's very presence in the pit was able to negate the evil forces represented by the snakes and the scorpions.

[90] See *Transforming Darkness into Light*, p. 102; *The Mystery of Marriage*, p. 49.

[91] Genesis 44:15.
[92] *Ibid.* 49:17.
[93] *Ibid.* 49:16.
[94] *Shabbat* 55b; *Bava Batra* 17a.
[95] Judges, chapters 13-16.
[96] *Sotah* 10a.
[97] Judges 14:14.
[98] Numbers 21:9.
[99] Exodus 25:3.
[100] As mentioned above, in the vision of the Divine chariot that opens the Book of Ezekiel, the lion is situated on the right and thus associated with *chesed*, which, in turn, is associated with the color white and the metal silver.
[101] *Igeret HaTiul, Remez* 7. See *Esa Einai*, pp. 116 ff.
[102] According to the sages, in any acute state of illness, one fears losing his mind and is quick to order those present to give of his assets as he desires. From this it is clear that the most dangerous state, the state of greatest fear, is that of copper, the fear of the snake, the fear of insanity.
[103] *Bereishit Rabbah* 30:6.
[104] While the three primary emotive attributes of the soul, *chesed*, *gevurah*, and *tiferet*, are themselves identified with the three metals silver, gold, and copper, respectively, we see here that from a deeper perspective the three primary emotions correspond to the inter-inclusion of the three primary metals in silver itself. Thus, *chesed* is here seen to be silver-within-silver; *gevurah* is seen to be gold-within-silver; *tiferet* is seen to be copper-within-silver. This accords with the teaching of Hassidism that spiritually, *chesed* is a natural "silver-white" state of love, whereas *gevurah* is a newborn "gold-fiery" state of love, and *tiferet*, compassion, is a "copper-lust" state of love. All are states of love—the emotion that in particular corresponds to silver.
[105] *Bava Kama* 92a.

Chapter Five

[1] However, this process of change for the sake of establishing stability is sometimes problematic. For example: the response mechanism may become too frequent; or it may fail to shut off with the cessation of the need to change; or it may initially be inadequate.

[2] See the opening of *Sifra diTzeniuta* in *Zohar* 2:176b.

[3] See *Tanya—Igeret HaKodesh* 1. The brain senses and directs the body to walk along its path of life with caution. It knows that "all paths are likely to be dangerous" (*Kohelet Rabbah* 3:3). While sincerely offering thanks (*hod*, the immune system) to God for each successful step, one proceeds with confidence (*netzach*, the endocrine system). In the words of Proverbs (10:9): "He who walks sincerely will walk confidently."

[4] See Supplementary Essay #12, "Spirituality and Reproduction" (p. 240).

[5] Psalms 133:1.

[6] *Tanya*, ch. 3. There it is explained that all the emotions of the heart are "born" of the intellect, but *da'at* in particular is what keeps them alive. Without the faculty of *da'at*, the emotion would be stillborn.

[7] Exodus 15:26.

[8] *Ibid.* 32:11.

[9] *Berachot* 32a.

[10] Judges 16:17.

[11] Genesis 3:16.

[12] Psalms 84:8.

[13] *Berachot* 5b.

[14] *Ibid.*

[15] *Bava Metzia* 107b.

[16] Significantly, the numerical value of the very first word of the Torah, "In the beginning," *bereishit*, is 913 = 11 times 83. The first three letters of *bereishit*, identical to the second word of the Torah, "created," *bara*, also imply "healed" (as noted above with regard to the root *b-r-a*). Thus, the very beginning of the Torah alludes to the healing of 11 levels of illness (*machalah* = 83), i.e., illness at all 11 levels of the soul (when both *keter* and *da'at* are included amongst the *sefirot*). The number 11 itself is the reduction of 83, whose digits, 8 and 3, add to equal 11.

[17] *Tikunei Zohar* 19b.

[18] Isaiah 53:3-4.

[19] *Ibid.* 65:20.

[20] Zechariah 13:2.

[21] Isaiah 25:8.

[22] *Tanya*, the seminal work of Chabad Hassidism, was authored by Rabbi Shneur Zalman of Liadi (1745-1812), the first Rebbe of Chabad. See in particular: *Igeret HaKodesh* 31.

[23] See *Derech Mitzvotecha* 29a.

[24] *Kohelet Rabbah* 3:22.

[25] *Bereishit Rabbah* 16:4.

[26] *Nidah* 30b.

[27] See Supplementary Essay #13, "Regularity and Health" (p. 242).

[28] At birth, miraculously, the *ductus arteriosus* closes off, thereby ending a shunt of blood from the pulmonary circulation that existed *in utero*. Fetal hemoglobin is changed to normal hemoglobin and the child initiates and continues breathing.

When man was created, "dust from the earth"—"[God] breathed into his nostrils the breath of life" (Genesis 2:7). This is the experience of every newborn.

[29] Genesis 32:25-33.

[30] Rashi on Genesis 32:31.

[31] See Supplementary Essay #14, "Six Permutations" (p. 247).

[32] See Nachmanides' introduction to his commentary on the Torah.

Even Moses, the greatest of all prophets, did not achieve the fiftieth gate of understanding in his lifetime (*Rosh Hashanah* 21b). If from this we may infer that he was "sick," then surely all of us are sick, and will remain sick until the coming of the Messiah who will reveal the knowledge of God to all. In truth, however, the concept of the fiftieth gate of understanding (as is the case with regard to all abstract concepts in Kabbalah) varies, relative to the individual and his particular condition. Every illness requires a certain degree of the fiftieth gate, the knowledge of God, to be revealed in order to be healed. Although the essence of the fiftieth gate, the knowledge of the essence of God, is not known now even to a man as great as Moses, we certainly may and should know now of God's providence over all. This is sufficient to heal most if not all of our illnesses.

[33] For the following, see *Likutei Torah—Torat Shmuel 5637*, pp. 92 ff.

[34] *Chagigah* 13a; see, at length, *Transforming Darkness into Light*, pp. 111 ff.

[35] The *yud* of God's Name corresponds to the world of *Atzilut*. Here one is never "sick," but continuously concerned and longing to manifest one's entire Divine potential in order to reveal God's infinite light and the mysteries of the Torah to all of reality.

[36] Song of Songs 2:5.

[37] Here, it is the estranged "I"—the "I" that longs to be together with "You"—who is sick. At this level, one is "self-conscious." At the previous level, in existential anxiety, one is relatively in a state of "nothingness" or "selflessness." The Hebrew word for "nothingness" (*ayin*) permutes to spell the word for "I" (*ani*)—"nothing" at the level of *chochmah*, and "I" or "something" at the level of *binah*.

[38] Song of Songs 7:7.

[39] Deuteronomy 29:28.
[40] *Ibid.*
[41] *Shabbat* 61a.
[42] See *Transforming Darkness into Light*, pp. 97-98.
[43] Genesis 36:31-39.
[44] Psalms 77:11.
[45] *Yahel Or ad loc.*
[46] *Metzudot Tzion ad loc.*
[47] Rashi *ad loc.*
[48] *Shemot Rabbah* 45:2.
[49] *Ibid.* 43:3.
[50] *Zohar* 3:129a.
[51] *Tikunei Zohar*, introduction (17a).
[52] Exodus 15:26: ‎כי אני י-הוה רפאך.
[53] ‎אמן כן יהי רצון.
[54] *Tzara'at* is a Biblical disease that affects the skin, and is therefore traditionally translated as "leprosy." Biblical *tzara'at* is unknown in modern times, and indeed, in Kabbalah and Hassidism, we are taught that it affects only people who have reached high spiritual levels, as were those in Biblical times.
[55] *Likutei Torah* 2:22b
[56] While *keter* oversees the union of *chochmah* and *binah*, it is *da'at* (the conscious counterpart of *keter*, whose higher manifestation—*da'at elyon*—is situated between *chochmah* and *binah* in the mind) that actualizes it. Indeed, the inner experience of *da'at* is unification (*yichud*). Above we saw that *da'at* (in particular, *da'at elyon*) corresponds to the "covenant of the tongue," whose blemish (the evil tongue) is responsible for the disease of *tzara'at*, the disassociation of *chochmah* from *binah*.
[57] *Likutei Sichot*, vol. 1, p. 150 ff.
[58] See the second commentary of Rabbi Hillel of Paritch on *Kuntres HaHitpa'alut*, end of ch. 1.

The combined numerical value of *bitul* ("selflessness," the inner experience of *chochmah*, 47) and *simchah* ("joy," the inner experience of *binah*, 353) is 400, or 20^2. (The fact that the sum of the numerical values of two words or concepts is a perfect square indicates that these two concepts complement each other, creating a perfect "marriage.") One other pair of the inner lights of the supernal *sefirot* has a combined numerical value of 400: *emunah* ("faith," the highest of the three "super-heads" of *keter*, 102) and *rachamim* ("mercy," the inner experience of *tiferet*, 298). And so we learn that linking the two "companion" mental faculties of *chochmah* and *binah* draws down healing energy from the soul's apex point, *emunah*, to its heart, *rachamim*, the central focus-point of the healing process.

Adding the numerical value of *temimut* ("sincerity," the inner experience of *hod*, 896) to 400 (*bitul* plus *simchah*), gives 1296, or 36^2 (6^4). This numerical phenomenon supports our description of the importance of the *chochmah-binah-hod* cycle in overcoming (and preventing) disease.

[59] Isaiah 5:20.

[60] An opposite form of the malfunctioning of the immune system is observed when it fights too hard against foreign invaders. Such an exaggerated response of the immune system is responsible for certain allergies. On the spiritual plane, such a response reflects a lack of simple trust in God, the ultimate healer and victor over all enemies of soul and body. What both forms of malfunctioning have in common is that ultimately they both attack the good, either alone or together with the bad.

As *hod* is the branch of *gevurah* whose inner spiritual property is fear, *hod* may experience exaggerated fear with respect to any foreign entity, whether dangerous or not, that enters the body. This problem comes to the fore in the medical treatment of certain diseases where bone-marrow or organ transplants are necessary. A hypersensitive immune system (*hod*) may reject such transplants.

Once more, on the spiritual plane, this reflects a lack of simple trust in God, Who sometimes intervenes in life by replacing an old part of oneself (whether injured or no longer present) with a new one.

[61] The blood corresponds to the *sefirah* of *binah*; the body corresponds to all the *sefirot* from *chesed* to *hod*.

[62] Daniel 10:8.

[63] *Sha'ar HaKavanot, Keriat Shema* 7.

[64] Leviticus 12:2.

[65] *Sha'ar HaKavanot, Chanukah* 1.

[66] Just as "she is in *hod*," so "he is in *netzach*." Thus, metaphorically, the male soul-mate of the feminine immune system (*hod*) is the endocrine system (*netzach*). The "third partner" that oversees the union of the endocrine system and the immune system is the nervous system, as explained above.

Chapter Six

¹ Lupus—Systemic Lupus Erythematosus (SLE) affects the inner organs; Discoid Lupus Erythematosus (DLE) affects only the skin, which develops a rash on the nose in the form of an "open-winged butterfly."

² 1795-1877.

³ We find in the Talmud that of the six orders of the Mishnah, the "Order of Women" (*Nashim*) is referred to as the "Order of Immunity" (*Chosen*)!

⁴ Most significantly, the root of the word for "sun," *shemesh*, is the same as that for "sexual intercourse," *tashmish*. The two-letter sub-root of these words, *mash*, means "to touch." In *Sefer Yetzirah*, *tashmish* is the seventh ("all sevenths are cherished") of the twelve senses of the soul, corresponding to the seventh month of the year, *Tishrei*, the month of the High Holidays and the festival of *Sukot*. It further corresponds to the tribe of Ephraim (whose name means "to be fruitful" and "reproduce"), to the letter *lamed* (associated with the lower covenant of the *brit milah*, as discussed above), and to the gall bladder. All of these associations may be seen to relate to Lupus, its cause and its cure.

⁵ Feelings of disconnection and alienation derive from mistaken identity, the inability to identify who is in truth "family" and related and who is not. As noted above, autoimmune disease is characterized by a sense of mistaken identity.

⁶ See Isaiah 40:31.

⁷ Ibid. 6:10.

⁸ Psalms 15:2.

⁹ Blessings Upon Arising, Morning Prayers (and elsewhere).

¹⁰ In Kabbalah, *hod*, the immune system, corresponds to the left kidney. The kidneys, according to the sages (*Berachot* 61a), and as alluded to in the Bible (Job 38:36), are the seats of innate

wisdom. The innate wisdom associated with the left kidney in particular is the wisdom to adapt oneself to every life situation by trial and error.

This is the secret of the survival of the Jewish people throughout its prolonged exile. A Jew, whose name [*yehudi*] is related to *hod*, is gifted more than any other human with the innate wisdom to adapt to any situation without assimilating to it. This innate wisdom is the Jew's spiritual adrenaline.

[11] *Akedah* 14 (*Milei d'Avot* 10).

[12] As noted above, *chochmah* is the life-force of all of the *sefirot*. Particularly with regard to *netzach* and *hod*, which, according to Kabbalah, are associated with the two kidneys (*Zohar* 3:296a; *Sha'arei Orah* 3, 4; *Pardes Rimonim* 8:24, s.v. *kelayot*, 8:11, s.v. *eitzah*; *Mevo She'arim* 3:2:7), it is said that innate wisdom resides in the kidneys (*Berachot* 61a). In relation to the physiological systems, this refers to the innate wisdom of the endocrine system and the immune system.

[13] This is alluded to in the term *hod*, related to *hed*, which means "echo"—that is, to respond. As noted above, *hod* relates to "confession." Sincere confession is a form of "echo," naturally reacting to one's inner sense of being accused from on high. Confession is thus a form of "reflected light" (*or chozer*), an intrinsically feminine phenomenon.

[14] Interestingly, when written in Hebrew, the numerical value of Lupus, 182, is identical to that of Jacob. Just as Jacob overcame the angel of Esau in his wrestle with him, so by identifying with Jacob and becoming inspired by him, may the disease of Lupus be overcome.

[15] The legs—our continual contact with the ground—"meet" or "touch" outer reality. The legs are the physical extension of the body that connects with the outer world. Interestingly, the word in Hebrew for the laws of the Torah—*halachah*—literally means "walking." The sages say that "a person does not properly

appreciate the laws until he has stumbled in them" (*Gitin* 43a, based on Isaiah 3:6). Even of the righteous it is written, "Seven times a righteous man falls, and rises up" (Proverbs 24:16). The righteous one is someone who, despite stumbling or falling, will always rise, having learned from the experience.

[16] Since while nursing women do not normally menstruate, there is an opinion of the sages that the menstrual blood becomes (at least on the spiritual plane) mother's milk (*Bechorot* 6b; *Nidah* 9a). This might suggest that nursing women, who not only release their "bad" blood but even convert it into milk (which is fed to the infant from the mother's breasts, her "place of understanding" [*Berachot* 10a], where illness is sweetened in its source), may be less susceptible to contracting Lupus.

[17] Leviticus 20:18.

[18] *Bava Metzia* 107b.

[19] It is also significant that the Code is divided into 14 books. 14 is the numerical value of "hand" (*yad*), for which reason Maimonides called his Code, "The Strong Hand" (*Yad Hachazakah*). Here is a further allusion to medical practice, for "hand" refers to the "hand of the physician," as will be described in Chapter 7.

[20] *Igrot Kodesh Admor HaRayatz*, vol. 2, p. 537; vol. 7, p. 197.

[21] In this section, we have outlined four practices that aid the healing process:
- meditation on the Divine
- meditation on the spiritual root of disease
- positive thinking
- words of encouragement

These four practices, in their given order, correspond to the four letters of God's essential Name, *Havayah*:

The two levels of meditation correspond to the two concealed levels, the two first letters of the Name *Havayah*, the *yud* and the higher *hei*. Meditation on the Divine corresponds to the *yud*, for

"God is in wisdom [*chochmah*, the *yud* of the Name *Havayah*]." (This is a paraphrase in Kabbalah of Proverbs 3:19.) Sweetening the disease at its source, by meditation on its spiritual roots, takes place in the realm of *binah*, the higher *hei* of the Name *Havayah*. Positive thinking the entire day is one's correct psychological response to all of one's daily experiences and feelings. By thinking positively, one rectifies the emotions of one's soul, the source of one's experiences and feelings, which correspond to the *vav* of the Name *Havayah*. Finally, words of encouragement, spoken by loved ones, gives full expression to the rectified state of *malchut*, "the world of speech," the final *hei* of the Name *Havayah*.

As stated, the highest of the four practices, meditation on the Divine, may either succeed, with God's help, to totally rid the body of disease or at least to produce a state of remission. In the former case, the meditation has reached the level of *keter*, the higher tip of the *yud* of *Havayah*; in the latter case, the meditation has reached the level of *chochmah*, the body of the *yud*.

To summarize:

י upper tip of *yud*	*keter* "crown"	meditation on the Divine (ridding the body of disease)
י *yud*	*chochmah* "wisdom"	meditation on the Divine (producing a state of remission)
ה *hei*	*binah* "understanding"	meditation on the spiritual root of disease
ו *vav*	*midot* "emotions"	positive thinking
ה *hei*	*malchut* "kingdom"	words of encouragement

Chapter Seven

1. It is the priest who diagnoses and treats the affliction of *tzara'at*, the only disease discussed at length in the Torah (Leviticus 13).

2. Job 4:21.

3. The third Lubavitcher Rebbe (1789-1866), author of *Tzemach Tzedek*.

4. Based on the verse, "he shall surely heal" (Exodus 21:19) and the sages' comment: "From here is derived the permission granted to the physician to heal, [for otherwise we would have thought that mortal man should not interfere with God's decrees]" (*Berachot* 60a).

5. Isaiah 65:20.

6. We are taught in Kabbalah that in general, when a soul has been incarnated several times, vested in several different bodies, in each body one of the spiritual levels of the soul (of which, in general, there are five: *nefesh, ruach, neshamah, chayah,* and *yechidah*) is rectified. Each of these levels (and each of the particular levels of their inter-inclusion) is sufficient to animate—forever—that body in which its rectification took place.

7. See Supplementary Essay #15, "Death and Life" (p. 249).

8. *Berachot* 17a. The whole passage reads: "When Rabbi Yochanan finished the Book of Job, he used to say the following: 'The end of man is to die, and the end of a beast is to be slaughtered, and all are doomed to die. Happy is he who was brought up in the Torah and whose labor was in the Torah and who has given pleasure to his Creator and who grew up with a good name and departed the world with a good name. Of him King Solomon said: "A good name is better than precious oil, and the day of death, than the day of one's birth" [Ecclesiastes 7:1].'"

9. Ecclesiastes 12:13.

[10] Psalms 23:4.

[11] The Divine Name associated in Kabbalah with *chochmah* is the Name *Havayah* spelled out such that its numerical value is 72, which is the numerical value of *chesed*.

[12] The three divisions of the Jewish people—priests, Levites, and Israelites—correspond to the three principal emotions of the heart: *chesed*, *gevurah*, and *tiferet*.

[13] *Chochmah* is associated with the life-force of the body, as seen in the verse quoted above, "they shall die, but not with *chochmah*" (Job 4:21). The intellectual process of *binah*, in contrast, is one of self-awareness, in which the insight of *chochmah* is analyzed and evaluated in the context of the individual's present thought patterns. Because of the self-awareness inherent in this process, *binah* may distort the original truth of *chochmah*, leading the mind to false conclusions and intellectual "dead-ends." It is therefore necessary to ensure that the analysis of *binah* remain true to the pristine vision of *chochmah*. This is done by periodically evaluating the conclusions reached by *binah* against the re-experience of the original insight of *chochmah*. In this way, the self-awareness of *binah* is neutralized and "healed" by the selflessness of *chochmah*.

There are fifty "gates," or levels, of *binah*; the highest, fiftieth gate is this presence or point of *chochmah* shining into *binah*. When *binah* is missing this fiftieth gate, one is "sick." (The word for "sick" in Hebrew is *choleh*, which is numerically equivalent to 49, indicating *binah* missing its fiftieth gate—the *bitul* of *chochmah* shining into *binah*, as explained in the text.)

[14] These are: Genesis 20:17, 50:2 (twice); Exodus 15:26, 21:19 (twice); Numbers 12:13; and Deuteronomy 28:27, 28:35, 32:39. The ten can be seen to correspond to the ten *sefirot*, as we have detailed elsewhere.

[15] Only in these four instances does the prefix-letter *nun* appear. *Nun* is the *fourteenth* letter of the alphabet; its numerical

value of 50 alludes to the source of healing, since a sick person is one who lacks the fiftieth gate of understanding, as explained above (p. 138).

[16] These are: Leviticus 13:18, 13:37, 14:3, 14:48. These four can be seen to correspond to the four stages of the investiture of the soul into the body and the world, corresponding to the four worlds and the four letters of the Name *Havayah*.

[17] The fourteen appearances divide into two groups of ten and four in another fashion, as well. In four instances (Genesis 20:17, Exodus 15:26, Numbers 12:13, Deuteronomy 32:39), the subject of the verb (the "healer") is explicitly stated to be God; in the other ten, healing occurs either (seemingly) by itself or through the efforts of a human doctor.

[18] Genesis 20:17.

[19] *Eiruvin* 41a.

[20] The numerical value of the first two letters of *Elokim* in reduced numbering is also 4, and that of the remaining three letters is 10. Inasmuch as the first two letters of *Elokim* are themselves the Name of God (*Kel*) from which the Name *Elokim* is derived, this division of *Elokim* into 4 and 10 aligns with the division of the fourteen appearances of the root "healing" described above, in note 17.

[21] See *Sod Hashem Lireiav*, pp. 552 ff.

[22] 2 Kings 3:15.

[23] Psalms 145:16.

[24] *Tikunei Zohar*, introduction (7b).

[25] A common expression in Rabbinic literature.

[26] Exodus 14:31.

[27] *Ibid.* 3:19, et al.

[28] *Ibid.* 14:8, et al.

[29] Deuteronomy 23:13.

[30] Proverbs 3:19.

[31] See *Lev LaDa'at*, p. 10, footnote 34, on the verse (Psalms 35:10), "All of my limbs shall say, 'GOD [*Havayah*, God's essential Name, which relates in particular to His attribute of mercy], who is like You?"

[32] Psalms 145:16.

[33] *Tikunei Zohar*, introduction (7b).

[34] 2 Kings, ch. 5.

[35] *Ibid.* 3:15.

[36] Before the advent of modern surgical technology, surgery was entirely hands-on. The doctor made the incision and operated. Surgical precision has been greatly enhanced by the use of endoscopes and "keyhole" surgery, in which the doctor makes a much smaller incision and inserts tiny surgical apparatuses (controlled by "joysticks") with which he operates. This technology requires virtually no tactile ability. It is interesting to note that recently even more advanced techniques have allowed the trend to swing back toward a more traditional form of surgery, in which a small incision is made but the surgeon does insert his hand to operate.

[37] See *The Torah Academy*.

[38] According to the sages, the first word of the Torah ("in the beginning") implies a concealed, implicit utterance (*Rosh Hashanah* 32a). The very first letter of the Torah is a large *beit*. The form of the letter *beit* is itself the white silhouette traced by the interior edges of the letter *pei*, whose name means "mouth." This is a most beautiful allusion to the fact that the large *beit* that begins the account of creation issues from the mouth of God.

[39] Genesis 1:2.

[40] *Berachot* 22a. This is an instruction to one who is impure. Nonetheless, he may and should study Torah, for "the words of the Torah cannot be defiled" (*ibid.*). Their light shines against any background, no matter how dark it be. This is identical with God's

creation of light on the first day against the background of primordial darkness.

⁴¹ They spell the word for "circumcision" (*milah*), which we have seen above to relate to the secret of the mouth.

⁴² *Zohar* 2:123a.

⁴³ "And Adam *knew* [*yada*] his wife, Eve" (Genesis 4:1).

⁴⁴ Proverbs 12:25.

⁴⁵ *Yoma* 75a. See *Transforming Darkness into Light*, ch. 3 ff.

⁴⁶ Just as it is said about God, "You open Your hands and satisfy the need of every living being" (Psalms 145:16), we are enjoined, "You shall surely open your hand and [give or] lend him whatever he needs" (Deuteronomy 15:8).

⁴⁷ "They are life to those who find them" (Proverbs 4:22); "Do not read 'who find them' [*motzeihem*] but 'who articulate them with their mouths' [*motzieihem (befeh)*]" (*Eiruvin* 54a).

⁴⁸ The eyes, associated with *chochmah* and *bitul*, project the energies of *chesed* and *ahavah*, for *chesed* is the branch or extension of *chochmah* on the right axis of the Tree of Life. The two hands, *chesed* (right) and *gevurah* (left), join, in perfect balance—"touching and not touching"—to project the energy of *tiferet* (the third, middle hand), *rachamim*. The mouth, *malchut*, projects the energy of the first of the *sefirot* that combine to rectify *malchut*—*netzach* and *bitachon*. (*Netzach* is the *sefirah* which enters *malchut* to rectify *malchut*'s own *sefirah* of *chochmah*, as explained in Kabbalah.)

⁴⁹ The sequence of submission, separation, and sweetening presented here is only an idealized order. In everyday life, the stages described can appear in any order as, indeed, each is inter-included within the other.

⁵⁰ *Avot* 3:13.

⁵¹ *Nidah* 66a.

⁵² See Nachmanides on Numbers 21:9.

⁵³ *Bereishit Rabbah* 77a.

[54] In the words of the sages, "[God] prepared the remedy before He brought on the disease" (*Megilah* 13b).

[55] Psalms 85:12.

[56] Deuteronomy 20:19. There it appears as a rhetorical question, but throughout Rabbinic literature it is read as in the text.

[57] *Tikunei Zohar*, introduction (17a).

[58] *Da'at* is referred to in Kabbalah as the soul of *tiferet*, indicating that the nervous system (*da'at*) lies at the core of the muscular system (*tiferet*), as explained above. In the form of the letter *vav*, the *yud* at the head of the *vav* alludes to *da'at* (the nervous system) while the straight and upright extension of the *vav* itself represents *tiferet* (the torso and muscular system).

[59] See Supplementary Essay #16, "Expert Healing" (p. 251).

[60] Deuteronomy 12:23.

[61] Genesis 1:26.

[62] For this reason as well, the numerical value of "snake," *nachash*, 358, is identical with that of "Messiah," *Mashiach*. The Messiah (who will kill the evil snake, i.e., eradicate the source of evil from the world) is the ultimate healer of all humanity. Even in the animal kingdom, in the time of the Messiah, "lamb and wolf" will dwell together in health and harmony (Isaiah 11:6).

[63] Singular: *segulah*. A *segulah* is an object (generally, a precious object) or act that possesses a specific property or power that renders it effective—indirectly, in a manner that does not obey natural rules of cause and effect—with regard to some given condition. The indirect manner in which a *segulah* works is reflected in the etymology of the word *segulah* itself, related to the concept of "circle" (rather than direct, linear sequence of causality).

In the Torah (Exodus 19:5), the Jewish people are the *segulah* of God—the Divine "treasure/charm" of creation, whose power it is to reveal God's presence and absolute unity throughout reality.

[64] The principle of the rectified Tree of Knowledge.

⁶⁵ Furthermore, in Kabbalah and Hassidism we are taught that the consummately rectified "power of imagination" borders on the power of prophecy. At the time of the exile of the Jewish people, the prophetic phenomenon disappeared, and was replaced by illusionary imagination. Speedily, with the redemption of the Jewish people and the entire world, true prophecy will return and God "will pour out His spirit on all flesh" (Joel 3:1).

⁶⁶ Psalms 121:5.

⁶⁷ See Supplementary Essay #17, "Healing and the Torah" (p. 253).

⁶⁸ *Ketubot* 111b.

⁶⁹ See *Tanya*, ch. 48 (67b ff).

⁷⁰ See *Zohar* 1:24a.

⁷¹ Liturgy, evening service.

⁷² *Mikva'ot* 6:8.

⁷³ In Kabbalah, we are taught that the *chayah* of the soul resides in the "air fluid" above the brain, beneath the skull. This corresponds to a true state of selflessness—as that which one experiences when immersing in the pure waters of the *mikveh*—infused with a sense of infinite serenity.

⁷⁴ Here, the light of the Torah blinds the eyes of the impure "shells" (*kelipot*) responsible for the ailment. The negative influence of the "shells" disappears and the body recovers.

⁷⁵ *Ta'anit* 11b.

⁷⁶ Of this level it is said, "the *tzadik* lives in his faith" (Habakkuk 2:4).

⁷⁷ See Supplementary Essay #18, "The Indestructible Bone" (p. 257).

⁷⁸ Daniel, chapter 3.

Chapter Eight

[1] 2 Kings 20:1

[2] The sages teach (*Bava Metzia* 87a) that before the time of the prophet Elisha, no one ever recovered from a mortal disease. Through the power of prayer, Elisha was the first man to recover from such a disease, thereby blazing the path for all.

[3] 2 Kings 20:5-6.

[4] 2 Samuel 23:1.

[5] *Berachot* 10a.

[6] *Bereishit Rabbah* 53:14.

[7] This was the case with Hezekiah, who, being the king, was most essentially identified with *malchut*. As cited above, Hezekiah learned to pray even in a seemingly hopeless situation from his ancestor, King David, the archetypal soul of *malchut*.

Ironically, the prophet Isaiah, the sage of the second level (to be discussed presently), had apparently lost hope of Hezchiah's recovery.

[8] *Yevamot* 63b.

[9] *Bava Batra* 116a.

[10] Praying for another is the essence of the *mitzvah* of "visiting the sick" (*Yalkut Shimoni*, Psalms 740).

[11] Genesis 29:11; see *Tanya*, ch. 45.

[12] Genesis 25:27; see Rashi *ad loc*.

[13] Cf. *Likutei Diburim*, vol. 1, pp. 1 ff.

[14] This redemptive power derives from the *sefirah* of *binah*, which corresponds to the first *hei* of God's Name *Havayah*. In the *Zohar* (2:186a), *binah* is referred to as "the world of freedom," the epitome of spiritual redemption.

This is the principle underlying the Jubilee year, the fiftieth year—corresponding to the fiftieth gate of understanding—when slaves are freed and lands return to their original owners.

[15] Isaiah 60:21.
[16] Numbers 6:22-23.
[17] *Zohar* 2:121a.
[18] Proverbs 3:19.
[19] See *Tikunei Zohar* 6b.
[20] *Shabbat* 88b, *et al.*
[21] *Asarah Ma'amarot*, Ha*Itim* 6.
[22] Indeed, the Aramaic term used for "prayer" throughout the Talmud is *rachamei* ("mercy"). This implies that any spiritual activity that arouses God's mercy may be referred to as "prayer."
[23] *Midrash Tehilim* 122. *Bava Batra* 16b recounts that Job's three friends felt his suffering telepathically and came to console him, albeit unsuccessfully.
[24] Malachi 3:6.
[25] We further observe, in contemplation of these five ascending levels of prayer for the sick, a definite order of self-other-self-other-self. The first and fifth levels explicitly pertain to one's own spiritual service to elicit Divine mercy. The second and fourth levels derive from the power of another, empathizing soul, "above" oneself (the wise man and the priest). The third level, that of the *tzadik*, the holy man, pertains to oneself as well (for, as noted above, at this level, all are equal—one relates to the other as to oneself and to oneself as to the other).
[26] *Yoma* 86a. This section is based on *Sod Hashem Lireiav*, pp. 456 ff.
[27] Here, the soul reaches the level of the supernal crown, *keter elyon*. Later we will explain, that this level is alluded to in the phrase "for I am God who heals you" (Exodus 15:26), whose initials spell *Arich* (literally, "the long, extended face," symbolizing infinite patience), as was mentioned above. This is an appellation for *keter elyon*, the source of "healing" (*aruchah*, from the word *arich*).
[28] Throughout the *Zohar*, *binah* ("understanding") is identified as the spiritual service of true and complete *teshuvah*.

[29] Isaiah 6:10.
[30] 57:19.
[31] *Berachot* 34b.

Glossary

Note: all foreign terms are Hebrew unless otherwise indicated. Terms preceded by an asterisk have their own entries.

Abba (אַבָּא, "father" [Aramaic]): the *partzuf* of *chochmah.

Adam Kadmon (אָדָם קַדְמוֹן, "primordial man"): the first *world.

Arich Anpin (אֲרִיךְ אַנְפִּין, "the long face" or "the infinitely patient one"): the external *partzuf* of *keter (the inner dimension is *Atik Yomin). In psychological terms, it is synonymous with will. It possesses its own *keter* (the *gulgalta), and its own *chochmah (*mocha stima'ah).

Asiyah (עֲשִׂיָּה, "action"): the lowest of the four *worlds.

Atbash: (אתב״ש): the simple reflective transformation. The first letter of the alphabet is paired with the last, the second with the second-to-last, and so on. Letters in each pair may then be interchanged.

א	ב	ג	ד	ה	ו	ז	ח	ט	י	כ
ת	ש	ר	ק	צ	פ	ע	ס	נ	מ	ל

Atik: short for *Atik Yomin.

Atik Yomin (עַתִּיק יוֹמִין, the ancient of days" [Aramaic]): the inner *partzuf* of *keter.

Atika Kadisha (עַתִּיקָא קַדִּישָׁא, "the holy ancient One" [Aramaic]): in some contexts, this term is a synonym for *Atik Yomin; in others, for *keter in general.

Atzilut (אֲצִילוּת, "Emanation"): First and highest of the four *worlds emanating from *Adam Kadmon.

Av (אָב, "father"): the fifth month of the Jewish calendar.

Ba'al Shem Tov (בַּעַל שֵׁם טוֹב, "Master of the Good Name [of God]"): Title of Rabbi Yisrael ben Eliezer (1698-1760), founder of the Chassidic movement (see *Chassidut*).

Ba'al Teshuvah (בַּעַל תְּשׁוּבָה, "one who returns"): one who returns to the ways of Judaism and adherence to Jewish law after a period of estrangement. Often used in contrast to a **tzadik*, who has not undergone such a period. The *ba'al teshuvah* strives continually to ascend, return and become subsumed within God's essence; the *tzadik* strives primarily to serve God by doing good deeds and thus drawing His light into the world. Ideally these two paths are meant to be inter-included, i.e. that every Jew should embody both the service of the *ba'al teshuvah* and that of the *tzadik*, as well. See also *teshuvah*.

Beriah (בְּרִיאָה, "creation"): the second of the four **worlds.

Binah (בִּינָה, "understanding"): the third of the ten **sefirot*.

Birur (בֵּרוּר, "separation," "choosing," or "refinement"): a type of **tikun* in which one must work to separate good from evil in any given entity, and then reject the evil and accept the good. This may be done actively or in one's consciousness. See **yichud*.

Bitachon (בִּטָּחוֹן, "confidence"): 1. the feeling of confidence in one's God-given power to take initiative and succeed in one's mission in life. See **emunah*. 2. The inner experience of the **sefirah* of **netzach*. 3. ("trust"): the feeling that God will orchestrate events in accord with the greatest revealed good. This passive *bitachon* is associated with the *sefirah* of **hod*.

Bitul (בִּטּוּל, "annihilation"): any of a number of states of selflessness or self-abnegation. The inner experience of the **sefirah* of **chochmah*.

Brit (בְּרִית, "covenant") or ***brit milah*** (בְּרִית מִילָה, "covenant of circumcision"): 1. the covenant or eternal bond God made with Abraham and the Jewish people, indicated by the circumcision of the male reproductive organ, usually on the eighth day after birth. 2. The ceremony at which this commandment is

Glossary

performed. 3. Euphemism for the male reproductive organ itself.

Chabad (חַבַּ״ד) acronym for *chochmah, *binah, *da'at (חָכְמָה בִּינָה דַּעַת, "wisdom, understanding, knowledge"): 1. the first triad of *sefirot, which constitute the intellect (see *Chagat, Nehi*). 2. the branch of *Chassidut founded by Rabbi Shneur Zalman of Liadi (1745-1812), emphasizing the role of the intellect and meditation in the service of God.

Chagat (חַגַ״ת) acronym for *chesed, *gevurah, *tiferet (חֶסֶד גְּבוּרָה תִּפְאֶרֶת, "loving-kindness, strength, and beauty"): the second triad of *sefirot, which together constitute the primary emotions (see *Chabad, Nehi*).

Chasadim: plural of *chesed (second sense).

Chassidut (חֲסִידוּת, "piety" or "loving-kindness"): 1. An attribute or way of life that goes beyond the letter of the law. 2. The movement within Judaism founded by Rabbi Yisrael Ba'al Shem Tov (1648-1760), the purpose of which is to awaken the Jewish people to its own inner self through the inner dimension of the Torah and thus to prepare the way for the advent of *Mashiach. 3. The oral and written teachings of this movement.

Chayah (חַיָּה, "living one"): the second highest of the five levels of the *soul.

Chesed (חֶסֶד, "loving-kindness"; pl. חֲסָדִים *chasadim*): 1. the fourth of the ten *sefirot. 2. a manifestation of this attribute, specifically in *da'at.

Chochmah (חָכְמָה, "wisdom" or "insight"): the second of the ten *sefirot.

Da'at (דַּעַת, "knowledge"): 1. the unifying force within the ten *sefirot. 2. the third *sefirah of the intellect, counted as one of the ten *sefirot* when *keter is not.

Din (דִּין, "judgment; pl. דִּינִים, *dinim*): 1. a synonym for *gevurah. 2. a manifestation of this attribute. 3. a synonym for *kal vechomer.

Emunah (אֱמוּנָה, "faith" or "belief"): 1. the belief that no matter what God does, it is all ultimately for the greatest good, even if it does not appear so to us presently; see *bitachon*. 2. the inner experience associated with *Reisha d'lo Ityada*.

Gedulah (גְּדֻלָה, "greatness"): a synonym for *chesed*.

Gematria (גִּימַטְרִיָּא, "numerology" [Aramaic]): the technique of comparing Hebrew words and phrases based on their numerical values.

Gevurah (גְּבוּרָה, "strength" or "might"; pl. גְּבוּרוֹת, *gevurot*): 1. the fifth of the ten *sefirot*. 2. a manifestation of this attribute, specifically in *da'at*.

Gevurot: plural of *gevurah* (second sense).

Gulgalta (גֻּלְגַּלְתָּא, "the skull" [Aramaic]): the *keter* of *Arich Anpin*. In psychological terms, the interface between pleasure and will, which serves as the origin of the super-conscious will.

Halachah (הֲלָכָה, "way" or "walking): 1. the entire corpus of Jewish law. 2. a specific Jewish law.

Havayah (יהו-ה): also known as the Tetragrammaton ("four-letter Name"). Due to its great sanctity, this Name may only be pronounced in the Holy Temple, and its correct pronunciation is not known today. When one is reciting a complete Scriptural verse or liturgy, it is read as if it were the Name *Adni*; otherwise one says *Hashem* (הַשֵּׁם, "the Name") or *Havayah* (הֲוָיָה, a permutation of the four letters of this Name).

Havayah is the most sacred of God's Names. Although no name can fully express God's essence, the Name *Havayah* in certain contexts *refers* to God's essence. In these cases it is called "the higher Name *Havayah*" and is termed "the essential Name" (שֵׁם הָעֶצֶם), "the unique Name" (שֵׁם הַמְיֻחָד), and "the explicit Name" (שֵׁם הַמְפֹרָשׁ).

Otherwise, the Name *Havayah* refers to God as He manifests Himself through creation. In these cases it is called "the lower Name *Havayah*," and its four letters are seen to depict in their form the creative process and allude to the worlds, ten *sefirot*, etc., as follows:

	creation	worlds	sefirot
׳ upper tip of *yud*	will to create	*Adam Kadmon*	*keter*
׳ *yud*	contraction	*Atzilut*	*chochmah*
ה *hei*	expansion	*Beriah*	*binah*
ו *vav*	extension	*Yetzirah*	the six *midot*
ה *hei*	expansion	*Asiyah*	*malchut*

The lower Name *Havayah* appears on several levels. It is first manifest as the light within all the *sefirot*. It thus possesses on this level ten iterations, which are indicated as ten vocalizations—each using one of the ten vowels. (These are only meditative "vocalizations," since it is forbidden to pronounce the Name *Havayah* with any vocalization, as we have said.) For example, when each of its four letters is vocalized with a *kamatz*, it signifies the light within the *sefirah* of *keter*; when they are each vocalized with a *patach*, it signifies the light within the *sefirah* of *chochmah*. The other Names of God (including the subsequent manifestations of the Name *Havayah*) refer to the vessels of the *sefirot*. In the world of *Atzilut*, where these Names are principally manifest, both the vessels and the lights of the *sefirot* are manifestations of Divinity.

The second manifestation of the lower Name *Havayah* is as the vessel of the *sefirah* of *chochmah*. (This is alluded to in the verse, "*Havayah* in *chochmah* founded the earth" [*Proverbs* 3:19].)

Its third manifestation is as the vessel of the *sefirah* of *binah*. This manifestation is indicated by the consonants of the Name vocalized with the vowels of (and read as) the Name *Elokim* (for example, *Deuteronomy* 3:24, etc.).

The most basic manifestation of the lower Name *Havayah* is in the *sefirah* of *tiferet*, whose inner experience is mercy. The Name

Havayah in general is associated with "the principle of mercy," since mercy is the most basic emotion through which God relates to His creation. In this, its most common sense, it is vocalized with the vowels of (and read as) the Name *Adnut*.

Hod (הוֹד, "splendor," "thanksgiving," "acknowledgment"): the eighth of the ten *sefirot*.

Ima (אִמָּא, "mother" [Aramaic]): the *partzuf* of *binah*.

Kabbalah (קַבָּלָה, "receiving" or "tradition"): the esoteric dimension of the Torah.

Kabbalat Shabbat (קַבָּלַת שַׁבָּת, "welcoming the Sabbath"): the series of psalms and hymns, etc. recited as a prelude to the Friday night prayer service, to mark the onset of the Sabbath.

Kav (קַו, "line"): the ray of light beamed into the vacated space created in consequence of the *tzimtzum*.

Keter (כֶּתֶר, "crown"): the first of the ten *sefirot*.

Lecha Dodi (לְכָה דוֹדִי, "Come, my beloved"): a hymn recited as part of *Kabbalat Shabbat*.

Lights: see *Sefirah*.

Lubavitch (לְיוּבַּאוִויטְשׁ, "City of Love" [Russian]): the town that served as the center of the *Chabad* movement from 1812 to 1915; the movement became known also after the name of this town.

Malchut (מַלְכוּת, "kingdom"): the last of the ten *sefirot*.

Mashiach (מָשִׁיחַ, "anointed one," "messiah"): the prophesied descendant of King David who will reinstate the Torah-ordained monarchy (which he will head), rebuild the Holy *Temple, and gather the exiled Jewish people to their homeland. This series of events (collectively called "the Redemption") will usher in an era of eternal, universal peace and true knowledge of God, called "the messianic era." There is also a prophesied messianic figure called *Mashiach ben* Joseph, who will rectify certain spiritual aspects of reality in preparation for the advent of *Mashiach ben* David.

Mazal (מַזָּל, pl. מַזָּלוֹת, *mazalot*): 1. a spiritual conduit of Divine beneficence (from the root נזל, "to flow"). 2. specifically, the thirteen tufts of the "beard" of *Arich Anpin. 3. a physical embodiment of such a spiritual conduit, such as a star, planet, constellation, etc. 4. specifically, the twelve constellations of the zodiac. 5. According to our sages, the Jewish people are not under the influence of the *mazalot* (Shabbat 156a). The Ba'al Shem Tov teaches that the Divine "nothingness" itself is the true *mazal* of the Jewish people.

Menorah (מְנוֹרָה, "candelabrum"): the seven-branched candelabrum that was lit daily in the sanctuary of the *Tabernacle and, afterwards, in the Holy *Temple.

Midah (מִדָּה, "measure" or "attribute," pl. מִדוֹת, *midot*): 1. an attribute of God. 2. specifically, one of the *sefirot* from *chesed* to *malchut*, in contrast to the higher *sefirot* of the intellect. 3. one of the thirteen attributes of mercy, which are part of the revelation of *keter.

Midot: plural of *midah.

Midrash (מִדְרָשׁ, "seeking"; pl. מִדְרָשִׁים, *Midrashim*): the second major body of the oral Torah (after the *Talmud*), consisting of halachic or homiletic material couched as linguistic analyses of the Biblical text. An individual work of midrashic material is also called a *Midrash*, as is a specific analysis in midrashic style.

The *Midrash* is a corpus of many works written over the span of several centuries (roughly the second to the eighth CE), mostly in the Holy Land. The chief collection of homiletic midrashic material is the *Rabbah* ("great") series, covering the five books of Moses and the five scrolls. Other important collections are *Midrash Tanchuma*, *Midrash Tehilim*, *Pesikta d'Rav Kahana*, *Pirkei d'Rabbi Eliezer* and *Tana d'vei Eliahu*. Several later collections contain material that has reached us in its original form. These include *Midrash HaGadol* and *Yalkut Shimoni*. There are many smaller, minor *Midrashim*, as well; some of these are to be found in the collection *Otzar HaMidrashim*. Halachic *Midrashim* include the *Mechilta*, the *Sifra* and the *Sifrei*.

Mikveh (מִקְוֶה, "gathering [of water]"): a specially constructed pool used for immersion as a stage of ritual purification. See *tumah* and *taharah*.

Mitzvah (מִצְוָה, "commandment"; pl. מִצְוֹת, *mitzvot*): one of the six hundred thirteen commandments given by God to the Jewish people, or seven commandments given by God to the nations of the world, at Mt. Sinai. 2. one of the seven commandments instituted by the sages. 3. idiomatically, any good deed.

Mitzvot: plural of *mitzvah.

Mocha Stima'ah (מוֹחָא סְתִימָאָה, "the hidden brain" [Aramaic]): the *chochmah of *Arich Anpin. In psychological terms, the power to generate new insight (כֹּחַ הַמַּשְׂכִּיל).

Mochin d'Abba (מוֹחִין דְּאַבָּא, "brains of *Abba" [Aramaic]): a state of consciousness, mentality, or cognitive life force in which one experiences *chochmah, or insight.

Mochin d'Ima (מוֹחִין דְּאִמָּא, "brains of *Ima" [Aramaic]): a state of consciousness or mentality, or cognitive life force in which one experiences *binah, or understanding or rationality.

Motzaei Shabbat (מוֹצָאֵי שַׁבָּת, "the outgoings of the Sabbath"): the night after the termination of *Shabbat; Saturday night.

Nefesh (נֶפֶשׁ, "creature," "soul"): 1. the soul in general. 2. the lowest of the five levels of the *soul.

Nehi (נְהִ״י) acronym for *netzach, *hod, *yesod (נֵצַח הוֹד יְסוֹד, "victory, splendor, foundation": the third triad of *sefirot, which together constitute the attributes of behavior (see *Chabad, Chagat*).

Nekudim (נְקֻדִים, "dotted," "spotted"): the second stage in the development of the *world of *Atzilut.

Neshamah (נְשָׁמָה, "soul"): 1. the soul in general. 2. the third of the five levels of the *soul.

Netzach (נֵצַח, "victory," "eternity"): the seventh of the ten *sefirot.

Notrikun (נוֹטָרִיקוֹן, "acronym"): a hermeneutic method in which the letters of a word are interpreted as the initials or main consonantal letters of a different word or phrase.

Nukvei d'Z'eir Anpin (נוּקְבֵיהּ דִזְעֵיר אַנְפִּין [Aramaic]): the *partzuf of *malchut.

Omer: see *Sefirat HaOmer*.

Partzuf (פַּרְצוּף, "profile," "persona"; pl. פַּרְצוּפִים, *partzufim*): the third and final stage in the development of a *sefirah, in which it metamorphoses from a tenfold articulation of sub-*sefirot* into a human-like figure possessing the full set of intellectual and emotional powers. As such, it may thus interact with the other *partzufim* (which could not occur before this transformation. This stage of development constitutes the transition from *Tohu to *Tikun (or from *Nekudim* to *Berudim*, see under Worlds).

Within any particular *partzuf*, the *sefirot* are arranged along three axes, right, left and middle, as follows:

left axis	center axis	right axis
	keter	
binah		chochmah
	da'at	
gevurah		chesed
	tiferet	
hod		netzach
	yesod	
	malchut	

In this arrangement, there are three triads of related *sefirot*: *chochmah-binah-da'at* (the intellect), *chesed-gevurah-tiferet* (the primary emotions) and *netzach-hod-yesod* (the behavioral attributes).

The *sefirot* develop into a primary and a secondary array of *partzufim*, as follows:

sefirah	primary *partzufim*		secondary *partzufim*	
keter	עַתִּיק יוֹמִין *Atik Yomin*	"The Ancient of Days"	עַתִּיק יוֹמִין *Atik Yomin*	[The male dimension of] "the Ancient of Days"
			נוּקְבֵיה דְעַתִּיק יוֹמִין *Nukvei d'Atik Yomin*	[The female dimension of] "the Ancient of Days"
	אֲרִיךְ אַנְפִּין *Arich Anpin*	"The Long Face"	אֲרִיךְ אַנְפִּין *Arich Anpin*	[The male dimension of] "the Long Face"
			נוּקְבֵיה דַאֲרִיךְ אַנְפִּין *Nukvei d'Arich Anpin*	[The female dimension of] "the Long Face"
chochmah	אַבָּא *Abba*	"Father"	אַבָּא עִילָאָה *Abba Ila'ah*	"Supernal Father"
			אִמָּא עִילָאָה *Ima Ila'ah*	"Supernal Mother"
binah	אִמָּא *Ima*	"Mother"	יִשְׂרָאֵל סַבָא *Yisrael Saba*	"Israel the Elder"
			תְּבוּנָה *Tevunah*	"Understanding"
the midot	זְעֵיר אַנְפִּין *Z'eir Anpin*	"The Small Face"	יִשְׂרָאֵל *Yisrael*	"Israel"
			לֵאָה *Leah*	"Leah"
malchut	נוּקְבֵיה דִזְעֵיר אַנְפִּין *Nukvei d'Z'eir Anpin*	"The Female of Z'eir Anpin"	יַעֲקֹב *Yaakov*	"Jacob"
			רָחֵל *Rachel*	"Rachel"

Both of the secondary, male and female *partzufim* of *Atik Yomin* and *Arich Anpin* exist within the same figure. There are thus actually only ten distinct secondary *partzufim*.

Pesach (פֶּסַח, "Passover"): the seven-day *yom tov (eight days in the Diaspora) commemorating the liberation of the Jewish people from Egyptian slavery.

Rachamim (רַחֲמִים, "mercy"): the inner experience of the *sefirah* of *tiferet.

Rasha (רָשָׁע, "wicked one," pl. רְשָׁעִים, *resha'im*): one who succumbs to his urge to do evil and commits a sin. He retains this status until he does *teshuvah, at which point he becomes a *ba'al teshuvah.

Reisha d'Arich (רֵישָׁא דַאֲרִיךְ, "the head of *Arich [Anpin]" [Aramaic]): the lowest of the three heads of the *keter, synonymous with the *partzuf of Arich Anpin. In psychological terms, super-conscious will.

Reisha d'Ayin (רֵישָׁא דְאַיִן, "the head of nothingness" [Aramaic]): the middle of the three heads of the *keter, related to the emotions of the *partzuf of *Atik Yomin. In psychological terms, super-conscious pleasure.

Reisha d'Lo Ityada (רֵישָׁא דְלֹא אִתְיָדַע, "the unknowable head" [Aramaic]): the highest of the three heads of the *keter, related to the keter and intellect of the *partzuf of *Atik Yomin. In psychological terms, super-conscious belief in God.

Rebbe (רַבִּי, "my teacher"): 1. a term used to describe or address a teacher of Torah. 2. leader of a branch of the Chassidic movement.

Reshimu (רְשִׁימוּ, "residue," "impression"): the residual impression of the infinite Divine light that God withdrew from the vacated space resulting from the *tzimtzum.

Rosh Chodesh (רֹאשׁ חֹדֶשׁ, "new month"): the first day of a Jewish month, a day of celebration.

Rosh HaShanah (רֹאשׁ הַשָּׁנָה, "beginning of the year"): the Jewish New Year, commemorating the creation of man on the sixth day of creation, a day of universal judgment.

Ruach (רוּחַ, "spirit"): a level of the *soul.

Sabbath: see *Shabbat*.

Sages: see *Torah*.

Sefirah (סְפִירָה, pl. סְפִירוֹת, *sefirot*): a channel of Divine energy or life force. It is via the *sefirot* that God interacts with creation; they may thus be considered His "attributes."

There are altogether eleven *sefirot* spoken of in Kabbalistic literature. Inasmuch as two of them (*keter* and *da'at*) are two dimensions of a single force, the tradition generally speaks of only ten *sefirot*. Each *sefirah* also possesses an inner experience, as discussed in *Chassidut. The order of the *sefirot* is depicted in the following chart:

	name			inner experience
keter	כֶּתֶר	"crown"	אֱמוּנָה תַּעֲנוּג רָצוֹן	1. "faith" 2. "pleasure" 3. "will"
chochmah	חָכְמָה	"wisdom," "insight"	בִּטוּל	"selflessness"
binah	בִּינָה	"understanding"	שִׂמְחָה	"joy"
da'at	דַּעַת	"knowledge"	יִחוּד	"union"
chesed	חֶסֶד	"loving-kindness"	אַהֲבָה	"love"
gevurah	גְּבוּרָה	"strength," "might"	יִרְאָה	"fear"
tiferet	תִּפְאֶרֶת	"beauty"	רַחֲמִים	"mercy"
netzach	נֶצַח	"victory," "eternity"	בִּטָּחוֹן	"confidence"
hod	הוֹד	"splendor," "thanksgiving"	תְּמִימוּת	"sincerity," "earnestness"
yesod	יְסוֹד	"foundation"	אֱמֶת	"truth"
malchut	מַלְכוּת	"kingdom"	שִׁפְלוּת	"lowliness"

Originally emanated as simple point-like forces, the *sefirot* at a certain stage develop into full spectrums of ten sub-*sefirot*. Subsequent to this, they metamorphose into *partzufim.

Sefirot are composed of "lights" and "vessels." The light of any *sefirah* is the Divine flow within it; the vessel is the identity that

Glossary

flow takes in order to relate to or create some aspect of the world in a specific way. Inasmuch as all reality is created by means of the *sefirot*, they constitute the conceptual paradigm for understanding all reality.

Sefirat HaOmer (סְפִירַת הָעֹמֶר, "counting the *Omer*"): an *omer* is a dry measure mentioned in the Torah, and refers specifically to the measure of barley offered in the *Temple on the second day of *Pesach*. Beginning with this day, the Jew is commanded to count the next forty-nine days, after which, on the fiftieth day, falls the holiday of *Shavuot*.

Sefirot: plural of *sefirah*.

Shabbat (שַׁבָּת, "Sabbath"): the day of rest beginning sunset on Friday and ending at nightfall on Saturday.

Shacharit (שַׁחֲרִית, "morning"): the morning prayer service.

Shavuot (שָׁבוּעוֹת, "weeks"): the *yom tov* celebrating the wheat harvest and commemorating the giving of the Torah at Mt. Sinai.

Shechinah (שְׁכִינָה, "indwelling"): the immanent Divine Presence that inheres within the universe, corresponding to the *sefirah* of *malchut*, the "feminine" aspect of Divinity.

Shema (שְׁמַע, "hear"): a compilation of three Biblical passages (*Deuteronomy* 6:4-9, 11:13-21, *Numbers* 15:37-41) beginning with this word, or sometimes, the first verse alone. The first verse is the fundamental profession of monotheism, "Hear O Israel, *God* is our God, *God* is one." We are commanded to recite the *Shema* twice daily, and it has been incorporated into the morning and evening services as well as the prayer said upon retiring at night. When reciting the first sentence, we are intended to consider ourselves ready to give up our lives rather than deny the oneness of God.

Shemini Atzeret (שְׁמִינִי עֲצֶרֶת, "the eighth-day gathering"): the *yom tov* immediately following *Sukot*, marking the end of the high-holiday season.

Soul: the animating life or consciousness within man (or any other creature, see *Sha'ar HaYichud VehaEmunah*, ch. 1). The Jew possesses an additional "Divine soul" which is focused on God's concerns in creation.

The essence of the soul possesses five manifestations ("names"), as follows:

name			experience
yechidah	יְחִידָה	"unique one"	unity with God
chayah	חַיָּה	"living being"	awareness of God as continually creating the world
neshamah	נְשָׁמָה	"breath"	vitality of intelligence
ruach	רוּחַ	"spirit"	vitality of emotion
nefesh	נֶפֶשׁ	"creature"	physical vitality

Sukot (סֻכּוֹת, "huts," "booths"): the **yom tov* celebrating the ingathering of the harvest and commemorating the clouds of glory that accompanied the Jewish people on their desert trek after the exodus from Egypt.

Taharah (טָהֳרָה, ritual "purity"): the spiritual state in which one purified himself from a specific degree of **tumah* (or from *tumah* altogether), and is thus allowed to enter areas or touch, be touched by, or consume things or food he otherwise may not. In general, the process of attaining *taharah* involves some type of reaffirmation of life, such as immersion in a **mikveh*. The spiritual correlate to *taharah* is optimistic elation or joy in the service of God. See *tumah*.

Talmud: (תַּלְמוּד, "learning"): the written version of the greater part of the Oral *Torah, comprising mostly legal but also much homiletic and even some explicitly mystical material.

The *Talmud* comprises the *Mishnah* (מִשְׁנָה, "repetition") and the *Gemara* (גְּמָרָא, "completion"). The *Mishnah* is the basic compendium of the laws (each known as a *mishnah*) comprising the Oral Torah, redacted by Rabbi Yehudah the Prince in the second century CE. The *Mishnah* was elaborated upon over the next few centuries in the academies of the Holy Land and Babylonia; this material is the *Gemara*.

There are thus two *Talmuds*: the one composed in the Holy Land, known as the *Talmud Yerushalmi* ("The Jerusalem *Talmud*"), completed in the third century, and the one composed in Babylonia, known as the *Talmud Bavli* ("The Babylonian *Talmud*), completed in the sixth century.

The *Mishnah*—and *ipso facto* the *Talmud*—is divided into tractates. References to the *Mishnah* are simply the name of the tractate followed by the number of the chapter and individual *mishnah*.

The Jerusalem Talmud was first printed in Venice, 1523-24. Although subsequent editions have generally followed the same pagination as this edition, it is nonetheless cited by chapter and *halachah* (i.e., individual *mishnah*) number, as is the *Mishnah*. References to it are therefore prefaced by "Y.," to distinguish them from references to the *Mishnah* itself. The Babylonian Talmud was first printed in its entirety in Venice, 1520-23, and subsequent editions have followed the same pagination as this edition. References to the tractates of the *Talmud Bavli* are simply by tractate name followed by leaf and page ("a" or "b").

Temimut (תְּמִימוּת, "sincerity"): 1. earnestness and sincerity, either in one's conduct with his fellow man or in his connection to God. 2. The inner experience of **hod*.

Temple (or "Holy Temple"; Hebrew: בֵּית הַמִּקְדָּשׁ, "house of the sanctuary"): The central sanctuary in Jerusalem which serves as the physical abode of the indwelling of God's Presence on earth and as the venue for the sacrificial service. The Temple is the focal point of one's spiritual consciousness. The first Temple was built by King Solomon (833 BCE) and destroyed by the Babylonians (423 BCE); the second Temple was built by Zerubabel (synonymous, according to some opinions, with Nehemiah, 353 BCE), remodeled by Herod and destroyed by the Romans (68 CE); the third, eternal Temple will be built by *Mashiach*.

Teshuvah (תְּשׁוּבָה, "return"): the return of the individual (or community), after a period of estrangement, to a state of oneness with and commitment to God and His Torah. See *Ba'al Teshuvah*.

Tevunah (תְּבוּנָה, "comprehension"): the lower of the two secondary *partzufim which develop from the *partzuf* of *Ima, the higher one being *Ima Ila'ah* (אִמָּא עִילָאָה).

Tiferet (תִּפְאֶרֶת, "beauty"): the sixth of the ten *sefirot*.

Tishah b'Av (תִּשְׁעָה בְּאָב, "the ninth of *Av*"): fast day commemorating the destruction of the two Temples, which occurred on this day.

Tikun (תִּקּוּן, "rectification," pl. תִּקּוּנִים, *tikunim*): 1. a state of perfection and order. 2. "The world of *Tikun*" is the *world that first manifests this state, which is synonymous with the world of *Atzilut* (and *Berudim*, see Worlds). 3. the spiritual process of liberating the fragments of Divine light trapped within the material realm, unconscious of God's presence, thereby restoring the world to its initially intended state of perfection. This is accomplished through the performance of *mitzvot. 4. a remedy prescribed against the effects of committing a specific sin.

Tikunim: plural of *tikun (fourth sense).

Tohu (תֹּהוּ, "chaos"): 1. the primordial, unrectified state of creation. 2. "The world of *Tohu*" is the *world which manifests this state, synonymous with the initial, premature form of the world of *Atzilut*. It itself develops in two stages: a stable form (*Akudim*) followed by an unstable form (*Nekudim*, see Worlds). The world of *Tohu* is characterized by "great lights" entering premature "vessels," resulting in the (שְׁבִירַת הַכֵּלִים) "breaking of the vessels." See *Tikun*.

Torah (תּוֹרָה, "teaching"): God's will and wisdom as communicated to man. It pre-existed creation, and God used the Torah as His blueprint in creating the world.

God certainly communicated the teachings of the Torah in some form to Adam, who then transmitted them orally from generation to generation. However, God "officially" gave the Torah to mankind c. 1313 BCE (and during the ensuing 40 years) at Mt. Sinai through Moses. The Ten Commandments were pronounced in the presence of the entire Jewish people.

God gave the Torah in two parts: the Written Torah and the Oral Torah. The Written Torah originally consisted of the Five Books of Moses (the "Pentateuch"), the other books being added later (see Bible). The Oral Torah was communicated together with the Five Books of Moses as an explanation of the laws and lore included in it. This material was later written down by the sages of the Oral Torah in the form of the *Talmud*, the *Midrash*, and the *Zohar*. (All references to "our sages" in this book refer to the sages who transmitted the Oral Torah as recorded in these works.)

Tumah (טֻמְאָה, ritual "impurity"): a spiritual state contracted by someone or something under various circumstances and to various degrees, in which he is prohibited from entering various holy areas or touching, being touched by, or consuming various holy objects or foods. In general, the sources of *tumah* are in some way associated with death (or a missed chance for potential life) and the purification process involves some type of reaffirmation of life. The spiritual correlate to *tumah* is depression or despair. See *taharah*.

Triangle (of n): the sum of the integers from 1 to a specific number, n. For example, the triangle of 5 (denoted $\Delta 5$) is $15 = 1 + 2 + 3 + 4 + 5$.

Tzadik (צַדִּיק, "righteous" person; pl. צַדִּיקִים, *tzadikim*): someone who has fully overcome the evil inclination of his animal soul (and converted its potential into good). See *beinoni, rasha*.

Tzadikim: plural of *tzadik*.

Tzimtzum (צִמְצוּם, "contraction"): the contraction and "removal" of God's infinite light in order to allow for creation of independent realities. The primordial *tzimtzum* produced the "vacated space" (חָלָל) devoid of direct awareness of God's presence. See *Kav* and *Reshimu*.

Vessels: see *sefirah*.

World (Hebrew: עוֹלָם): a spiritual level of creation, representing a rung on the continuum of consciousness or awareness of God. In general, there are four worlds: *Atzilut, *Beriah, *Yetzirah, and *Asiyah. In particular, however, these four worlds originate from a fifth, higher world, *Adam Kadmon. All ten *sefirot and twelve *partzufim are manifest in each world; however, since there is a one-to-one correspondence between the worlds and the *sefirot*, a particular *sefirah* dominates in each world.

The world of *Atzilut* is fundamentally different from the three subsequent worlds in that in it there is no awareness of self *per se*, while the three lower worlds are progressive stages in the development of self-awareness.

The worlds correspond to the Name *Havayah* and the *sefirot* as follows:

the Name *Havayah*	world	dominant sefirah	level of consciousness
׳ upper tip of *yud*	אָדָם קַדְמוֹן *Adam Kadmon* "Primordial Man"	*keter*	Divine will to create; plan of creation
י	אֲצִילוּת *Atzilut* "Emanation"	*chochmah*	solely of God; no self-awareness
ה	בְּרִיאָה *Beriah* "Creation"	*binah*	potential existence; formless substance
ו	יְצִירָה *Yetzirah* "Formation"	*midot*	general existence: archetypes, species
ה	עֲשִׂיָּה *Asiyah* "Action"	*malchut*	particular existence; individual creatures

Glossary

In particular, the world of *Atzilut* develops out of *Adam Kadmon* in three stages (the names of which are taken from *Genesis* 30:10):

world		developmental stage	description	
עֲקֻדִּים *Akudim*	"bound," "striped"	ten lights in one vessel	stable chaos	תֹּהוּ *Tohu*
נְקֻדִּים *Nekudim*	"dotted," "spotted"	ten lights in ten vessels, unstable	unstable chaos, collapse	
בְּרֻדִּים *Berudim*	"patterned," "speckled"	ten lights in ten inter-included vessels; stable	stable, mature rectification	תִּקּוּן *Tikun*

Whenever unqualified reference is made to the world of *Atzilut*, its final, mature stage is meant. It should be noted as well that our physical universe is *below* and "enclothes" the final two *sefirot* (**yesod* and **malchut*) of the spiritual world of *Asiyah* referred to above.

Yechidah (יְחִידָה, "single one"): the highest of the five levels of the **soul.

Yesod (יְסוֹד, "foundation"): the ninth of the ten **sefirot*.

Yetzirah (יְצִירָה, "formation"): one of the four **worlds.

Yisrael Saba (יִשְׂרָאֵל סָבָא, "Israel the Elder" [Aramaic]): the lower of the two secondary **partzufim* which develop from the *partzuf* of **Abba*, the higher being *Abba Ila'ah* (אַבָּא עִלָּאָה, "the higher *Abba*").

Yom Kippur (יוֹם כִּפּוּר, "Day of Atonement"): the holiest day of the Jewish year, marked by fasting and **teshuvah*, particularly through confession of sin.

Yom Tov (יוֹם טוֹב, "good day" or "holiday"): a festive holiday on which, with certain exceptions, weekday work is prohibited just as on **Shabbat.

Z'eir Anpin (זְעֵיר אַנְפִּין, "the small face" [Aramaic]): the **partzuf* of the **midot*, corresponding to the emotive faculties of the soul. In general, the concept of "finitude" or "finite power" is identified with *Z'eir Anpin*.

Zohar (זֹהַר, "Brilliance"): one of the basic texts of the oral *Torah and Kabbalah, recording the mystical teachings of Rabbi Shimon bar Yochai (2nd century). The Zoharic literature includes the *Zohar* proper, the **Tikunei Zohar*, and the **Zohar Chadash*. The *Zohar* was printed in 1558 in both Mantua and Cremona, but standard pagination follows the Mantua edition.

Index

Aaron
    hod, 125
Abimelech, 243
Abraham, 240
    and Abimelech, 243
    priest, 244
    twofold covenant, 62
Acupuncture and
    acupressure, 180
Adam, 49, 223
AIDS, 147
Allopathy, 179
Allostasis, 123
Alphabet, 28
    and body parts, 29
    and eyesight, 40
    and human anatomy, 58
    beginning, middle, and end, 232
    pathways of wisdom, 225
    phonetic origins, 52
Altar, 109
Altar, Temple, 102
Amalek, 113
Amidah
    blessing for healing, 242
Amulets, 189
Angels, 53, 235
Antibodies, 147, 157
Anxiety, 176

Arich Anpin, 144
Ariel, 109
Atbash, 230
Ba'al Peor, 99
Balance, 41
Bees, 108
Benayah ben Jehoyada, 110
Benjamin, tribe of, 101
Bile, 129
Binah, 14, 20, 24
    allopathy, 182
    and *chochmah*, 144
    and *hod*, 107
    blood, 76
    deficiency in, 140
    Egypt, 135
    fifty gates of, 138
    fire, 212
    hand, 170
    healing, 199
    heart, 211
    in mouth, 66
    in the eye, 34
    love of fellow Jew, 135
    sphere of the ears, 213
    teshuvah, 156
    this world, 226
Birth, 136
    healing, 243
Blessing vs. prayer, 203

Blood
    and *nefesh*, 186
Bloodletting, 158
Body
    and mind, 161
    and soul, 11
    division into spheres, 213
    division into three's, 27
Books of Creation, 31
Brain, 24
Brainstem, 211
Bride, 34
Brit, 52, 60
    and fingers, 228
    nakedness, 222
Caduceus, 118
Careers, 83
Cazenave
    Pierre Louis Alphe, 151
Chariot, Divine, 34
Charity, 177
Charms, 187
Chashmal, 56, 177
Chashmalim (angels), 235
Chayah
    level of healing, 191
Cherubim, 223
Chesed, 15, 25
    agility, 112
    and priest, 167
    and *yesod*, 247
    in mouth, 67
    skeletal system, 77

Chest, 53
Chinese medicine, 180
Chiropractic, 180
Chochmah, 14, 20, 24
    and *binah*, 144
    and DNA, 257
    and lungs, 211
    and priest, 165
    bone marrow, 75
    deficiency in, 139
    hand, 170
    homeopathy, 182
    in mouth, 65
    in the eye, 34
    Moab and Midian, 110
    power of "what," 246
    priestly blessing, 200
    sphere of the eyes, 213
    water, 212
    Word to Come, 226
Chronic Fatigue Syndrome, 155
Circumcision, 62, 83, 222
    and and speech, 55
Clapping, 51
Collagens, 154
Color, 217
    and fingers, 228
Colors
    in the eye, 34
Commandments
    and sexuality, 241
Compassion, 82

Concubine of Gibeah, 101
Constipation, 245
Copper, 118
Covenant between the Pieces
    twofold covenant, 62
Da'at, 15, 24
    and diagnosis, 173
    and fear of insanity, 97
    balance, 41
    good and evil, 79
    higher and lower, 54
    higher covenant, 48
    in mouth, 66
    in the eye, 35
    nervous system, 79
    only in human beings, 49
    sensitivity and equilibrium, 125
    sphere of the nose and mouth, 214
    subdivision into *chesed* and *gevurah*, 42
Dan, tribe of, 111
Daniel, 111
Daughter, 37
David, King, 117, 196
    and the *brit*, 222
    character of, 37
David, Star of, 125, 240
Death, 126, 131, 180
    and *chochmah*, 165
Diagnosis, 173
Digestion, 67

Disease
    and evil, 91
    and sin, 127
    autoimmune, 147
    collagen, 154
Divination, 116
DNA, 257
Doubt, 113
Dry Bones, 69
Eating, 67
Education, 63
Elisha, 171
Emet veyatziv (prayer), 232
Endocrine system
    and allostasis, 123
Epstein, Rabbi Yitzchak Isaac HaLevi of Homil, 184
Esther, 103
Eve, 187, 254
Evil
    and disease, 91
Exile
    allegory for fear, 93
    disease, 126
    left thigh, 137
Eye, 33
    colors, 34
    Shabbat, 220
Eyes, 214
    healing, 40
Family, raising a, 83
Fatigue, 155

Fear, 91
Fingers, 41, 228
Free choice, 81
Friend, 204
Gall bladder, 129
Gevurah, 16, 25
    and *netzach*, 247
    circulatory system, 78
    courage, 112
    in mouth, 67
    in the eye, 34
Gideon, 100
Goat, 100
God
    (apparent) contraction of Infinite Light, 154
    72 Names of, 166, 249
    belief in, 11
    Divine Providence, 76
    doubt, 113
    estrangement from, 142
    love of, 77
    Name *Chet-tav-chaf*, 250
    Names of, 6, 189
    referred to as a lion, 109
    seeing, 40
    transcendent and immanent light, 63
    trust in, 157
Gold, 118
Golden Calf, 127
Gonorrhea, 105
Good and evil, 79

Hadrian, 113
Haman, 103
Hananiah, Mishael, and Azariah, 193
Hand, 169, 229
Hannah, 59
Hassidism
    and positive thinking, 161
    and tumors, 145
Havayah, Name, 20
    and Vision of Dry Bones, 70
    as healing process, 21
    blemish in, 206
    colors in the eye, 34
    four spellings, 229
    healing through Torah, 256
    human model, 52
    permutations, 247
    Priestly blessing, 200
Healers, 188
Healing
    and creation, 175
    miracle, 192
Health
    and eating, 67
    and speech, 67
Heart
    and soul essence, 238
    muscular and circulatory systems, 81
    two *lamed*'s, 51
Hebrew letters
    in *Sefer Yetzirah*, 28

Herbs, 181
Hezekiah, 195
Hod, 17, 25
   Aaron, 125
   and *binah*, 107
   and women, 151
   between hidden and revealed worlds, 160
   equilibrium, 125
   estrangement, 142
   fatigue, 156
   immune system, 85
   teshuvah, 156
   vulnerability, 137
Homeopathy, 179
Honey, 108
Hypochondria, 157
Immune system
   and allostasis, 123
Insanity, 94
Inspirational numbers, 229
Intellect, 14
Inter-inclusion, 2, 33, 216
Inversion, 212
Isaiah, 195
Israel Ba'al Shem Tov
   amulets, 190
   analysis of doubt, 113
   chashmal, 56
   spiritual healing, 251
Jacob
   immortality, 258
   tiferet, 198
   wrestled with angel, 137
Japhet, 222
Jesse, 117
Jewish identity, 152
Jewish people, 105
Jordan river, 171
Joseph, 82, 116
Judah, tribe of, 111
Jugular vein, 212
Kabbalah
   and Hassidism, 23
   and healing, 190
   and medicine, 2
   as treatment for bone marrow, 75
   meaning of, 2, 27
Kel, Name of God, 59
Kelipat nogah, 130
Keter, 13, 20, 24
   50th gate, 206
   Arich Anpin, 144
   left and right in, 144
   mouth, 175
   patience, 202
   respiratory system, 74
Kissing, 53
Lactation, 107
Lamed, 51
Land of Israel, 62, 105
Laziness, 112
Leo, zodiac sign, 109
Leprosy, 145, *See Tzara'at*
Light

and healing, 252
and lion, 119
from fingers, 228
Light, Water, Firmament, 237
Lion, 94
Liquids, 106
Livelihood, 250
Love, 201
   antidote to exile, 135
   in physician, 168
Lovesickness, 140
Lungs, 211
Lupus, 147
Luz bone, 257
Magen David. *See* David, Star of
Maimonides, 159, 245
Malchut, 18, 20, 26
   deficiency in, 141
   digestive system, 84, 242
   hand, 171
   in mouth, 66
   in the eye, 37
   naturopathy, 182
   prayer, 197
   womb of, 105
Man
   created in God's image, 11
Ma'on, 235
Marital relations, 53, 55, 66, 107
Medicine
   and Kabbalah, 2

   and spirituality, 1
Meditation, 160
Menachem Mendel of Lubavitch, Rabbi, 145, 165
Menstrual cycle, 128
Menstruation, 158
Mercy, thirteen attributes of, 200
Messiah
   and tribe of Dan, 111
   Daniel, 111
   individual spark of, 131
   sick, 131
   snake, 111
   son of Joseph, 116
Messianic Era, 105, 131
   and death, 166
Midian, 110
Midot, 20, 247, *See also Tiferet*
   and Creation week, 49
   and liquids, 106
   deficiency in, 141
   hand, 171
   in mouth, 66
   in the eye, 36
   osteopathy, 182
Mikveh, 191
Mind
   and body, 161
Moab, 110
Months of year, 217
Mordechai, 103
Moses, 54

netzach, 125
Mosquito, 113
Mother's milk, 107
Mouth
    five parts, 52
Murder, 94
Music, 172
Na'aman, 171
Nachash, king of Ammon, 114
Naturopathy, 180
Nebuchadnezzar, 109
Nefesh
    level of healing, 185
Nervous system
    and allostasis, 123
Neshamah
    level of healing, 189
Netzach, 17, 25
    endocrine system, 85
    equilibrium, 125
    Moses, 125
Neuro-endocrine-immune mechanism, 123
Noah, 222
Orev, officer of Midian, 100
Osteopathy, 180
Partzufim, 231
Peor, 99
Perfect number, 216
Philistines, 244
Plasmapheresis, 158
Pleasure
    worldly, 141
Pleasure principle, 130
Positive thinking, 199
Prayer, 196
    on another's behalf, 244
Prayer vs. blessing, 203
Priest
    as physician, 165
    chesed, 167
Priestly Blessing, 50
Primordial Sin, 94, 114, 254
Quacks, 188
Rachel, 198
Rape, 93
Raphael (angel), 247
Raven, 100, 103
Red, 218
Remission, 159
Reproduction, physiology of, 238
Resurrection, 70, 166, 193, 258
Ruach
    level of healing, 187
Run and return, 107
Sacrifices, 109
Sages
    "eyes of the congregation," 34
Samson, 117
Sarah, 243
Saul, King, 103, 115
Sciatic nerve, 137

Sefirot
    and fingers, 41
    and letters, 28
    and subdivisions of *da'at*, 46
    and the Name *Havayah*, 20
    estrangement between, 143
    in Kabbalah and Hassidism, 23
    meaning of, 12
    pathways of wisdom, 225
    three axes, 26
Self, sense of, 147
Self-awareness, 167
Selflessness, 250
Senses, 50
Sexuality, 84, 116, 241
Shabbat, 220
Shechinah, 197
    sick, 132
Shem, 222
Shema, 229
Shlomit bat Divri, 99
Sickness, purpose of, 131
Silver, 118
Skin, 84
Sleep, 223
Snake, 94, 186
    and mosquito, 114
    copper, 118
Soul
    and body, 11
    holy of holies, 194
    immortality of, 166

super-conscious, 13
Speech, 55
Stress, 124
Submission, separation, and sweetening, 57, 177
Sun
    and Lupus, 152
Syphilis, 106, 153
Teeth, 67, 214
Temple, 109
Ten Commandments, 47
Teshuvah, 156
    and healing, 205
Thought, positive, 161
Throne, Divine, 34
Tiferet, 16, 25
    and diagnosis, 173
    and fear of murder, 97
    and *hod*, 247
    compassion, 82
    healing, 247
    in the eye, 36
    muscular system, 81
    prayer, 198
Time
    and circulatory system, 78
Tishah b'Av, 109
Titus, 113
Toes, 43
Tohu
    world of, 132
Tongue, 60
Torah

Index

and healing, 254
healer, 191
Touch, 42
Trachea, 212
Tree, 181
Tree of Knowledge, 79, 188
Truth, 180, 239
immortality, 258
Tumors, 145
Twenty-eight changing Times, 251
Tzadik, 198
36, 215
Tzalmuna, king of Midian, 101
Tzara'at, 145, 245
Tzimtzum, 154
Understanding, Fifty gates of, 205
Vaccination, 251
Water

higher and lower, 129
White, 218
Wisdom, 32 pathways of, 225
Wolf, 93
Woman, 108
and *hod*, 151
of Valor, 84
Word
and circumcision, 55
Yechidah
level of healing, 192
Yesod, 17, 25
and fear of rape, 96
and truth, 239
ateret hayesod, 83
lower covenant, 48
reproductive system, 82
Yud, 170
Ze'ev, officer of Midian, 100
Zevach, king of Midian, 101

Printed by BoD™ in Norderstedt, Germany